MOM'S UPDATED
Quick Meals Recipe Box

250 Family Favorites in Thirty Minutes or Less

Donna L. Weihofen, R.D.

Adams Media
Avon, Massachusetts

Published by Adams Media, an F+W Publications Company
57 Littlefield Street
Avon, MA 02322
www.adamsmedia.com

ISBN: 1-59337-377-5
Printed in Canada.
J I H G F E D C B A

Library of Congress Cataloging-in-Publication Data

Weihofen, Donna L.

Mom's updated quick meals recipe box : 250 family favorites in thirty minutes or less / Donna L. Weihofen.

p.   cm.   ISBN 1-59337-377-5

1. Quick and easy cookery. I. Title: Updated quick meals recipe box. II. Title: Quick meals recipe box. III. Title.

TX833.5.W453 2006

641.5'55--dc22

2005026442

This publication is designed to provide accurate and authoritative information with regard to the subject matter covered. It is sold with the understanding that the publisher is not engaged in rendering legal, accounting, or other professional advice. If legal advice or other expert assistance is required, the services of a competent professional person should be sought.
—From a Declaration of Principles jointly adopted by a Committee of the American Bar Association and a Committee of Publishers and Associations

This book is available at quantity discounts for bulk purchases.
For information, please call 1-800-872-5627.

Contents

Acknowledgments...xi
Introduction...xii
General Cooking Tips xii

Chapter 1
Soups and Stews...1

Soup and Stew Cooking Tips..................................2
Apple Butternut Squash Soup with Brandy.............4
Bacon and Potato Soup...5
Bacon Corn Chowder 6
Black Bean Soup with a Secret Ingredient..............7
Broccoli Cheese Soup...8
Cajun Chicken Soup..9
Carrot Soup with Fresh Mint 10
Chicken Chili 11
Chicken Noodle Soup with Spinach 12
Chicken, Sausage, and Bean Stew 13
Chili Con Crazy 14
Chilled Spinach and Tarragon Soup.....................15
Chunky Gazpacho Garden Soup 16
Cod Chowder with Black Beans and Corn 17

Country Vegetable Soup 18
Crab Bisque Florentine...19
Crab Potato Soup..20
Cream of Spinach Soup 21
Curried Lentil Soup..22
Gingered Carrot Soup 23
Ham and Bean Soup for Two..................................24
Hamburger Soup 25
Irish Stew with Stout Beer......................................26
Jamaican Chicken Stew 27
Lazy Day White Bean Chili.....................................28
Mediterranean Beef Stew 29
Mexican Chicken Chili..30
Mexican Pork Chili 31
Minestrone-Style Stew 32
Orange and Yellow Pepper Soup...........................33
Oriental Beef and Noodle Soup.............................34
Pork and Butternut Squash Stew...........................35
Posole...36
Santa Fe Soup 37
Scallop, Mushroom, and Potato Soup....................38
Shrimp Basil Soup 39
Southwestern Chili 40
Spicy Asian Chicken Noodle Soup........................41

Split Pea Soup in an Hour 42
Squash Bisque with Rum 43
Tortellini Soup 44

Chapter 2
Salads 45

Salad Preparation Tips 46
Bacon, Swiss, and Grape Salad 48
Beet and Orange Salad with Blue Cheese
    and Walnuts 49
Blueberry, Walnut, and Wild Rice
    Chicken Salad 50
Broccoli, Roasted Red Peppers,
    and Artichoke Salad 51
Cherry Chicken Salad 52
Colorful Bean and Cheddar Salad 53
Crunchy Cole Slaw with Cashews 54
Festive Apple Pear Salad 55
Green Beans with Gorgonzola 56
Make Ahead Coleslaw 57
Mexican Macaroni Salad 58
Moroccan Rice Salad with Feta 59
Peanut Raisin Slaw 60
Quinoa, Pepper, and Peanut Salad 61

Raspberry Pecan Spinach Salad 62
Red Cabbage and Apple Salad 63
Salmon Mousse 64
South of the Border Bean and Corn Salad 65
Spinach Salad with Bacon Dressing 66
Spinach Salad with Honey Cranberry Dressing 67
Spinach Salad with Oranges and
    Pomegranates 68
Spinach, Kiwi, and Strawberry Salad
    with Poppy Seed Dressing 69
Strawberry and Spinach Salad
    with Apple Mustard Dressing 70
Swiss Apple Grape Salad 71
Tortellini and Shrimp Salad 72
Tuscan Pasta Salad with Artichokes
    and Sun Dried Tomatoes 73

Chapter 3
Eggs and Breakfast 75

Eggs and Breakfast Cooking Tips 76
Artichoke and Red Pepper Pie 77
Bacon and Egg Pizza 78

Cheesy Sausage Bake 79
Crustless Mexican Quiche 80
Italian Egg Puff 81
Mushroom and Artichoke Frittata Squares 82
Orange Marmalade French Toast 83
Sausage and Spinach Breakfast Casserole 84
Scotch Eggs 85
Strawberry Breakfast Salsa 86
Swedish Pancakes 87
Swiss Sweet Onion Pie 88
Vegetable Frittata 89

Chapter 4
Beef and Pork 91

Beef and Pork Cooking Tips 92
Apple and Kraut Pork Chops 93
Beef Fillets Crusted with Blue Cheese 94
Beef Merlot 95
Beef Strip Steak with Soy Maple Mustard Glaze ... 96
Beef Stroganoff with Mushrooms and Peppers 97
Beef Tenderloin with Soy Ginger Marinade 98
Old-Fashioned Sweet Brandy Pork Medallions 99
Burger Stuffed Bundles 100
Chicken-Fried Steak 101

Curried Pork and Rice 102
Grilled Ham Steak with Raisin Sauce 103
Ham with Maple Syrup, Pineapple
    Ginger Sauce 104
Honey and Soy Marinated Flank Steak 105
Honey Apricot Glazed Ham 106
Hungarian Pork Chops 107
Molasses Grilled Pork Chops
    with Horseradish Sauce 108
Moroccan Beef Kabobs 109
Pork and Vegetable Stir-Fry on the Grill 110
Pork Chops and Apricots in Curry Sauce 111
Pork Chops with Orange Cranberry Sauce 112
Pork Chops, Potatoes, and Cabbage 113
Pork Loin with Fruit Pilaf 114
Pork Medallions with Port Wine Cherry Sauce ... 115
Pork Ribs and Sauerkraut 116
Pork Tenderloin with Cinnamon Apples 117
Spanish Beef and Mushrooms—Estofado 118
Spicy Orange Marinated Beef Roast 119
Swiss Steak 120
Two-Meal Slow Roasted Pork Shoulder 121

Chapter 5
Chicken and Poultry 123

Chicken and Poultry Cooking Tips 124
Apple Raisin Rum Stuffed Chicken Breasts 125
Apricot Chicken with Pecans 126
Artichoke and Mushroom Chicken Bake 127
Chicken Breast with Port Wine Plum Sauce 128
Chicken Breasts in Apricot Brandy Sauce 129
Chicken California Style 130
Chicken Parmesan 131
Chicken with Brandy Orange Sauce 132
Chicken with Mushrooms, Roasted Peppers,
    and Olives 133
Chicken, Cashew, and Apple Stir-Fry 134
Chicken, Vegetables, and Stuffing Bake 135
Creamy Swiss Chicken Bake 136
Grilled Chicken with Raspberry and
    Blueberry Grand Marnier Sauce 137
Honey Mustard Chicken
    with Dried Cranberries 138
Indian Chicken Curry 139
Italian Chicken Rolls 140
Maple Mustard Grilled Chicken 141
Orange Glazed Chicken Strips 142

Pineapple Cranberry Chicken 143
Raspberry Chicken 144
Soy Glazed Chicken and Dried Fruit Pilaf 145
Turkey Piccata 146
Turkey Tenderloins with
    Mustard Cranberry Sauce 147
Tuscan Chicken with Pistachio Rice 148

Chapter 6
Fish and Seafood 149

Fish and Seafood Cooking Tips 150
Apple Glazed Salmon 151
Bacon Wrapped Scallops in Brandy Marinade 152
Baked Sea Bass with Walnut Crumb Crust 153
Broiled Shrimp and Cheese on French Bread 154
Cod with Parmesan Dill Topping 155
Cornflake Crusted Cod 156
Crab Imperial 157
Grilled Tuna Steak with Roasted Vegetables 158
Honey Mustard Haddock 159
Lemon Tuna Spread 160
Orange Glazed Salmon 161
Pecan Crusted Sea Bass 162
Salmon Loaf with Creamy Dill Sauce 163

Shrimp and Feta with Italian Tomato Sauce....... 164
Shrimp in Tomato Cream Sauce on Linguine 165
Shrimp with Couscous, Roasted Red
    Peppers, and Pine Nuts.................................. 166
Smoked Salmon with Sun-Dried
    Tomatoes on Fettuccine................................ 167
Southwestern Tuna
    with Avocado Butter Sauce............................ 168

Chapter 7
Casseroles and Pasta................................... 169

Casseroles and Pastas Tips 170
Cheddar Veggie Pasta Toss............................. 173
Chicken and Biscuit Casserole 174
Chicken Tetrazzini Casserole........................... 175
Chilies and Refried Bean Casserole................... 176
Country Italian Penne..................................... 177
Creamy Chicken Linguine................................ 178
Enchilada Casserole 179
Ham and Asparagus Casserole........................ 180
Hamburger Pie 181
Italian Baked Mostaccioli 182
Italian Beef and Spinach Pie 183
Lasagna with No-Cook Noodles 184

Linguine with Chicken, Spinach,
    and Tomatoes 185
Meat and Potatoes Skillet Dinner 186
Mushroom Stroganoff..................................... 187
Pasta Alfredo—Create Your Own 188
Pasta with Broccoli and
    Red Peppers in Peanut Sauce 189
Pasta with Spinach, Olives, and Pine Nuts.......... 190
Pasta with Tomato and White Bean Sauce—
    A Build Your Own Pasta Dish........................ 191
Pork and Noodles 192
Reuben Casserole 193
Russian Beef, Mushrooms, and Noodles.............. 194
Seafood and Red Pepper Couscous.................... 195
Shrimp and Pasta in Creamy
    Swiss Cheese Sauce.................................... 196
Spaghetti and Italian Sausage Pie 197
Spaghetti with Beef and Bacon Tomato Sauce 198
Spanish Rice with Chicken and Red Peppers 199
Spicy Seafood Rice 200
Tamale Pie.. 201
Tortilla and Bean Casserole 202
Tuna Noodle Casserole 203
Turkey and Dressing Casserole.......................... 204

Chapter 8
Side Dishes 205

Side Dishes Cooking Tips 206
Apple Apricot Bread Dressing 207
BLT Mashed Potatoes 208
Colcannon—Irish Mashed Potatoes
    and Cabbage 209
Cornbread 210
Grilled Potato Salad 211
Hot German Potato Salad 212
Irish Soda Bread 213
Mediterranean Rice with Pine Nuts
    and Dried Cranberries 214
Mexican Rice 215
Orange Persian Barley 216
Orzo with Parmesan and Basil 217
Oven Roasted Red Potatoes with Rosemary 218
Parmesan Potatoes 219
Pasta with Pesto Sauce 220
Pilaf with Spinach and Walnuts 221
Spice It Up with Lentils 222
Tuscan White Beans with Herbs 223
Wild Rice with Cranberries and Cashews 224
Yellow Rice with Golden Raisins 225

Chapter 9
Vegetables 227

Vegetable Cooking Tips 228
Asparagus Blue Cheese Bundles 231
Asparagus with Black Olives and Bacon 232
Baked Stuffed Sweet Potatoes 233
Broccoli with Honey Sesame Topping 234
Brussels Sprouts in Creamy Dijon Sauce 235
Brussels Sprouts with Apricot Glaze 236
Carrots with Dried Cranberries and Walnuts 237
Green Beans with Blue Cheese and
    Bacon Dressing 238
Green Beans with Pecans 239
Green Beans with Tomatoes and Onions 240
Honey and Parmesan Topped Asparagus 241
Marmalade Glazed Carrots 242
Roasted Red and Yellow Peppers
    with Green Beans 243
Sweet Potatoes and Apples in Ginger
    Orange Sauce 244
Swiss Spinach Soufflé 245
Wilted Spinach with Balsamic Mustard Sauce ... 246
Zucchini Bake 247

Chapter 10
Snacks 249

Avocado Olive Dip 250
Banana Oatmeal Bread 251
Bean Salsa Dip 252
Black Bean and Red Pepper Dip 253
Bruschetta and Crostini 254
Feta and Red Pepper Cheesecake 255
Light Guacamole 256
Mushroom Bacon Spread 257
Rhubarb Bread 258
Roasted Red Pepper and Olive Tapenade 259
Spinach and Artichoke Dip 260

Chapter 11
Desserts 261

Desserts Cooking Tips 262
Apple Cake—the Best Ever 264
Apple Tart 265
Apple, Brie, and Pecan Dessert Quesadillas 266
Blueberry Peach Crostata 267
Chocolate Chip Peanut Butter Cake 268
Chocolate Silk Pie 269

Chocolate Wonder Bars 270
Creamy Rice Pudding 271
Crème Brulée 272
Dutch Apple Crumble 273
Fudge Brownies (with a Secret Ingredient) 274
Nectarine-Berry Crisp 275
Oatmeal Chocolate Chip Cake 276
Oatmeal Toffee Bars 277
Peach and Raspberry Cobbler 278
Pecan Chocolate Bourbon Pie 279
Raspberry Rhubarb Pie 280
Raspberry Sauce 281
Rhubarb Cake 282
Rocky Road S'Mores 283

Recipe Index 284

Acknowledgments

My cookbook is done and I am wondering who had more fun—the writer of the book, who is me, or my husband, friends, and neighbors who helped me by eating my recipe creations. I loved every minute of developing and testing these great recipes. Oh, I guess all the typing and proofreading were not that much fun, but then I had the help of my friend Judith Neese, who found mistakes even though I promised her it was a mistake-free manuscript.

The biggest kudos go to one of those special friends—the kind you have only once in a lifetime. This book would not have been half the fun without Mary Risgaard. She helped me create and test recipes, and she has a special knack for practical and insightful advice.

A special thanks to my husband, Ray, who never knew what to expect for dinner for the past year. He learned that if I was in a recipe-testing mode, he might come home to a dinner with five entrees and six unexpected guests. Other nights it was leftovers or nothing if I was in the typing mode. He really did enjoy the many testing parties we hosted and the wonderful bottles of wine our guests would bring as gifts. I think he secretly hopes I will do another book so we can continue to have those parties and enjoy more wine.

Introduction

The first *Mom's Recipe Box Cookbook* was full of great recipes. It was easy to follow and well received by both veteran and not-so-veteran cooks. The most common response over the years has been, "More recipes, please, *Mom*." Well, here they are! *Mom's Updated Quick Meals Recipe Box* has lots of well-loved recipes from past and present generations, seasoned with my experience as a nutritionist. Many of the recipes have been featured on my regular television show on WISC TV 3 (CBS) in Madison, Wisconsin.

These are recipes you will want to make for both family and friends. Each dish was adapted to make it as quick to prepare as possible while keeping the appearance and flavor you will be proud to serve. All of the recipes have been tested and fine-tuned to perfection by me and my cooking friends, Mary Risgaard and Barry Greenberg. You will succeed the first time you try them. Each section also has many cooking and baking tips that will enhance your experience in the kitchen.

Recipes that successfully made it into this book had to qualify in two major areas: they had to be good and tasty, *and* they had to require no more than 30 minutes of your time in the kitchen. A recipe may need to bake or cook longer than that, but you don't have to be around. Each recipe was adapted, whenever possible, to use lower fat and lower calorie ingredients but never at the expense of good taste.

This recipe collection offers an uncomplicated way to make impressive, fun dinners that will please your family and friends. When you find that entertaining is easy, you will be more likely to entertain again and again. And remember, serving a simply delicious dinner to your family, gathered around the supper table, is a priceless investment.

General Cooking Tips

Spices and herbs are essential ingredients in most recipes. The general guideline to use when converting between dry and fresh herbs is to use one-third the amount of dried herbs as you would fresh. If a recipe calls for 1 tablespoon fresh oregano, use 1 teaspoon dried oregano. When cooking with fresh herbs, it is best to add them at the end of the recipe so the heat does not destroy their color and flavor. If using dried herbs, add them at the beginning. The dried herbs need to be rehydrated and it takes time for their flavor to be infused in the dish.

You can adjust any seasoning to suit your own taste. It is very important to remember that you can always add a little more spice but you can never take it out. If you are preparing a new recipe and you are not sure you love a particular spice or herb, I recommend that you use less than the recipe calls for. For instance, if a pork dish calls for 2 teaspoons of thyme, try 1 teaspoon and then taste it.

Red pepper and red pepper flakes add a significant amount of heat to a dish. Red pepper is the same as cayenne pepper or ground red pepper. Red pepper flakes are from whole dried cayenne peppers that have been crushed and not ground.

Specific amounts of salt and pepper are not often specified in these recipes. The recipe will often call for "sprinkle with salt and pepper" or "add salt and pepper to taste." There is a big difference in the amount of salt and pepper people enjoy or want to use in their own cooking.

When a recipe calls for salt, it refers to common table salt. Both common table salt and kosher salt come from underground rock salt. Table salt is dried into sugarlike grains that are usually mixed with an additive to prevent clumping. Kosher salt is made into flakes without any additives. Sea salt is basically what remains after ocean water has evaporated. Additional rinsing and drying will make the salt even whiter. The salt crystals have a different shape and texture than the finely ground table salt. Sea salts may have varying tastes due to small amounts of trace minerals. Do not bake with sea salt because it will not dissolve evenly and its trace mineral might clash with certain flavors.

Canola oil and olive oils are used extensively throughout this book. Canola oil consists of mainly monounsaturated fats (62%) and the rest is polyunsaturated with a very small amount of saturated fat. Canola oil is also a source of the important omega-3 fats. Olive oil is also high in monounsaturated fat (72%) and has 17% saturated fat.

Recipes often call for butter or margarine. It is your choice. I recommend using a margarine that is labeled "free of trans fats." Do not substitute light or reduced-fat margarines for regular margarines in recipes. Light margarines are often whipped or have water added. This would change the baking or cooking properties of the margarine.

You may need a little more or a little less oil than the recipe calls for when cooking meats or vegetables, depending on the size of the skillet you use.

Cooking sprays can sometimes be used in place of greasing a pan or adding fat to a skillet. The label states the spray contains no calories. Actually there are no calories in a ⅓-second spray of Pam or other cooking sprays, but to cover a 10-inch skillet, you need at least a 1-second spray, and that contains 7 calories. You will still cut calories since a teaspoon of oil poured from a bottle has 40 calories, and a tablespoon has 120 calories.

Whenever possible, I substitute fat-free half-and-half for cream in recipes. It does not work in every recipe to substitute this in the place of cream, so the recipe must be adapted for this change. Fat-free half-and-half is made primarily from skim milk with carrageenan added to give it body and thickness. Carrageenan is a healthy seaweed extract. Fat-free half-and-half has only 10 calories per tablespoon, compared to heavy cream, which has 50 calories per tablespoon. (That is 800 calories per cup!)

To make muffins and quick breads extra moist, add a little more sugar or oil and cut out an egg white. Egg whites are drying agents. For example, if your recipes call for 3 eggs, use 2 whole eggs and 1 egg yolk. Discard the one egg white.

If a recipe calls for coconut milk, a substitution can be evaporated milk with a small amount of coconut extract.

If adding an alcohol product to a cream-based sauce, it is best to add it near the end of the cooking process. Heat slowly and avoid boiling the mixture. It is important to note that not all alcohol content evaporates during cooking. The amount of alcohol retained depends on the preparation method and the length of cooking or baking.

When recipes call for wine, beer, or liquor, it may be possible to use a nonalcoholic substitution. Choose the option that best matches the flavor of the dish you are making. The following are suggestions for substitutions:

WHITE WINE	white grape juice, chicken broth, ginger ale
RED WINE	grape juice; cranberry juice; chicken, meat, or vegetable broth; flavored vinegar
BRANDY	white grape juice, apple juice, peach or apricot syrup, brandy extract
BOURBON	vanilla extract
GRAND MARNIER	orange juice concentrate, orange extract
BEER	chicken or beef broth, white grape juice, ginger ale
RUM	pineapple juice with almond extract, vanilla extract, rum extract
SHERRY	vanilla extract, orange or pineapple juice, coffee

CHAPTER 1

Soups and Stews

Apple Butternut Squash Soup with Brandy

Bacon and Potato Soup

Bacon Corn Chowder

Black Bean Soup with a Secret Ingredient

Broccoli Cheese Soup

Cajun Chicken Soup

Carrot Soup with Fresh Mint

Chicken Chili

Chicken Noodle Soup with Spinach

Chicken, Sausage, and Bean Stew

Chili Con Crazy

Chilled Spinach and Tarragon Soup

Chunky Gazpacho Garden Soup

Cod Chowder with Black Beans and Corn

Country Vegetable Soup

Crab Bisque Florentine

Crab Potato Soup

Cream of Spinach Soup

Curried Lentil Soup

Gingered Carrot Soup

Ham and Bean Soup for Two

Hamburger Soup

Irish Stew with Stout Beer

Jamaican Chicken Stew

Lazy Day White Bean Chili

Mediterranean Beef Stew

Mexican Chicken Chili

Mexican Pork Chili

Minestrone-Style Stew

Orange and Yellow Pepper Soup

Oriental Beef and Noodle Soup

Pork and Butternut Squash Stew

Posole

Santa Fe Soup

Scallop, Mushroom, and Potato Soup

Shrimp Basil Soup

Southwestern Chili

Spicy Asian Chicken Noodle Soup

Split Pea Soup in an Hour

Squash Bisque with Rum

Tortellini Soup

Soup and Stew Cooking Tips

Soups are usually a liquid base with added ingredients such as meat and vegetables. Light soups are served as a first course, and heartier soups can be the main course. There are some common names related to soups:

- **Bisque**—a thick, rich soup that is often partially pureed. Often cream is added to make it smooth and thick.

- **Fricassee**—a thick, chunky vegetable-and-meat stew. It is usually thickened with a roux and finished with egg yolk and cream.

- **Chowder**—a thick and chunky type of milk-, cream-, or tomato-based soup.

- **Stew**—a mixture of chunky vegetables and meat, poultry, or seafood with less liquid than most soups.

Everyone likes their soup, stew, bisque, and chili at a different consistency. You can adjust the liquid in any of the recipes according to your preference.

A handheld immersion blender is an important piece of kitchen equipment. It makes it easy to puree part or all of the soup without having to pour hot soup into a regular blender.

Soups can be thickened in several ways. The easiest is to use a handheld immersion blender to partially puree the vegetables in the soup. Mashed potato flakes can be added. Cornstarch or flour mixed with water also can be used. Cornstarch always has to be mixed in cold water before adding to a hot liquid. It gives the broth or sauce a glossy appearance. Flour also has to be mixed with water. Use a shaker or jar with a lid to get a smooth paste. Add small amounts to a hot liquid while stirring constantly. After the mixture boils, continue adding flour and water until it reaches the desired consistency.

When leftover soups, stews, or sauces are rewarmed, additional liquid will probably need to be added.

The most common ingredient used in this section is chicken broth or beef broth. Large and small cans of broth are great to keep on hand. Often the fat-free broth is much more expensive. You can buy the regular broth, chill it, and remove the fat that floats to the top. It may be easier and more cost effective to use good-quality chicken and beef base in concentrated paste form. One brand is Better Than Bouillon. One teaspoon mixed with 1 cup of water makes a tasty broth. The concentrate needs to be stored in the refrigerator after opening.

Canned tomatoes are a staple ingredient for recipes in this section and throughout this book. Keep a variety of seasoned diced and stewed tomatoes on hand. If a recipe calls for "seasoned canned tomatoes," choose the seasoning you like best or the one that will complement the recipe you are making.

Worcestershire sauce is a dark, flavorful sauce that was developed in India. It was named after the English town Worcester, where it was first bottled. It is made from secret ingredients, including anchovies, tamarind paste, molasses, onions, garlic, and soy sauce.

Soy sauce is a dark, salty liquid made by fermenting boiled soybeans and wheat or barley together.

Chili powder is a combination of spices that can vary with the brand. It usually contains a mixture of ground dried chilies, cloves, coriander, cumin, garlic, salt, and oregano.

The bitter taste in tomato-based sauces, soups, stews, and chili may be caused by several factors. Overcooked or browned garlic will turn bitter. If you add too much tomato paste, it will be bitter. If you heat the sauce back to a boil after adding wine, it may create bitterness. Cooking tomatoes with their skins contributes to a bitter taste. If it is appropriate for the dish, try adding some shredded carrots while cooking the dish. If cooked for quite a while, the carrots disappear into the sauce and sweeten the dish. You may also try adding a touch of sugar to tomato-based dishes just before serving. Adjust the amount of sugar to suit your taste.

If family members or guests do not like onions, wrap and tie onions in a cheesecloth bag. Place the bag in your soup or sauce while it is cooking. Remove the onion when ready to serve the dish.

Apple Butternut Squash Soup with Brandy

1 tablespoon butter or margarine
1 medium onion, chopped
3 cups fat-free chicken broth
1 package (10 ounces) frozen winter
   squash
1 large Granny Smith apple, peeled,
   cored, and diced
½ tablespoon brown sugar
¼ teaspoon cumin
¼ teaspoon cinnamon
¼ teaspoon curry powder
2 tablespoons brandy, optional
Salt and freshly ground pepper to taste
4 tablespoons fat-free sour cream

Nutritional information per serving:

Calories	120
Fat, gm.	3
Protein, gm.	3
Carbs, gm.	20
Cholesterol, mg.	10
Fiber, gm.	2.2

The great part of this recipe is the time you will save by using frozen squash instead of having to peel, cook, and mash the fresh squash yourself. Serve a small amount of this soup as a first course. It has a touch of sweetness from the apples and brown sugar. The brandy is optional but it adds fullness to the flavor.

❖ In a large cooking pot, melt butter and cook onion until translucent. Add chicken broth, squash, apple, brown sugar, cumin, curry powder, and cinnamon Bring to a boil, reduce heat, and simmer until apples are very tender. Remove from heat. Using a handheld immersion blender, mix soup until smooth. Add brandy if desired. Adjust seasoning with salt and pepper. Serve with a dollop of sour cream in each bowl.

Bacon and Potato Soup

What could be more comforting than a bowl of this hearty, creamy soup? The bacon and onion toppings add lively flavor and color.

❖ In a large soup pot, melt butter. Add onions and cook over medium heat until lightly brown. Add potatoes and chicken broth. Bring to a boil, reduce heat, and boil gently for 30 minutes or until potatoes are very tender. Add milk, white pepper, and thyme. Using an immersion blender, mix soup until smooth. (Soup may also be transferred to a blender to puree.) Adjust seasoning with salt and pepper to taste. Serve in individual bowls and top with crumbled bacon and chopped onions.

Serves 4

1 tablespoon butter or margarine
2 large onions, chopped
4 large potatoes, peeled and chopped
6 cups fat-free chicken broth
1 can (12 ounces) fat-free evaporated
  milk
¼ teaspoon white pepper
¼ teaspoon ground thyme
Salt and pepper to taste
6 slices precooked bacon, crumbled
½ cup chopped green onions

Nutritional information per serving:

Calories	230
Fat, gm.	6
Protein, gm.	12
Carbs, gm.	32
Cholesterol, mg.	15
Fiber, gm.	2.6

Bacon Corn Chowder

Serves 6

½ tablespoon canola oil
6 slices turkey bacon, diced
1 medium onion, finely chopped
1 cup finely chopped carrots
3 cups fat-free chicken broth
1 large potato, peeled and diced
1 cup corn, frozen or canned
1 can (14 ounces) cream-style corn
1 can (12 ounces) fat-free evaporated
  milk
¼ teaspoon ground thyme
¼ teaspoon white pepper
Salt and freshly ground pepper to taste

Nutritional information per serving:

Calories	175
Fat, gm.	2
Protein, gm.	10
Carbs, gm.	30
Cholesterol, mg.	10
Fiber, gm.	2.9

If you are looking for a soup that kids will like, this should be the one. Most kids like bacon, potatoes, corn, and carrots. Those are the healthful ingredients they will see in this soup.

❖ In a large soup pot, combine oil, bacon, and onion. Cook until bacon begins to brown and onion is tender. Add carrots, broth, and potato. Bring to a boil. Reduce heat, cover pan, and boil gently for 20 minutes or until potato is tender. Add corn, creamed-style corn, milk, thyme, and white pepper. Heat through. Adjust seasoning with salt and pepper. Makes 9 cups.

_____

Note: *Ham could be substituted for the bacon in this recipe.*

Black Bean Soup with a Secret Ingredient

Pumpkin is the special secret ingredient. This soup has a wonderful, full flavor and is loaded with nutrients. It is high in protein, fiber, vitamin A, and folate, and yet is low in fat and calories.

❖ In a large soup pot, heat oil. Add onion and cook over medium heat until lightly brown. Add garlic, cumin, cinnamon, and cayenne pepper. Cook for 1 minute. Add all remaining ingredients except cheese. Bring to a boil, reduce heat, and simmer for 30 to 40 minutes or until ready to serve. Add extra water or chicken broth if it gets too thick. Add salt and pepper to taste. Top with grated Parmesan cheese if desired.

---

*For extra flavor, use canned Southwestern-flavored black beans.

Serves 10

1 tablespoon canola oil
1 large onion, chopped
2 teaspoons minced garlic
1 tablespoon ground cumin
½ teaspoon cinnamon
¼ teaspoon cayenne pepper
4 cups fat-free chicken broth
3 cans (15 ounces each) black beans*, drained
1 can (16 ounces) pumpkin
1 can (28 ounces) garlic-flavored diced tomatoes
2 tablespoons apple cider vinegar
1 pound low-fat kielbasa or ham, diced
Salt and pepper to taste
½ cup shredded Parmesan cheese, optional

Nutritional information per serving:

Calories	240
Fat, gm.	5
Protein, gm.	18
Carbs, gm.	29
Cholesterol, mg.	20
Fiber, gm.	8

Broccoli Cheese Soup

Serves 6

½ tablespoon canola oil
1 medium onion, finely chopped
3 medium potatoes, peeled and finely
  diced
2 cups chopped fresh broccoli
4 cups fat-free chicken broth
1 bay leaf
1 can (12 ounces) evaporated skim milk
4 ounces (6 single slices) fat-free
  processed Cheddar-type cheese*
¼ teaspoon white pepper
Salt and freshly ground pepper to taste

Nutritional information per serving:

Calories	135
Fat, gm.	1
Protein, gm.	13
Carbs, gm.	18
Cholesterol, mg.	5
Fiber, gm.	3.1

Wow—you won't believe that this creamy, flavorful soup could be so low in fat and calories!

❖ In a large, heavy soup pot, heat oil. Add onion and cook over medium heat until translucent. Add potatoes, broccoli, chicken broth, and bay leaf. Bring to a boil and reduce heat. Cover pan and simmer for 20 to 30 minutes or until vegetables are tender. Discard bay leaf. Use an immersion blender and blend until desired consistency. You can make it completely smooth or leave a few lumps for texture. Add milk, cheese, and white pepper. Heat until cheese has melted. Add salt and pepper to taste.

_____

Fat-free processed cheese will be labeled "Nonfat pasteurized process cheese product." It is better known as fat-free cheese singles. You can use regular Cheddar cheese in this soup, but a processed cheese will melt better. Other cheeses sometimes get stringy when melted.

Cajun Chicken Soup

In just a few minutes you can have a full-flavored soup. Serve it with crunchy bread and some fresh fruit for a completely satisfying meal.

❖ In a large soup pot, heat oil. Add chicken, chili powder, and cumin. Cook over medium-high heat until browned. Add garlic and cook 1 minute. Add broth, tomatoes, lemon juice, corn, and black beans. Bring to a boil, reduce heat, and simmer for 10 to 30 minutes or until desired. Adjust seasoning with salt and pepper. Serve in individual bowls and top with shredded cheese if desired.

------

*For a more flavorful soup, use the Southwestern-seasoned black beans with cumin and chili spices.

Serves 6

1 tablespoon canola oil
1 pound boneless chicken breasts, thinly
   sliced
1 tablespoon chili powder
1 teaspoon cumin
2 teaspoons minced garlic
6 cups fat free chicken broth
1 can (28 ounces) Cajun-seasoned diced
   tomatoes
¼ cup lemon juice
2 cups frozen or canned corn
2 cans (15 ounces each) black beans*,
   drained and rinsed
Salt and pepper to taste
½ cup shredded Cheddar cheese, optional

Nutritional information per serving:

Calories	330
Fat, gm.	5
Protein, gm.	29
Carbs, gm.	42
Cholesterol, mg.	45
Fiber, gm.	9.5

Carrot Soup with Fresh Mint

Serves 8

1 tablespoon butter or margarine
1 medium onion, chopped
2 pounds baby carrots
¼ cup rice
6 cups fat-free chicken or vegetable broth,
  divided
⅛ teaspoon white pepper
1 tablespoon balsamic vinegar
½ teaspoon sugar
Salt and freshly ground pepper to taste
6 fresh mint leaves
½ cup fat-free sour cream, optional

Nutritional information per serving:

Calories	80
Fat, gm.	1
Protein, gm.	2
Carbs, gm.	16
Cholesterol, mg.	5
Fiber, gm.	3.4

This is a wonderful, mild-flavored soup that would be a great first course at a dinner party. It can also be served at a family meal as an option to a vegetable. It tastes so good kids may not even recognize it as carrots.

❖ In a medium heavy soup pot, melt butter. Add onion and cook over medium heat until translucent. Add whole carrots, raw rice, and 5 cups broth. Bring to a boil, reduce heat, cover, and boil gently for 20 minutes or until rice is tender. Place soup in a food processor or use an immersion blender to process soup until smooth.* Add additional broth if soup is too thick. Add white pepper, vinegar, and sugar. Add salt, and freshly ground pepper to taste. Serve in individual soup bowls and add either whole or chopped mint leaves to each bowl. Add a dollop of sour cream to each bowl if desired.

─────

*It really is a lot easier to use a handheld immersion blender than to transfer the hot soup to a food processor.

Chicken Chili

This recipe is easily made with a purchased rotisserie chicken. Use the dark meat in this recipe and save the breast meat for another use. If you don't have access to cooked chicken, use any boneless pieces of chicken.

❖ In a large saucepan or soup pot, heat oil. Add onion and cook until translucent. If using a rotisserie chicken, remove the dark meat, cut into bite-sized pieces, and place in the pan. If using raw chicken, add to pan and cook until brown. Add all remaining ingredients. Bring to a boil, reduce heat, and simmer for 30 minutes or until soup reaches desired consistency. Soup may remain on very low heat for 1 to 3 hours or until ready to serve.

Serves 4

1 tablespoon canola oil
1 large onion, chopped
½ pound cooked skinless dark-meat chicken
1 teaspoon minced garlic
1 can (15 ounces) great northern beans, partially drained
1 can (15 ounces) garbanzo beans, partially drained
1 can (11 ounces) corn, drained
1 can (4 ounces) green chilies
1 teaspoon chili powder
1 teaspoon cumin
1 tablespoon balsamic vinegar
4 cups fat-free chicken broth

Nutritional information per serving:

Calories	390
Fat, gm.	8
Protein, gm.	26
Carbs, gm.	54
Cholesterol, mg.	45
Fiber, gm.	13.6

Chicken Noodle Soup with Spinach

Serves 4

1 tablespoon canola oil
2 boned and skinned chicken breast
   halves, thinly sliced
Salt and pepper
1 medium onion, finely chopped
1 cup chopped carrots
1 teaspoon minced garlic
5 cups fat-free chicken broth
⅛ teaspoon nutmeg
¼ teaspoon allspice
½ cup noodles or pasta shells
3 cups fresh spinach, chopped
Salt and pepper to taste
½ cup grated Parmesan cheese

Nutritional information per serving:

Calories	200
Fat, gm.	7
Protein, gm.	18
Carbs, gm.	16
Cholesterol, mg.	30
Fiber, gm.	2.4

This is a light soup, mild flavored but very attractive with the fresh spinach added right before serving.

❖ In a medium soup pan, heat oil. Add chicken, sprinkle with salt and pepper, and cook over medium-high heat until brown. Add onion and cook until translucent. Add carrots and garlic. Cook 2 minutes. Add broth, nutmeg, and allspice. Bring to a boil, reduce heat, and simmer for 10 minutes or until carrots are tender. Add pasta and boil gently for 10 minutes or until pasta is tender. When ready to serve, add spinach and boil for 1 to 2 minutes or just until spinach is wilted. Add salt and pepper to taste. Serve in individual bowls and top each serving with Parmesan cheese.

Note: *Other vegetables of your choice may be added. Cooked chicken pieces can be substituted for the chicken breasts.*

Chicken, Sausage, and Bean Stew

This is one of those wonderful full-flavored meals that will warm you on a cold winter night.

❖ In a large, deep, heavy skillet, heat oil. Add chicken and sausage. Cook over medium-high heat until browned. Remove chicken and sausage from pan and set aside. Add onion and carrots to the skillet and cook until tender. Add garlic, thyme, and pepper flakes and cook 1 minute. Add 1 cup of the broth and bring to a boil. Stir to deglaze the pan. Add tomatoes, beans, and reserved meat. Bring to a boil, reduce heat, and simmer for 30 minutes or until it reaches desired consistency. Stir occasionally. For a thinner consistency, add additional broth. Add salt and pepper to taste.

Note: This dish can be thinned or thickened to desired consistency. You can serve it as a soup or allow it to thicken and serve it on top of noodles or rice.

Serves 4

1 tablespoon canola oil
3 skinless, boneless chicken breasts, cubed
½ pound low-fat turkey sausage links, cut into 1-inch slices
1 medium onion, chopped
3 large carrots, peeled and diced
2 teaspoons minced garlic
½ teaspoon ground thyme
¼ teaspoon red pepper flakes
2 cups fat-free chicken broth, divided
1 can (15 ounces) seasoned petite diced tomatoes
1 can (15 ounces) great northern beans, drained
Salt and pepper to taste

Nutritional information per serving:

Calories	445
Fat, gm.	11
Protein, gm.	51
Carbs, gm.	36
Cholesterol, mg.	100
Fiber, gm.	8.2

Chili Con Crazy

Serves 8

1 tablespoon canola oil
1 medium onion, diced
1 large red pepper, diced
1 tablespoon minced garlic
½ cup grated carrots
2 medium sweet potatoes, peeled and
    diced
6 cups fat-free chicken broth
1 can (28 ounces) crushed tomatoes
1 can (6 ounces) tomato paste
2 cans (4 ounces each) chopped green
    chilies
2 tablespoons chili powder
2 teaspoons cumin
1 tablespoon honey
1 cup dry-roasted peanuts
Salt and pepper to taste

Nutritional information per serving:

Calories	310
Fat, gm.	14
Protein, gm.	11
Carbs, gm.	35
Cholesterol, mg.	0
Fiber, gm.	7.8

Be ready for a taste surprise with this unusual meatless chili. A friend brought this to a couples tennis party and it was a hit!

❖ In a large, heavy soup pot, heat oil. Add onion and cook until translucent. Add pepper, garlic, and carrots. Cook until tender. Add all remaining ingredients except salt and pepper. Bring to a boil. Reduce heat and boil gently 30 to 40 minutes or until sweet potatoes are tender and soup reaches desired consistency. Adjust seasoning to your taste.

_____

Note: *Cooked and crumbled Italian sausage can be added to the soup if desired.*

Chilled Spinach and Tarragon Soup

Serve this cold or hot if you enjoy spinach.

❖ In a large, heavy soup pot, melt butter. Add onion and cook over medium heat until translucent. Add garlic and cook 1 minute. Add 5 cups chicken broth and potatoes. Cook until potatoes are tender. Add spinach, lemon juice, and tarragon and simmer for 10 minutes. Remove from heat. Using an immersion blender or a food processor, process soup until smooth. Add hot pepper sauce and salt and pepper to taste. Add additional chicken broth to thin if desired. Chill soup in the refrigerator. Serve with a dollop of sour cream.

Serves 4

1 tablespoon butter or margarine
1 large sweet onion, finely chopped
2 teaspoons minced garlic
6 cups fat-free chicken broth, divided
2 medium potatoes, diced
1 package (10 ounces) frozen spinach
1 tablespoon lemon juice
1 teaspoon dried tarragon
Dash hot pepper sauce
Salt and pepper to taste
½ cup fat-free sour cream

Nutritional Information per serving:

Calories	135
Fat, gm.	3
Protein, gm.	6
Carbs, gm.	20
Cholesterol, mg.	15
Fiber, gm.	3.8

Chunky Gazpacho Garden Soup

Serves 6

6 medium tomatoes, seeded and chopped
1 clove garlic, minced
1 large cucumber, peeled, seeded,
   and chopped
1 cup diced green onions
1 tablespoon olive oil
1 tablespoon cider vinegar
1 can (46 ounces) tomato-vegetable juice
2 teaspoons Worcestershire sauce
1 tablespoon lemon juice
1 teaspoon lime juice
2 dashes hot pepper sauce
Salt and pepper to taste

Nutritional information per serving:

Calories	100
Fat, gm.	3
Protein, gm.	3
Carbs, gm.	18
Cholesterol, mg.	0
Fiber, gm.	3.8

Save this for a refreshing treat on a hot summer day.

❖ Combine all ingredients in a large bowl. Cover tightly and refrigerate at least 8 hours. It will thicken slightly from the vegetable pectin. Serve cold.

Cod Chowder with Black Beans and Corn

I served this recipe on a winter Friday night when my brother-in-law did not want to eat meat. Use any firm mild white fish or even shrimp if you prefer. It is a good, hearty soup that is fairly spicy, with the green chilies, chili powder, and cumin.

❖ In a large saucepan or soup pot, heat oil. Add cod and cook over medium heat until lightly brown on all sides. Remove cod from pan, cut into bite-sized pieces, and set aside. Add onion to pan and cook until translucent. Add garlic and cook 1 minute. Add all remaining ingredients. Bring to a boil, reduce heat, and simmer for 10 to 15 minutes or until soup reaches desired consistency. When ready to serve, add reserved cod and cook until heated through.

Serves 4

2 tablespoons canola oil
½ pound cod fillet
1 cup chopped onion
2 cloves garlic, minced
1 can (14 ounces) diced tomatoes
1 can (15 ounces) cumin-seasoned black beans, drained
1 can (11 ounces) corn
1 can (4 ounces) diced green chilies
5 cups fat-free chicken broth
1 tablespoon lime juice
1 teaspoon chili powder
½ teaspoon cumin

Nutritional information per serving:

Calories	310
Fat, gm.	6
Protein, gm.	21
Carbs, gm.	43
Cholesterol, mg.	25
Fiber, gm.	10.7

Serves 8

1 tablespoon olive or canola oil
1 large onion, diced
1 tablespoon minced garlic
½ teaspoon ground cumin
¼ teaspoon cinnamon
¼ teaspoon turmeric
1 large sweet potato, peeled and diced
3 medium kohlrabies or turnips,
*   peeled and diced*
1 cup fresh green beans, cut in 1-inch pieces
6 cups fat-free chicken broth
1 can (15 ounces) garlic-seasoned diced
*   tomatoes*
1 can (15 ounces) great northern beans,
*   undrained*
1 pound cooked and crumbled Italian
*   sausage, optional*
Salt and pepper to taste

Topping:
½ cup fat-free sour cream
Dash hot pepper sauce, to taste
¼ cup sliced black olives

Nutritional information per serving (without the sausage):

Calories	260
Fat, gm.	2
Protein, gm.	15
Carbs, gm.	46
Cholesterol, mg.	2
Fiber, gm.	2.1

Country Vegetable Soup

Use the best of the fall vegetables to make this great soup. There is a blend of unusual seasonings in this recipe that gives it a fantastic flavor.

❖ In a large soup pot, heat oil. Add onion and cook until translucent. Add garlic, cumin, cinnamon, and turmeric. Cook 1 minute. Add sweet potato, kohlrabies, green beans, chicken broth, tomatoes, and great northern beans. Bring to a boil. Reduce heat and simmer until vegetables are tender and soup is desired consistency. Add Italian sausage if desired. Season with salt and pepper to taste. For the topping, mix sour cream and hot pepper sauce in a small bowl. Add a dollop to each bowl of soup. Garnish with olives.

Crab Bisque Florentine

Impress your guests with this elegant soup. It tastes rich and creamy but it is surprisingly low in calories.

❖ In a large saucepan, melt butter. Add onion and cook over medium heat until translucent. Add flour and cook, stirring constantly, for 2 minutes. Add broth and half-and-half. Bring to a boil, stirring constantly. Boil for 2 minutes or until mixture thickens. Add spinach and Worcestershire sauce. Cook 3 minutes. When ready to serve, add sherry and crab. Heat through. Season with salt and pepper. Thin with additional broth if desired.

Serves 6

3 tablespoons butter or margarine
1 medium onion, finely chopped
3 tablespoons flour
3 cups fat-free chicken broth
2 cups fat-free half-and-half
1 package (10 ounces) frozen chopped
  spinach, thawed and squeezed dry
1 teaspoon Worcestershire sauce
½ cup sherry
1 can (6 ounces) crabmeat
Salt and pepper to taste

Nutritional information per serving:

Calories	165
Fat, gm.	6
Protein, gm.	11
Carbs, gm.	16
Cholesterol, mg.	40
Fiber, gm.	1.7

Crab Potato Soup

Serves 6

1 medium onion, finely chopped
3 tablespoons butter or margarine
3 tablespoons flour
1 can (12 ounces) fat-free evaporated
  milk
5 cups fat-free chicken broth, divided
3 medium potatoes, peeled and diced
1 teaspoon dry mustard
2 teaspoons Worcestershire sauce
¼ teaspoon white pepper
½ pound crab or surimi seafood chunks
¼ cup dry sherry
¼ teaspoon Tabasco sauce
Salt and pepper to taste
⅓ cup chopped green onions to garnish

Nutritional information per serving:

Calories	185
Fat, gm.	6
Protein, gm.	12
Carbs, gm.	22
Cholesterol, mg.	30
Fiber, gm.	1.1

The texture is smooth and the taste is elegant. Make this with imitation crab, real crab, or other seafood of your choice.

❖ In heavy soup pan, cook onion in butter over medium heat. Stir in flour and cook until bubbly. Add evaporated milk and 4 cups of the broth. Bring to a boil, stirring constantly, until mixture thickens. Add potatoes, dry mustard, Worcestershire sauce, and white pepper. Bring to a boil, reduce heat, and cook 20 to 30 minutes or until potatoes are tender. Remove from heat. Using an immersion blender or a hand mixer, blend soup until smooth. Return to the stove and add crab and sherry. Heat through. Add Tabasco and salt and pepper to taste. If soup is too thick, add extra broth to thin. Serve in individual bowls and garnish with green onions.

Cream of Spinach Soup

Combine this soup with your favorite sandwich for a light supper. Serve it hot in the winter and chilled in the summer.

❖ In a large saucepan, melt butter. Add onion and cook until translucent. Add flour and stir over medium heat for 2 minutes. Add broth and evaporated milk. Bring to a boil, stirring constantly, until mixture thickens. Add nutmeg, thyme, and white pepper. Add spinach and bring to a boil. Reduce heat and simmer for 10 minutes. Using an immersion blender or a regular blender, blend soup until smooth. Adjust seasoning with salt and pepper. If soup is too thick, add additional milk or broth to thin. Serve in individual bowls with a dollop of sour cream.

Serves 4

2 tablespoons butter or margarine
1 medium onion, finely chopped
3 tablespoons flour
2 cups fat-free chicken broth
1 can (12 ounces) fat-free evaporated milk
½ teaspoon nutmeg
¼ teaspoon ground thyme
¼ teaspoon white pepper
1 package (10 ounces) frozen chopped spinach (thawed and drained)
Salt and pepper to taste
1 cup fat-free milk, to thin if needed
¼ cup fat-free sour cream

Nutritional Information per serving:

Calories	165
Fat, gm.	8
Protein, gm.	8
Carbs, gm.	15
Cholesterol, mg.	30
Fiber, gm.	1.8

Curried Lentil Soup

Serves 4

1 tablespoon canola oil
1 large onion, finely chopped
2 large leeks, white part only, finely
   chopped
2 large carrots, peeled and chopped
1 teaspoon garam masala curry or hot
   curry powder
½ teaspoon cumin
¼ teaspoon turmeric
Dash hot pepper sauce, optional
2 cloves garlic, minced
6 cups fat-free chicken broth, divided
8 ounces (1 cup) lentils, washed and
   sorted
Salt and pepper to taste

Nutritional information per serving:

Calories	290
Fat, gm.	4
Protein, gm.	20
Carbs, gm.	45
Cholesterol, mg.	0
Fiber, gm.	22

The lentils are seasoned with just the right amount curry, cumin, and turmeric to make this a very tasty meatless soup.

❖ In a large soup pot, heat oil. Add onion and leeks. Cook over medium heat until onion and leeks are translucent. Add carrots, curry powder, cumin, turmeric, and pepper sauce. Cook for about 5 minutes, stirring occasionally. Add garlic and cook 1 minute. Add 5 cups of chicken broth and lentils. Bring to a boil. Reduce heat, cover pot, and cook for about 35 minutes or until lentils are very tender. Using an immersion blender, puree part of the soup to desired consistency. If soup is too thick, add additional broth. Add salt and pepper to taste.

Gingered Carrot Soup

Serve this in place of a vegetable. What a good way to eat your carrots!

❖ In a large, heavy saucepan, heat oil. Cook bacon and onion until onion is translucent. Add carrots and garlic. Cook for 5 minutes, stirring occasionally. Add all remaining ingredients except salt, pepper, and sour cream. Bring to a boil, reduce heat, and simmer for 30 minutes or until vegetables are very tender. Use an immersion blender or place soup in batches in a food processor or blender. Blend until smooth. Return pureed soup to pot and heat through. (This may be prepared a day in advance. Refrigerate until ready to serve, then reheat to boiling.) Add salt and pepper to taste. Serve in individual bowls and garnish with a dollop of sour cream.

Serves 8

½ tablespoon canola oil
6 slices turkey bacon
1 cup chopped onion
4 cups baby carrots
2 teaspoons minced garlic
6 cups fat-free chicken broth
1 can (15 ounces) diced or stewed tomatoes
2 medium potatoes, peeled and diced
½ teaspoon white pepper
½ teaspoon ground ginger
¼ teaspoon cinnamon
½ teaspoon coriander, optional
Salt and pepper to taste
½ cup fat-free sour cream

Nutritional information per serving:

Calories	90
Fat, gm.	0.5
Protein, gm.	5
Carbs, gm.	16
Cholesterol, mg.	10
Fiber, gm.	2.7

Ham and Bean Soup for Two

Serves 2

6 ounces extra-lean ham, cut into
  small cubes
1 cup salsa, mild or medium to
  suit your taste
1 can (15 ounces) black beans, drained
  and rinsed
2 cups fat-free chicken broth
¼ cup chopped green onions for garnish

Nutritional information per serving:

Calories	340
Fat, gm.	10
Protein, gm.	29
Carbs, gm.	33
Cholesterol, mg.	33
Fiber, gm.	12.4

This has to be the easiest soup you will ever make. It is one of the few soup recipes that is actually designed to be made in a small enough quantity to serve just two people. Double the recipe for a family meal.

❖ In a medium saucepan, combine ham, salsa, beans, and broth. Bring to a boil over medium heat. Reduce heat and simmer for 10 to 15 minutes to blend flavors. Garnish with onions if desired.

———

Note: *If you would like to prepare this for 4 servings, another suggestion is to add an extra can of white or black beans and an extra cup of broth. My husband thought this soup would also be good with pieces of leftover bratwurst or Italian sausage.*

Hamburger Soup

If you like a soup full of vegetables and flavor, you will like this one.

❖ In a large soup pot, cook beef over medium-high heat until browned. Sprinkle with salt and pepper. Add onion and cook until translucent. Add all remaining ingredients except the extra salt and pepper. Bring to a boil, reduce heat, and simmer for about 45 minutes or longer if desired. If soup gets too thick, add extra broth or water. When ready to serve, season with salt and pepper to taste. Remove bay leaf before serving.

Serves 8

1 pound 95% lean ground beef
Salt and pepper
1 large onion, chopped
3 medium potatoes, peeled and diced
3 large carrots, peeled and diced
2 cups shredded cabbage
1 can (28 ounces) stewed tomatoes
¼ cup rice
½ teaspoon basil
¼ teaspoon ground thyme
1 bay leaf
6 cups fat-free beef or chicken broth
Salt and pepper to taste

Nutritional information per serving:

Calories	245
Fat, gm.	5
Protein, gm.	16
Carbs, gm.	34
Cholesterol, mg.	40
Fiber, gm.	4.0

Irish Stew with Stout Beer

Serves 4

1 tablespoon canola oil
1½ pounds beef top round, cubed
Salt and pepper
2 cups low-fat beef broth, divided
1 can (12 ounces) Stout beer or a dark
   beer of your choice*
1 tablespoon dry mustard
1 tablespoon Worcestershire sauce
2 tablespoons honey mustard**
3 large potatoes, peeled and diced
4 large carrots, peeled and diced
1 pound frozen pearl onions
Salt and pepper to taste
¼ cup flour, optional
1 cup frozen peas

Nutritional information per serving:

Calories	520
Fat, gm.	20
Protein, gm.	47
Carbs, gm.	39
Cholesterol, mg.	100
Fiber, gm.	6.1

Picture yourself in an old pub in Ireland when you enjoy this country-comfort meal. It can be put together quickly, but it needs some time in the oven or in a slow cooker to develop the flavor and tenderize the meat.

❖ Preheat oven to 325°F. Heat oil in a heavy Dutch oven. Add meat and brown on all sides. Sprinkle with salt and pepper. Remove from heat. Add broth, beer, dry mustard, Worcestershire sauce, honey mustard, potatoes, and carrots. Cover and bake for 1½ to 2 hours or until beef is very tender. Add onions 10 minutes before serving. Adjust seasoning with salt and pepper to taste. If a thicker sauce is desired, mix flour in ¾ cup cold water. Stir into stew and bring to a boil. Continue stirring until it thickens to desired consistency. Stir peas into the stew right before serving.

---

*The beer gives the broth a distinctive flavor. It tastes best with a smooth dark beer rather than a sharp or bitter beer. Tomato juice could be substituted for the beer if you prefer.
**The honey mustard is an important ingredient. If you do not have honey mustard on hand, use Dijon mustard and add a teaspoon or two of honey.

Jamaican Chicken Stew

When I tested this recipe, my husband gave this one a 9.5 out of 10. He likes meals with lots of flavor! This is a perfect recipe to cut in half for 2 or 3 servings.

❖ In a large nonstick skillet, heat oil. Add onion and cook over medium heat until translucent. Add chicken, sprinkle with salt and pepper, and cook until lightly browned. Add garlic, curry powder, thyme, and allspice. Cook for 2 minutes, stirring constantly. Add wine, capers, beans, and tomatoes. Bring to a boil, reduce heat, and simmer until sauce reaches desired consistency. Add chicken broth to thin if desired. Season with salt and pepper to taste. For a more intense flavor, add additional curry powder. Serve over cooked rice.

_____

Note: Start out with the amount of spices recommended in this recipe. If desired, add more curry powder. I think this tastes best with a hot curry powder. This recipe can also be made with pork or beef.

Serves 4

1 tablespoon canola oil
1 medium onion, chopped
4 boned and skinned chicken breasts, thinly sliced
Salt and pepper
2 teaspoons minced garlic
1 teaspoon hot curry powder
½ teaspoon dried thyme
¼ teaspoon allspice
½ cup dry red wine
2 tablespoons capers
2 cans (15 ounces each) black beans, drained and rinsed
1 can (28 ounces) seasoned diced tomatoes
½ cup fat-free chicken broth, optional
Salt and pepper to taste

Nutritional information per serving:

Calories	380
Fat, gm.	7
Protein, gm.	40
Carbs, gm.	40
Cholesterol, mg.	65
Fiber, gm.	14

Lazy Day White Bean Chili

Serves 8

1 can (29 ounces) seasoned diced
  tomatoes
2 cans (15 ounces each) great northern
  beans
2 cans (10 ounces each) chicken breast
  in water
4 cups fat-free chicken broth
1 teaspoon Italian seasoning
½ teaspoon cumin
1 can (4 ounces) green chilies, optional
2 tablespoons lime juice
Dash hot pepper sauce
Salt and pepper to taste

Nutritional information per serving:

Calories	200
Fat, gm.	2
Protein, gm.	23
Carbs, gm.	23
Cholesterol, mg.	45
Fiber, gm.	6.8

This truly is a soup anyone can make successfully. My friend Nancy Goyings shared this recipe with me. It is almost magical that opening a few cans and simmering the mixture together on the stove can make such a good-tasting soup. Keep these ingredients on hand and you can put together a lunch or supper in just minutes.

❖ In a large saucepan or soup pot, combine all ingredients except salt and pepper. Bring to a boil. Reduce heat and simmer for 30 minutes or until flavors are blended and soup reaches desired consistency. If soup gets too thick, add additional chicken broth or water to thin. Add salt and pepper to taste.

Mediterranean Beef Stew

Most stews are good, but this one is extra good. You will love the blend of flavors.

1. Heat oil in a large Dutch oven. Add beef and cook over medium-high heat until brown on all sides. Sprinkle meat with salt and pepper. Add onion to the pan and cook until translucent. Add mushrooms, carrots, and garlic. Cook for 5 minutes, stirring occasionally. Add broth to deglaze the pan. Add thyme, bay leaf, tomatoes, and wine. Bring to a boil. Reduce heat, cover pan, and simmer for 1 to 1½ hours or until meat is very tender. Before serving, discard bay leaf and add olives. In a shaker or jar, mix flour in ¾ cup water. Shake to mix. Pour flour mixture slowly into stew as it boils. Stir constantly. Add additional flour mixture until stew reaches desired consistency.

2. Serve with cooked noodles or mashed potatoes.

_____

Note: *This recipe should be doubled for 6 to 8 servings.*

Serves 4

1 tablespoon canola oil
1 pound lean beef, cubed
Salt and pepper
1 medium onion, sliced
½ pound sliced mushrooms
2 cups baby carrots
1 teaspoon minced garlic
2 cups fat-free beef broth
½ teaspoon thyme
1 bay leaf
1 can (15 ounces) seasoned stewed or
    diced tomatoes
1 cup dry red wine
½ cup pitted black olives, optional
¼ cup flour

Nutritional information per serving:

Calories	375
Fat, gm.	12
Protein, gm.	35
Carbs, gm.	32
Cholesterol, mg.	65
Fiber, gm.	2.6

Mexican Chicken Chili

Serves 4

¾ pound cooked chicken, boneless dark
* meat*
6 cups fat-free chicken broth
1½ cups chopped carrots
½ cup brown or white rice
1 cup salsa
1 cup frozen or canned corn
1 can (15 ounces) great northern beans,
* undrained*
½ teaspoon cumin
salt and pepper, to taste

Nutritional information per serving:

Calories	365
Fat, gm.	7
Protein, gm.	28
Carbs, gm.	47
Cholesterol, mg.	70
Fiber, gm.	8.7

This is a good way to get two meals from a purchased rotisserie chicken. Cut off the good breast meat and save it for another meal. Use all the other meat on the chicken for this zesty chili. The soup is given more body with the pureed carrots and there is extra flavor from the salsa.

❖ Purchase a rotisserie chicken. Remove and discard skin. Cut off the breast meat and save it for another meal. Pick off all remaining good meat and place it in a bowl. Set it aside. Discard bones. In a soup pot, combine broth and carrots. Cook until carrots are tender. Using a handheld immersion blender, puree carrots. Add all remaining ingredients and reserved chicken. Bring to a boil, reduce heat, and simmer for 30 to 45 minutes or until rice is tender. Add salt and pepper to taste

Note: *It is not necessary to use a rotisserie chicken for this recipe. Cook any raw chicken, or use purchased cooked chicken or leftover chicken.*

Mexican Pork Chili

Using a very tender cut of meat such as pork tenderloin makes this a fast-cooking chili. Combine the ingredients and simmer just long enough to blend the flavors.

❖ Cut pork into 1-inch cubes. Sprinkle with salt and pepper. In a large heavy skillet, heat oil over medium-high heat. Add pork and brown on all sides. Reduce heat to medium. Add onion and cook until translucent. Add garlic and cook 1 minute. Add chili powder, cumin, cinnamon, tomatoes, kidney beans, and chicken broth. Bring to a boil. Reduce heat, cover, and simmer for 30 minutes. Adjust seasoning with hot pepper sauce and extra salt and pepper if desired. Serve in individual bowls and top with green onions and cheese.

Serves 6

1½ pounds pork tenderloin
Salt and pepper, divided
1 tablespoon canola oil
1 large onion, chopped
2 teaspoons minced garlic
2 teaspoons chili powder
½ teaspoon cumin
¼ teaspoon cinnamon
1 can (28 ounces) diced tomatoes with green chilies
2 cans (15 ounces each) kidney beans, partially drained
1½ cups fat-free chicken broth
Dash hot pepper sauce
2 green onions, chopped
¾ cup (3 ounces) shredded mozzarella cheese

Nutritional Information per serving:

Calories	370
Fat, gm.	10
Protein, gm.	39
Carbs, gm.	31
Cholesterol, mg.	85
Fiber, gm.	11.4

Minestrone-Style Stew

Serves 6

1 tablespoon canola oil
2 pounds round steak, cut into
  1-inch cubes
Salt and pepper
1 tablespoon Italian seasoning
1 large onion, chopped
6 large carrots, peeled and diced (about
  4 cups)
1 teaspoon minced garlic
4 cups fat-free beef broth
1 can (28 ounces) Italian-seasoned diced
  tomatoes
1 cup pasta shells
1-pound package frozen mixed vegetables
½ cup grated Parmesan cheese, optional

Nutritional information per serving:

Calories	480
Fat, gm.	21
Protein, gm.	41
Carbs, gm.	32
Cholesterol, mg.	90
Fiber, gm.	6.0

This is a real comfort-food meal with wonderful flavor. It is the kind of meal that everyone loves.

❖ Preheat oven to 325°F. In a large Dutch oven, heat oil. Add meat and cook over medium-high heat until brown on all sides. Sprinkle with salt, pepper, and Italian seasoning. Add onion and carrots. Cook until onions are translucent. Add garlic, broth, and tomatoes. Bring to a boil. Remove from heat and cover pan. Place in oven and bake for 50 to 90 minutes or until meat is very tender. Check occasionally and add additional broth or water if it gets too dry. Add the pasta and mixed vegetables 15 minutes before ready to serve. Boil gently until pasta and vegetables are tender. Serve in individual bowls and sprinkle each with Parmesan cheese if desired.

Note: *This can also be cooked on the stove top instead of using the oven.*

Orange and Yellow Pepper Soup

There are significant health benefits to eating peppers, and this recipe will make it enjoyable to eat them. I made this recipe for a cooking class featuring soups, and everyone liked it.

❖ In a large, heavy saucepan, heat oil. Add onion and cook until translucent. Add peppers and carrot. Cook until tender. Add garlic and cook 1 minute. Add potatoes and broth. Bring to a boil. Reduce heat, cover, and simmer for 30 to 40 minutes or until vegetables are tender. Place mixture into food processor and process until smooth or use an immersion blender and process until the desired consistency. Add extra broth if thinner consistency is desired. Add white pepper. Add salt, pepper, and Tabasco to taste. Serve in individual soup bowls and garnish with cilantro or chives.

Serves 6

1 tablespoon olive oil
1 large onion, diced
2 medium orange peppers, diced
2 medium yellow peppers, diced
1 large carrot, peeled and diced
2 cloves garlic, minced
2 large potatoes, peeled and diced
4 cups fat-free chicken broth
¼ teaspoon white pepper
Salt and pepper to taste
Dash Tabasco sauce, optional
¼ cup chopped cilantro or chives for garnish

Nutritional information per serving:

Calories	145
Fat, gm.	3
Protein, gm.	4
Carbs, gm.	27
Cholesterol, mg.	0
Fiber, gm.	4.2

Oriental Beef and Noodle Soup

Serves 4

1 tablespoon canola oil
¾ pound beef tenderloin, cut into thin
    strips
1 teaspoon sesame oil
2 leeks, white part only, thinly sliced
1 medium red pepper, thinly sliced
6 cups fat-free beef broth
3 ounces (1½ cups) egg noodles
1 cup canned baby corn, optional
3 cups fresh broccoli florets
2 tablespoons soy sauce
Dash hot chili sauce
Salt and pepper to taste

Nutritional information per serving:

Calories	460
Fat, gm.	20
Protein, gm.	39
Carbs, gm.	29
Cholesterol, mg.	80
Fiber, gm.	5.0

Thinly sliced beef tenderloin and oriental-style vegetables make this a special soup that can be made very quickly.

❖ In a large soup pot, heat oil. Add beef and cook over medium-high heat until brown. Add sesame oil, leeks, and red pepper. Cook until tender. Add broth and noodles. Bring to a boil. Cover pan, reduce heat, and boil gently until noodles are tender. When ready to serve, add corn, broccoli, soy sauce, and chili sauce. Cook 5 minutes or just until broccoli is tender. Add salt and pepper to taste.

Note: *In place of the corn and broccoli, you might use a package of frozen oriental vegetable mix.*

Pork and Butternut Squash Stew

This is a hearty-flavored dish seasoned with thyme and rosemary. I love the squash and pork cooked together with beer. When fall arrives, this is a recipe you will really enjoy.

1. Combine flour, salt, pepper, and thyme in a plastic bag. Add pork cubes. Close bag and shake until meat is coated. Set aside. In a large skillet or cooking pan, heat 1 tablespoon oil. Add half of the pork cubes and cook over medium-high heat until brown. Remove from skillet and add remaining pork to brown. Add additional oil as needed. Remove pork and set aside. Add onion to skillet and cook until translucent. Add beer and stir to deglaze the pan. Add squash and rosemary. Cover, and gently boil for 25 to 35 minutes or until squash is tender. Return pork to the skillet and heat through. If a thicker broth is desired, mix cornstarch in ¼ cup cold water. Add cornstarch mixture to pan. Stir constantly until mixture thickens. Add salt and pepper to taste. Garnish with parsley.

2. Serve with cooked noodles or mashed potatoes.

Serves 6

1/3 cup flour
1 teaspoon salt
½ teaspoon pepper
1 teaspoon thyme
2 pounds lean pork loin, cut into 1-inch cubes
2 tablespoons canola oil, divided
1 large onion, diced
1 can (12 ounces) beer
4 cups butternut squash, peeled and cubed
1 teaspoon crushed rosemary
1 tablespoon cornstarch, optional
Salt and pepper to taste
¼ cup chopped fresh parsley

Nutritional information per serving:

Calories	290
Fat, gm.	11
Protein, gm.	28
Carbs, gm.	19
Cholesterol, mg.	70
Fiber, gm.	0.6

Posole

Hominy resembles corn but it is softer in texture. It may be unfamiliar to many people but it is a traditional ingredient in this tasty Mexican soup.

Serves 4

1 tablespoon canola oil
1 medium onion, chopped
½ teaspoon cumin
½ teaspoon oregano
1 skinless, boneless chicken breast,
    cut into 1-inch cubes
2 teaspoons minced garlic
1 can (4 ounces) chopped green chilies
1 can (15 ounces) hominy
1 can (15 ounces) seasoned petite diced
    tomatoes
2 cups fat-free chicken broth

Nutritional information per serving:

Calories	185
Fat, gm.	5
Protein, gm.	12
Carbs, gm.	21
Cholesterol, mg.	25
Fiber, gm.	5.4

❖ In a medium saucepan or soup pot, heat oil. Add onion, cumin, and oregano and cook over medium heat until translucent. Add chicken and cook until brown. Add garlic and green chilies and cook 1 minute. Add remaining ingredients. Bring to a boil, reduce heat, and simmer for 10 to 30 minutes or until it reaches desired consistency.

Santa Fe Soup

This is sure to be a family favorite, and it is very easy to make.

❖ In a large, heavy skillet, cook ground beef until browned. Add all remaining ingredients. Stir to blend. Bring to a boil, reduce heat, and simmer for 10 to 20 minutes or until it reaches desired consistency. Add extra water to thin if needed. If desired, serve in individual bowls topped with shredded cheese and a dollop of sour cream. Pass a bowl of corn chips on the side.

Serves 4

1 pound extra-lean ground beef
1 can (15 ounces) black beans, drained and rinsed
1 can (28 ounces) seasoned diced tomatoes
1 can (11 ounces) corn, drained
1 package (1.25 ounces) taco seasoning mix
1 package (1 ounce) dry ranch salad dressing mix
⅔ cup water

Optional Topping:
½ cup shredded cheese
¼ cup fat-free sour cream

Nutritional information per serving:

Calories	485
Fat, gm.	21
Protein, gm.	31
Carbs, gm.	44
Cholesterol, mg.	80
Fiber, gm.	10

Scallop, Mushroom, and Potato Soup

Serves 8

1 tablespoon olive oil
1 large onion, chopped
4 medium potatoes, peeled and chopped
3 large carrots, peeled and thinly sliced
6 cups fat-free chicken broth
¼ teaspoon ground thyme
1 tablespoon butter or margarine
½ pound mushrooms, sliced
1½ pounds sea scallops, cut in half
1 cup white wine
*1 can (12 ounces) fat-free evaporated
  milk*
Salt and pepper to taste

Nutritional information per serving:

Calories	195
Fat, gm.	4
Protein, gm.	20
Carbs, gm.	20
Cholesterol, mg.	30
Fiber, gm.	2.0

This soup is elegant yet full of comfort-food flavor. It is creamy and delicious, with a rich taste, but it is very low in fat. If scallops are unavailable or very expensive, substitute cooked shrimp for part or all of the scallops.

❖ In a large soup pot, heat oil. Add onion and cook until translucent. Add potatoes, carrots, chicken broth, and thyme. Bring to a boil, cover, and reduce heat. Boil gently for 30 minutes or until potatoes are very tender. While vegetables are cooking, melt butter in a medium skillet. Add mushrooms and cook over medium heat until tender. Add scallops and wine. Cook for 3 to 5 minutes or until scallops are opaque. Remove from heat and set aside. When vegetables are tender in soup pot, use an immersion blender and blend just until about half of the vegetables are pureed or until the soup is creamy in texture. (The pureed vegetables thicken the soup.) Pour scallop mixture and evaporate milk into soup pot. Gently heat through. Add salt and pepper to taste.

Shrimp Basil Soup

Impress your family and friends with this super easy, flavorful soup. This is one of my favorite recipes.

❖ In a large saucepan or soup pot, heat oil. Add onion and carrots. Cook until onion is translucent. Add garlic and cook 1 minute. Add parsley, basil, and chicken broth. Bring to a boil. Add pasta shells and boil gently until pasta is al dente. Add shrimp, half-and-half, and sherry. Heat through. Add salt and pepper to taste. Just before serving, add spinach if desired. Heat while stirring just until spinach is wilted.

Serves 4

1 tablespoon olive oil
1 medium onion, thinly sliced
3 large carrots, finely chopped
2 teaspoons minced garlic
¼ cup chopped fresh parsley
2 tablespoons fresh or 2 teaspoons dry basil
6 cups fat-free chicken broth
3 ounces (1 cup) pasta shells
1 pound shrimp, cooked and peeled, tails removed
¾ cup fat-free half-and-half
¼ cup dry sherry
Salt and freshly ground pepper to taste
2 cups fresh baby spinach leaves, optional

Nutritional information per serving:

Calories	295
Fat, gm.	5
Protein, gm.	30
Carbs, gm.	32
Cholesterol, mg.	175
Fiber, gm.	2.7

Southwestern Chili

Serves 6

1 pound extra-lean ground beef
Salt and pepper
1 large onion, finely chopped
1 can (28 ounces) seasoned diced
*   tomatoes*
1 can (15 ounces) fat-free refried beans
2 cups water
2 teaspoons chili powder
1 teaspoon cumin
1 can (15 ounces) black beans, drained
1 can (4 ounces) chopped green chilies
1 teaspoon sugar or molasses, optional

Nutritional information per serving:

Calories	325
Fat, gm.	14
Protein, gm.	23
Carbs, gm.	27
Cholesterol, mg.	50
Fiber, gm.	9

This is a full-flavored chili with a rich, creamy consistency. The refried beans are the secret ingredient.

❖ In a large, heavy saucepan, brown meat. Stir meat as it cooks to break up into small pieces. Sprinkle with salt and pepper. Add onion and cook until translucent. Add all remaining ingredients except sugar. Bring to a boil. Reduce heat and simmer until flavors blend and it reaches the desired consistency. Add extra water if needed. Add sugar if desired.

Spicy Asian Chicken Noodle Soup

The combination of unique ingredients including chicken, ginger, curry, peanuts, and coconut make this a soup to remember.

❖ In a medium saucepan, cook noodles in boiling water until al dente. Drain well and set aside. In a large soup pot, heat oil. Add chicken and cook over medium heat until browned. Add onions, mushrooms, red pepper, garlic, and gingerroot. Cook until onions and mushrooms are tender. Add broth, coconut milk, curry powder, peanut butter, and soy sauce. Bring to a boil. Reduce heat and simmer for 10 minutes. Just before serving, add peas and reserved noodles. Heat through. Add salt, pepper, and hot sauce to taste. If a thinner soup is desired, add additional chicken broth.

Serves 6

4 ounces (2½ cups) egg noodles
1 tablespoon canola oil
1 pound boned and skinned chicken
  breast, cut into thin strips
½ cup chopped green onions
1 pound sliced mushrooms
1 medium red pepper, chopped
2 teaspoons minced garlic
1 tablespoon grated fresh gingerroot
6 cups fat-free chicken broth
1 cup light coconut milk
1 teaspoon hot curry powder
3 tablespoons smooth peanut butter
3 tablespoons soy sauce
1 cup frozen green peas
Salt and pepper to taste
Hot pepper sauce to taste

Nutritional information per serving:

Calories	310
Fat, gm.	11
Protein, gm.	26
Carbs, gm.	27
Cholesterol, mg.	60
Fiber, gm.	3.8

Split Pea Soup in an Hour

Serves 8

1 pound (2½ cups) dry green split peas
6 cups fat-free chicken broth
2 large potatoes, peeled and diced
1 tablespoon canola oil
1 large onion, chopped
3 large carrots, peeled and diced
3 teaspoons minced garlic
¼ teaspoon thyme
1 pound lean ham, diced
Water to thin
Salt and pepper to taste

Nutritional information per serving:

Calories	310
Fat, gm.	4
Protein, gm.	27
Carbs, gm.	50
Cholesterol, mg.	25
Fiber, gm.	15

Fill your kitchen with the fantastic aroma of a homemade soup in just an hour!

❖ Wash and sort split peas. Combine peas and chicken broth in large soup pot. Bring to a boil. Reduce heat and simmer for 30 minutes. Add potatoes, cover, and continue to simmer for an additional 20 to 30 minutes or until potatoes are very tender. While peas are cooking, heat oil in medium skillet. Add onion and cook until translucent. Add carrots, garlic, and thyme and cook until tender. Remove from heat and set aside. When peas and potatoes are done, add onion-and-carrot mixture to the pot. Add ham. Heat through and continue to simmer on very low heat until ready to serve. If soup gets too thick, add water to thin to desired consistency. Add salt and pepper to taste.

_____

Note: *For a smoother soup, use an immersion blender to blend the peas and potatoes before adding the vegetables and ham.*

Squash Bisque with Rum

My husband liked this soup so much that he suggested I change the serving size to 2 instead of 4 so he could eat more. If this soup is your main course, double the recipe for meal size servings.

❖ Peel butternut squash. Cut open and discard seeds. Cut squash into small cubes. Set aside. In a large saucepan, heat oil. Add leek and cook until tender. Add squash cubes, 3 cups of broth, thyme, and white pepper. Bring to a boil. Cover pan, reduce heat, and simmer for 20 to 30 minutes or until squash is very tender. Remove from stove. Using an immersion blender, blend soup until smooth. Return to the stove and add half-and-half. Add additional broth if needed to thin to desired consistency. Heat through. When ready to serve, add rum and adjust seasoning with salt and pepper to taste.

---

*This recipe can be made even easier using frozen mashed squash.

Serves 4

*1 pound (4 cups cubed) butternut squash**
1 tablespoon olive oil
1 large leek, white part only, thinly sliced
4 cups fat-free chicken broth, divided
¼ teaspoon ground thyme
⅛ teaspoon white pepper
½ cup fat-free half-and-half
2 tablespoons rum
Salt and pepper to taste

Nutritional information per serving:

Calories	110
Fat, gm.	3
Protein, gm.	3
Carbs, gm.	17
Cholesterol, mg.	0
Fiber, gm.	0.3

Tortellini Soup

Serves 4

1 tablespoon canola oil
1 boned and skinned chicken breast half,
cubed
1 medium onion, chopped
2 large carrots, peeled and chopped
2 stalks celery, diced
½ teaspoon cumin
½ teaspoon Chinese five-spice powder
1 can (28 ounces) seasoned diced tomatoes
4 cups fat-free chicken broth
3 cups tomato-vegetable juice
1 package (10 ounces) frozen spinach,
thawed and drained
3 ounces (¾ cup) dried tortellini

Nutritional information per serving:

Calories	275
Fat, gm.	6
Protein, gm.	15
Carbs, gm.	40
Cholesterol, mg.	25
Fiber, gm.	8.2

Try this when you are in the mood for something light.

❖ In a large, heavy soup pot, heat oil. Add chicken and cook over medium-high heat until brown on all sides. Remove chicken from pan and set aside. Add onion and cook until translucent. Add carrots, celery, cumin, and Chinese five-spice powder. Cook for 5 minutes, stirring occasionally. Add reserved chicken, tomatoes, broth, and vegetable juice. Bring to a boil, reduce heat, and simmer for 10 minutes to blend flavors. Add spinach and tortellini. Boil gently for 20 minutes or just until tortellini are tender.

CHAPTER 2
Salads

Bacon, Swiss, and Grape Salad

Beet and Orange Salad with Blue Cheese and Walnuts

Blueberry, Walnut, and Wild Rice Chicken Salad

Broccoli, Roasted Red Peppers, and Artichoke Salad

Cherry Chicken Salad

Colorful Bean and Cheddar Salad

Crunchy Cole Slaw with Cashews

Festive Apple Pear Salad

Green Beans with Gorgonzola

Make Ahead Coleslaw

Mexican Macaroni Salad

Moroccan Rice Salad with Feta

Peanut Raisin Slaw

Quinoa, Pepper, and Peanut Salad

Raspberry Pecan Spinach Salad

Red Cabbage and Apple Salad

Salmon Mousse

South of the Border Bean and Corn Salad

Spinach Salad with Bacon Dressing

Spinach Salad with Honey Cranberry Dressing

Spinach Salad with Oranges and Pomegranates

Spinach, Kiwi, and Strawberry Salad with Poppy Seed Dressing

Strawberry and Spinach Salad with Apple Mustard Dressing

Swiss Apple Grape Salad

Tortellini and Shrimp Salad

Tuscan Pasta Salad with Artichokes and Sun Dried Tomatoes

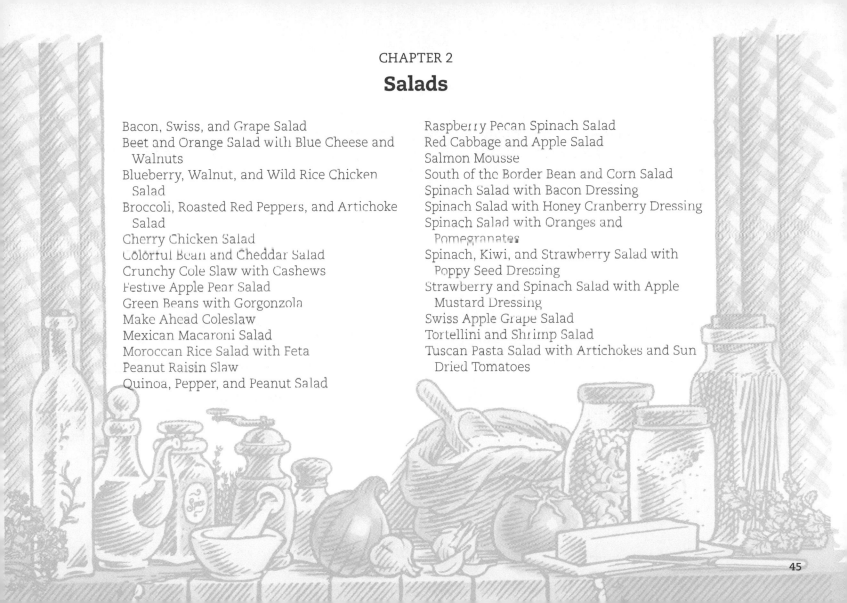

Salad Preparation Tips

Lettuce, spinach, greens, and herbs should be thoroughly washed and then spun dry before using them in a recipe. Greens for salads should be crisped in the refrigerator.

Spinach salads are best made with baby spinach. If baby spinach is not available, remove any long stems from mature spinach and tear leaves into bite-sized pieces. Try to be creative and use spinach wherever you can. It is full of important nutrients, including vitamin A, vitamin C, lutein, iron, and trace minerals.

Some salad recipes call for cooked, diced bacon. It is helpful to keep a clean pair of scissors to use in the kitchen. It works well to use the scissors to cut the raw bacon in small pieces directly into the frying pan.

Fresh tomatoes should never be refrigerated because the cold temperature causes their flesh to become mealy and lose flavor. Store them at room temperature.

To peel peaches or tomatoes easily, cut a small X in the bottom. Drop the fruit into a pot of boiling water for 10 to 20 seconds. Remove the fruit with a slotted spoon and immediately transfer it to ice water to stop the cooking. When cool, gently pinch the cut on the bottom of the fruit. The peel should slip right off. Trim off any stubborn peel with a knife.

Olive oil is the oil of choice for most salads. It contains the highest proportion of monounsaturated fat of all vegetable oils, and it is rich in phytochemicals, which act as potent antioxidants. Studies have shown that diets rich in olive oil decrease the risk of heart disease and certain cancers. Although olive oil has health benefits, it is still a fat, with 120 calories per tablespoon.

Olive oils vary in taste and color according to the variety of olive used, the region where the olives were grown, and the processing.

- **Extra-virgin olive oil** contains oil from the first cold pressing of the olive without the use of heat or chemicals. It is the most expensive and has the most distinctive taste. Because it has a low smoking temperature, it is not suitable for frying. Use it in your salads and other cold foods.

- **100% olive oil** is usually expressed from olives through chemical extraction. It is less flavorful and less expensive. It has a higher smoking temperature and can be used for frying.

- **Extra-light olive oil** refers to the color and flavor, not the calories. It also has a higher smoking temperature and can be used in frying and in foods where you do not want an olive oil taste. This oil is sold only in the United States to accommodate Americans' taste preferences.

Olive oil keeps for up to two years if stored in a tightly sealed container and kept away from light and heat. You can store it in the refrigerator, but I prefer not to because the oil turns cloudy and partially hardens. That will not affect the oil's flavor or quality, however, and it does clear up when brought to room temperature.

Avocados are high in fat, but it is the good fat—mainly monounsaturated. If you buy an avocado that is not fully ripe, it will ripen more quickly if you put it in a brown paper bag and keep it at room temperature.

Bacon, Swiss, and Grape Salad

Serves 6

6 cups fresh baby spinach
4 ounces Swiss cheese, cut in matchstick
  strips
2 cups seedless grapes
6 slices cooked bacon, diced

Dressing:
¼ cup cider vinegar
3 tablespoons olive oil
2 teaspoons Dijon mustard
1 tablespoon brown sugar
1 teaspoon seasoned salt*
¼ teaspoon black pepper
2 tablespoons minced onion

Nutritional information per serving:

Calories	220
Fat, gm.	15
Protein, gm.	9
Carbs, gm.	13
Cholesterol, mg.	25
Fiber, gm.	2.0

This sound great and it is great!

❖ In a large salad bowl, combine spinach, cheese, grapes, and bacon. In a small food processor, combine all dressing ingredients. Process until well blended. Pour dressing into salad bowl and toss to mix.

———

*One brand of seasoned salt is Lawry's.

Beet and Orange Salad with Blue Cheese and Walnuts

My friend Mary created this recipe with her favorite salad ingredients. If you like beets, this is an absolute winner. Combine them with oranges, blue cheese, and walnuts with a creamy red wine vinegar and blue cheese dressing. The salad can even be prepared ahead of time and refrigerated until ready to serve. It is awesome!

❖ Arrange salad greens on 4 individual salad plates. Cut each piece of beet into ¼-inch matchstick-style slices and place over lettuce. Arrange oranges on top. Reserve 1 tablespoon blue cheese for the dressing and set aside. Sprinkle remaining blue cheese and walnuts on top of the salad. In a small jar, combine all dressing ingredients. Mix until smooth with a spoon or use a small blender. Drizzle dressing over salad.

Serves 4

4 cups mixed greens
1 can (15 ounces) sliced beets
½ cup mandarin oranges
2 ounces crumbled blue cheese, divided
¼ cup chopped walnuts

Dressing:
2 tablespoons olive oil
1 tablespoon orange juice
1 tablespoon red wine vinegar
1 teaspoon sugar
1 tablespoon fat-free sour cream
1 tablespoon blue cheese
Salt and pepper to taste

Nutritional information per serving:

Calories	190
Fat, gm.	12
Protein, gm.	6
Carbs, gm.	14
Cholesterol, mg.	10
Fiber, gm.	2.7

Serves 8

2 cups cooked wild rice
2 cups cooked basmati rice or long-grain
  white rice
1 pound cooked chicken breast, cut into
  bite-sized pieces
2 cups fresh blueberries or seedless red
  grapes
1 can (20 ounces) pineapple tidbits,
  drained
2 medium oranges, peeled and sectioned
1 cup chopped walnuts

Dressing:
12 ounces fat-free vanilla yogurt
½ cup low-fat mayonnaise
2 tablespoons lemon juice
½ teaspoon allspice
½ teaspoon cinnamon
¼ teaspoon nutmeg
½ teaspoon salt
1 tablespoon orange zest

Nutritional information per serving:

Calories	350
Fat, gm.	11
Protein, gm.	20
Carbs, gm.	43
Cholesterol, mg.	40
Fiber, gm.	2.9

Blueberry, Walnut, and Wild Rice Chicken Salad

Enjoy this great salad with different colors and textures and a great blend of flavors for a special luncheon party or a light supper. This recipe makes enough for about 8 servings, but it keeps well for days in the refrigerator. In fact, it is even better after a day or two, when the flavors have blended.

❖ In a large bowl, combine wild rice, basmati rice, chicken pieces, blueberries, pineapple tidbits, orange sections, and walnuts. In a small bowl, combine all dressing ingredients. Add dressing to rice mixture and stir gently to mix well. Adjust seasoning with extra salt if desired.

Note: *Cook the rice ahead of time and cool it before combining with the other ingredients. One-half cup of raw wild rice will make 2 cups of cooked rice. One cup of raw basmati rice will make 2 cups of cooked rice. The chicken may be omitted if desired. This salad is good with or without the chicken.*

Broccoli, Roasted Red Peppers, and Artichoke Salad

Make dinnertime even easier by putting this salad together ahead of time.

❖ In a large resealable plastic bag, combine broccoli, red pepper, and artichoke hearts. In a small jar, combine dressing ingredients. Shake to mix. Pour over vegetables and toss to mix. Refrigerate for several hours before serving.

------

*To blanch the broccoli, plunge the florets into a large pan of boiling water for 30 to 45 seconds. Drain and cool rapidly under cold running water. Drain well and pat dry.

Serves 4

4 cups broccoli florets, blanched*
1 large roasted red pepper, thinly sliced
1 can (14 ounces) quartered artichoke
   hearts

Dressing:
½ cup fat-free Italian Parmesan salad
   dressing
¼ cup balsamic vinegar
1 tablespoon Dijon mustard
2 tablespoons honey

Nutritional information per serving:

Calories	155
Fat, gm.	0
Protein, gm.	7
Carbs, gm.	33
Cholesterol, mg.	0
Fiber, gm.	10.4

Cherry Chicken Salad

Serves 4

8 ounces cooked chicken, white meat
1 cup dried cherries
3 stalks celery, diced
2 large Granny Smith apples,
  cored and diced
1 cup chopped walnuts or pecans

Dressing:
¾ cup low-fat mayonnaise
¾ cup fat-free sour cream
4 tablespoons raspberry vinegar
4 teaspoons sugar

Nutritional information per serving:

Calories	360
Fat, gm.	20
Protein, gm.	10
Carbs, gm.	35
Cholesterol, mg.	25
Fiber, gm.	1.9

Choose this recipe when you need an easy but tasty luncheon salad. I love the combination of chicken with crunchy apples and celery, flavorful dried cherries, and walnuts. The dressing pulls it all together with a subtle hint of raspberry.

❖ Cut chicken into bite-sized pieces. In a large bowl, combine chicken, cherries, celery, apples, and nuts. In a small bowl, combine mayonnaise, sour cream, vinegar, and sugar. Spoon dressing into chicken mixture. Toss gently to blend.

Colorful Bean and Cheddar Salad

Make this ahead and keep it on hand for a quick meatless lunch or light supper. It can also be served in smaller portions for a salad or side dish. You will love the way it looks on your table!

❖ In a large bowl, combine beans, corn, onion, pepper, cheese, and parsley. In a small jar, combine all dressing ingredients. Pour dressing into bean mixture and stir to blend. Cover and refrigerate until ready to serve.

Note: Use any cheese of your choice. You can save calories by choosing a lower-fat cheese.

Serves 6 (1-cup servings)

2 cans (15 ounces each) black beans, drained and rinsed
1 can (11 ounces) corn, drained
½ small red onion, finely diced
1 large red pepper, finely chopped
6 ounces Cheddar cheese, cut into ¼-inch cubes
½ cup chopped parsley

Dressing:
2 tablespoons olive oil
2 tablespoons lime juice
½ teaspoon ground cumin
⅛ teaspoon black pepper
¼ teaspoon salt

Nutritional information per serving:

Calories	310
Fat, gm.	15
Protein, gm.	16
Carbs, gm.	28
Cholesterol, mg.	30
Fiber, gm.	9.8

Crunchy Cole Slaw with Cashews

Serves 12

1 bag (16 ounces) shredded cabbage
1 package (3 ounces) chicken-flavor ramen noodles, crumbled
6 green onions, thinly sliced
1 cup cashews, peanuts, or almonds

Dressing:
½ cup water
1 teaspoon cornstarch
½ cup sugar
⅓ cup white vinegar
¼ cup olive oil
Flavoring packet from ramen noodles*

Nutritional information per serving:

Calories	205
Fat, gm.	11
Protein, gm.	5
Carbs, gm.	22
Cholesterol, mg.	0
Fiber, gm.	4.1

This is an old recipe adapted to make it lower in calories and fat. The original recipe had twice the amount of fat. The trick is to replace some of the fat with water thickened with cornstarch. It works!

❖ In a large bowl, combine cabbage, ramen noodles, onions, and nuts. Set aside. In a small saucepan, combine water and cornstarch. Bring mixture to a rolling boil, stirring constantly. Continue to boil 1 to 2 minutes. Add sugar and stir until dissolved. Remove from heat. Add vinegar, oil, and flavoring packet. Stir to mix. Add dressing to cabbage mixture and stir until well mixed. Refrigerate until ready to serve.

_____

*I tested this recipe with and without the flavoring packet added to the dressing. It does taste better with the flavoring packet added, but if you need to watch your sodium, you can omit the flavoring packet.

Festive Apple Pear Salad

This is a light, refreshing salad that goes well with turkey or ham. It can be made the day before serving.

❖ In a small cup, mix lemon juice and corn syrup. Set aside. In a large bowl, combine apples and pears. Add lemon juice mixture and stir to mix well. Add cranberries, cabbage, and yogurt. Stir to mix. Cover and refrigerate until ready to serve. (The lemon juice and yogurt prevent the fruit from turning brown.) Add walnuts immediately before serving.

Serves 10

3 tablespoons fresh lemon juice
2 tablespoons corn syrup, Splenda, or sugar
4 large red apples, cored and diced
2 large fresh pears, cored and diced
1 cup dried orange-flavored cranberries
2 cups shredded cabbage
6 ounces fat free lemon flavored yogurt
½ cup chopped walnuts, optional

Nutritional information per serving:

Calories	100
Fat, gm.	0
Protein, gm.	1
Carbs, gm.	24
Cholesterol, mg.	0
Fiber, gm.	3.4

Green Beans with Gorgonzola

Serves 4

1½ pounds fresh green beans,
  ends snipped
½ cup diced red onion
¼ cup fat-free Italian salad dressing
½ cup crumbled Gorgonzola or
  blue cheese
Salt and pepper to taste

Nutritional information per serving:

Calories	110
Fat, gm.	4
Protein, gm.	6
Carbs, gm.	13
Cholesterol, mg.	10
Fiber, gm.	5.4

When green beans are in season, give them some extra zest with this dressing.

❖ In a large saucepan, cook beans and onion in salted water until tender-crisp. Drain and cool quickly under cold running water. Drain well. Add dressing and cheese. Toss to mix. Add salt and pepper to taste.

Make Ahead Coleslaw

This is a low-calorie adaptation of an old recipe that most of us remember from our childhood. Cabbage is a very healthy vegetable from the cruciferous family.

❖ In a large bowl, combine shredded cabbage mix, green pepper, red pepper, and onion. Spoon into a large resealable bag. In a small saucepan, combine all dressing ingredients. Bring to a boil and remove from heat. Pour hot dressing into the bag over salad. Toss to mix well. Refrigerate several hours before serving. It also keeps well for days in the refrigerator.

Serves 6

1 bag (16 ounces; 8 cups) shredded cabbage slaw mix
½ medium green pepper, finely chopped
½ medium red pepper, finely chopped
1 medium sweet onion, finely chopped

Dressing:
½ cup granular Splenda or sugar
½ teaspoon salt
½ teaspoon dry mustard
½ teaspoon celery seed or celery salt
½ cup cider vinegar
¼ cup olive oil

Nutritional information per serving:

Calories	125
Fat, gm.	8
Protein, gm.	2
Carbs, gm.	10
Cholesterol, mg.	0
Fiber, gm.	3.0

Serves 10

8 ounces elbow macaroni or small pasta
   of your choice
1 can (15 ounces) black beans, drained
   and rinsed
1 can (4 ounces) green chilies, drained
2 medium roasted red peppers, diced
1 teaspoon minced garlic
½ cup chopped green onions
6 ounces mozzarella or Swiss cheese,
   cubed

Dressing:
½ cup low-fat mayonnaise
¼ cup fat-free sour cream
1 teaspoon chili powder
¼ teaspoon cumin
Dash hot pepper sauce
Salt and pepper to taste

Nutritional information per serving:

Calories	210
Fat, gm.	7
Protein, gm.	10
Carbs, gm.	27
Cholesterol, mg.	10
Fiber, gm.	3.4

Mexican Macaroni Salad

This is not your ordinary bland pasta salad. It has a full flavor, with the green chilies, chili powder, and cumin seasonings. Serve in small portions for a side dish or in larger portions for a luncheon salad.

❖ In a large saucepan, cook macaroni in boiling salted water until al dente. Drain and rinse under cold water. Drain well and place in a large bowl. Add beans, green chilies, roasted peppers, garlic, onions, and cheese. Set aside. In a small bowl, combine mayonnaise, sour cream, chili powder, cumin, and pepper sauce. Add to macaroni mixture. Mix gently. Add salt and pepper to taste. Refrigerate until ready to serve.

Moroccan Rice Salad with Feta

The basmati rice, beans, colorful vegetables, and the special flavor of feta cheese make this a memorable meatless salad. And then, the mint in the dressing adds just the right seasoning!

❖ In a small, heavy saucepan, cook rice in broth for 20 minutes or until tender. Chill rice. In a large bowl, combine cold rice, tomatoes, cucumber, carrots, onion, garbanzo beans, and feta cheese. In a small jar, combine all dressing ingredients. Shake to mix and pour into rice mixture. Stir to blend. Refrigerate until ready to serve.

Note: *Although white rice could be used in this recipe, I think the basmati rice gives it a special flavor.*

**This recipe would be even better with fresh mint in place of the dried mint. Use 1 to 2 tablespoons of chopped fresh mint.

1 cup basmati rice or long-grained white rice*
2 cups vegetable broth or chicken broth
1½ cups cherry tomatoes, cut in half
1 medium cucumber, seeded and diced
1 cup finely chopped carrots
⅓ cup thinly sliced red onion
1 can (15 ounces) garbanzo beans, drained and rinsed
4 ounces (½ cup) fat-free tomato-basil feta cheese, crumbled

Dressing:
2 tablespoons lemon juice
2 tablespoons olive oil
½ teaspoon dried mint flakes**
½ teaspoon minced garlic
¼ teaspoon salt
⅛ teaspoon pepper
¼ teaspoon sugar

Nutritional information per serving:

Calories	330
Fat, gm.	7
Protein, gm.	11
Carbs, gm.	56
Cholesterol, mg.	20
Fiber, gm.	5.4

Peanut Raisin Slaw

Serves 10

1 bag (16 ounces) shredded cabbage
1 cup golden raisins
1 cup peanuts
1 cup frozen peas
1 cup low-fat mayonnaise
1 teaspoon curry powder

Nutritional information per serving:

Calories	235
Fat, gm.	15
Protein, gm.	5
Carbs, gm.	25
Cholesterol, mg.	0
Fiber, gm.	3.6

This recipe has a very interesting combination of ingredients that come together to make it a great-tasting salad.

❖ Mix all ingredients together in a large bowl. The salad will look dry but will become moist as it sits. It is best made several hours before serving. Refrigerate until ready to serve.

Quinoa, Pepper, and Peanut Salad

Quinoa (pronounced keen-wa) is an ancient grain that is high in protein and has a great nutty flavor and texture. When I tested this salad at a neighborhood party, everyone asked for the recipe. The soy sauce and cumin are the surprising ingredients in the dressing.

❖ Combine quinoa and water in small saucepan. Bring to a boil, cover pan, and boil gently for 15 to 20 minutes or until quinoa is tender and liquid has been absorbed. Remove from heat. Spoon grain onto a plate and chill. In a large bowl, combine quinoa, peppers, broccoli, onions, and dried fruit. Set peanuts aside. Combine all dressing ingredients in a small jar. Shake to mix well. Pour over quinoa and vegetables. Toss to mix. Refrigerate until ready to serve. Top with peanuts when ready to serve.

Serves 10

1 cup quinoa
2 cups water
1 large red pepper, thinly sliced
1 large yellow pepper, thinly sliced
2 cups broccoli florets
½ cup chopped green onions
1 cup bite-sized mixed dried fruit
½ cup dry-roasted peanuts

Dressing:
¼ cup soy sauce
¼ cup cider vinegar
¼ cup granular Splenda or sugar
2 tablespoons olive oil
1 teaspoon cumin
½ teaspoon salt
1 tablespoon orange zest

Nutritional information per serving:

Calories	125
Fat, gm.	11
Protein, gm.	7
Carbs, gm.	25
Cholesterol, mg.	0
Fiber, gm.	3.5

Raspberry Pecan Spinach Salad

Serves 10

1 pound fresh spinach
2 cups fresh raspberries

Dressing:
1 cup water
1 teaspoon cornstarch
½ cup granular Splenda or sugar
1 teaspoon dry mustard
⅓ cup raspberry vinegar
⅓ cup olive oil
1 tablespoon poppy seeds, optional
Salt to taste
½ cup chopped pecans

Nutritional information per serving:

Calories	110
Fat, gm.	8
Protein, gm.	1
Carbs, gm.	6
Cholesterol, mg.	0
Fiber, gm.	2.2

There is a big secret to this recipe. The dressing has lots of body without much oil because it is prepared with water slightly thickened with cornstarch. Calories are also saved by sweetening the dressing with Splenda instead of sugar. The salad is beautiful and healthy too!

❖ Wash and spin-dry spinach leaves. Combine spinach and raspberries in large salad bowl. Cover and refrigerate until ready to serve. For dressing, combine water and cornstarch in small saucepan. Bring to a rolling boil. Cook for 1 minute. Remove from heat and cool to room temperature. Add Splenda, mustard, vinegar, and oil. Add poppy seeds and salt if desired. To serve, toss spinach and raspberries with desired amount of dressing. Sprinkle pecans on top.

Note: *Strawberries or other fruit may be substituted for the raspberries.*

Red Cabbage and Apple Salad

At a salad luncheon I attended where there were about twenty different salads, this was my favorite. It was so refreshing, with the perfect blend of sweet-sour taste. It was also attractive and low in calories. This salad can be prepared ahead of time and refrigerated until ready to serve. If desired, toss all ingredients together except the apples. Add the apples right before serving.

❖ In a large salad bowl, combine cabbage, dried cranberries, apples, and walnuts. In a small jar or shaker, combine all dressing ingredients. Shake to mix. Pour over cabbage mixture and toss until well combined.

___

Note: The rice vinegar is good in this recipe because it has a very mild flavor. For the cranberries, plain sweetened dried cranberries can be used but the orange-flavored dried cranberries are extra special.

Serves 6

6 cups thinly sliced red cabbage
¾ cup dried orange-flavored cranberries
2 medium Granny Smith apples, cored
   and thinly sliced
¼ cup chopped walnuts, peanuts, or
   other nuts of your choice

Dressing:
¼ cup rice vinegar
¼ cup white wine vinegar
⅓ cup granular Splenda or sugar
1 tablespoon olive oil
½ teaspoon salt
¼ teaspoon pepper

Nutritional information per serving:

Calories	125
Fat, gm.	3
Protein, gm.	1
Carbs, gm.	24
Cholesterol, mg.	0
Fiber, gm.	2.9

Salmon Mousse

Serves 4

1 envelope (7 grams) unflavored gelatin
¼ cup cold water
½ cup boiling water
½ cup low-fat mayonnaise
1 tablespoon lemon juice
1 tablespoon grated onion
Dash Tabasco sauce
¼ teaspoon paprika
1 teaspoon salt
1 teaspoon dried dill weed
1 can (15 ounces) salmon, flaked
½ cup whipping cream

Nutritional information per serving:

Calories	420
Fat, gm.	27
Protein, gm.	23
Carbs, gm.	22
Cholesterol, mg.	100
Fiber, gm.	0.1

My friend Mary gave me this recipe. She served it at her New Year's Eve party. It received rave reviews. I rarely use heavy cream in any of my recipes, but this one is an exception. The whipped cream is really needed to make a delectably light mousse, and it is paired with healthy salmon.

1. In a small custard cup, combine gelatin and cold water. Add boiling water and stir until gelatin dissolves. Cool to room temperature. In a medium bowl, combine gelatin, mayonnaise, lemon juice, onion, Tabasco, paprika, salt, and dill weed. Stir to blend. Refrigerate for about 15 minutes or until mixture begins to thicken slightly.

Remove large bones and skin from the canned salmon. Fold finely flaked salmon into the gelatin mixture. In a small chilled bowl, whip cream with chilled beaters until peaks form. Fold cream gently into the salmon mixture. Transfer to an attractive serving bowl or a decorative mold. Cover and chill for several hours.

2. Serve on lettuce leaves as a luncheon salad. This mousse is also a great appetizer served as a spread for crackers or toast.

South of the Border Bean and Corn Salad

You will love the colors and the flavors of this salad. Choose a medium or hot salsa if you like a little heat. Serve it as a side dish or in larger portions for a luncheon meal.

❖ In a large saucepan, cook pasta in boiling salted water until al dente. Drain and rinse under cold water. Drain well. In a large bowl, combine pasta with all remaining ingredients. Stir to mix. Refrigerate until ready to serve.

_____

Note: *If leftovers are saved in the refrigerator, you may need to add extra salsa when ready to serve.*

Serves 8

1 cup pasta shells
1 can (15 ounces) black beans, drained and rinsed
1 can (15 ounces) great northern beans, drained and rinsed
1 can (11 ounces) corn, drained
1 cup chopped zucchini
1 cup chopped seeded tomatoes
¼ cup chopped cilantro
1 tablespoon lime juice
1 cup chunky salsa
½ cup fat-free sour cream
Salt and pepper to taste

Nutritional information per serving:

Calories	320
Fat, gm.	2
Protein, gm.	19
Carbs, gm.	57
Cholesterol, mg.	0
Fiber, gm.	5.0

Spinach Salad with Bacon Dressing

Serves 6

*10 ounces fresh baby spinach, washed
and dried*

Dressing:
6 slices bacon, diced
1 cup chopped green onions
3 tablespoons water
2 tablespoons cider vinegar
1 tablespoon sugar
1 tablespoon brown sugar
½ teaspoon salt

Nutritional information per serving:

Calories	60
Fat, gm.	3
Protein, gm.	3
Carbs, gm.	6
Cholesterol, mg.	5
Fiber, gm.	1.4

This recipe was given to me by my son-in-law, Steve, who is a fabulous cook. The proportions of bacon, vinegar, and sugar are just right.

❖ Break spinach leaves into bite-sized pieces. Place in a large salad bowl. In a small skillet, cook bacon over medium heat. Cook until crisp. Remove all but 2 tablespoons of bacon grease. Discard excess grease. Add onions to skillet. Cook 1 minute. Add all remaining ingredients and bring to a boil. Pour dressing over spinach leaves and serve immediately.

Spinach Salad with Honey Cranberry Dressing

By using canned cranberry sauce, you can create a fabulous dressing in just a few minutes.

❖ Wash spinach and drain well. Combine apples with orange juice. Set aside. In a small jar, combine all dressing ingredients. Cover and shake well. Arrange spinach leaves on individual serving plates. Top with fruit. Drizzle salads with dressing.

Note: Use any fresh fruit of your choice, such as apples, oranges, strawberries, kiwi, or melon.

Serves 6

10 ounces fresh spinach
1 large apple, cored and thinly sliced*
1 tablespoon orange juice

Dressing:
½ cup whole cranberry sauce
2 tablespoons honey
¼ cup olive oil
2 tablespoons balsamic vinegar
¼ teaspoon salt

Nutritional information per serving:

Calories	125
Fat, gm.	7
Protein, gm.	1
Carbs, gm.	17
Cholesterol, mg.	0
Fiber, gm.	1.8

Spinach Salad
with Oranges and Pomegranates

Serves 6

10 ounces fresh spinach
1 medium pomegranate
½ cup thinly sliced red onion
1 medium orange, peeled and sectioned

Dressing:
¼ cup olive oil
2 tablespoons balsamic vinegar
1 tablespoon sugar
¼ teaspoon salt

Nutritional information per serving:

Calories	125
Fat, gm.	9
Protein, gm.	1
Carbs, gm.	10
Cholesterol, mg.	0
Fiber, gm.	1.7

Pomegranate seeds dress up the traditional spinach salad. Check out the note below for an easy way to remove the seeds from the fruit.

❖ Place washed and dried spinach in large salad bowl. Remove seeds from pomegranate* and add to salad bowl. Add onion and orange sections. Combine dressing ingredients in a cup or small jar. Pour over spinach and toss to coat.

*An easy way to remove seeds from the pomegranate is to cut the fruit into sections. Take each section and place in a large bowl of water. Using your fingers, working under water, scrape seeds from the fruit. The seeds will fall to the bottom and the light membrane parts will float to the top. By removing the seeds this way, you will prevent the red juice from flying all over you and the kitchen cupboards.

Spinach, Kiwi, and Strawberry Salad with Poppy Seed Dressing

This received rave reviews when I served it for a large dinner party, but it is so easy, you can enjoy it at a simple family meal too.

❖ Wash and spin dry the spinach leaves. Place in a large salad bowl. Add strawberries and kiwi. In a pint jar, combine all dressing ingredients. Cover and shake to mix. Pour into salad bowl. Toss to coat leaves.

___

Note: *This is a perfect place to use Splenda and save a few calories.*

Serves 8

8 cups spinach leaves
2 cups sliced fresh strawberries
4 small kiwi, peeled and sliced

Dressing:
⅓ cup granular Splenda or sugar
⅓ cup olive oil
¼ cup cider vinegar
2 tablespoons chopped green onions
¼ teaspoon Worcestershire sauce
¼ teaspoon paprika
2 teaspoons poppy seeds

Nutritional information per serving:

Calories	120
Fat, gm.	9
Protein, gm.	1
Carbs, gm.	8
Cholesterol, mg.	0
Fiber, gm.	2.2

Strawberry and Spinach Salad with Apple Mustard Dressing

Serves 6

10 ounces mixed greens
1 pint fresh strawberries, sliced

Dressing:
¼ cup unsweetened applesauce
1 tablespoon Dijon mustard
2 tablespoons canola oil
¼ cup cider vinegar
⅓ cup granular Splenda or sugar
⅓ cup chopped onion
2 tablespoons water
½ teaspoon pepper

Nutritional information per serving:

Calories	80
Fat, gm.	4
Protein, gm.	2
Carbs, gm.	9
Cholesterol, mg.	0
Fiber, gm.	2.4

The dressing for this salad is made with a surprising blend of ingredients. It is thickened with applesauce, sweetened with Splenda, and seasoned with a good mustard. The calories are low yet the flavor is wonderful.

❖ Place greens and strawberries in large salad bowl. In a small food processor or blender, combine all dressing ingredients. Blend to mix well. Pour desired amount of dressing on salad. Store any leftover dressing in the refrigerator. (Makes 1 cup of dressing.)

Swiss Apple Grape Salad

I like the combination of fruit and cheese in this salad.

❖ In a large bowl, combine apples and lemon juice. Add remaining ingredients and stir to mix. Refrigerate until ready to serve.

Serves 4

2 large red apples, cored and diced
2 teaspoons lemon juice
1 cup grapes
½ cup chopped celery
4 ounces Swiss cheese, diced
⅓ cup fat-free sour cream
¼ teaspoon cinnamon
Salt to taste

Nutritional information per serving:

Calories	200
Fat, gm.	8
Protein, gm.	9
Carbs, gm.	23
Cholesterol, mg.	30
Fiber, gm.	2.5

Tortellini and Shrimp Salad

Serves 6

8 ounces dried tortellini
1 pound cooked shrimp, shelled and deveined
1 cup julienned fresh carrots
2 medium tomatoes, seeded and chopped
1 cup frozen peas
½ cup chopped red or green onion

Dressing:
¼ cup red wine vinegar
¼ cup olive oil
2 tablespoons Dijon mustard
2 tablespoons lemon juice
1 tablespoon minced garlic
Salt and pepper to taste

Nutritional information per serving:

Calories	340
Fat, gm.	13
Protein, gm.	23
Carbs, gm.	32
Cholesterol, mg.	170
Fiber, gm.	3.7

When a dish turns out beautiful, tasty, and healthful, too, it is a winning recipe. This is a winning recipe! Serve it as a luncheon salad or a light supper meal.

❖ In a large saucepan, cook tortellini in boiling salted water until al dente. Chill quickly under cold running water. Drain well. In a large bowl, combine tortellini, shrimp, carrots, tomatoes, peas, and onion. In a jar, combine all dressing ingredients. Cover and shake to mix. Pour dressing over salad and toss gently to mix. Cover and refrigerate until ready to serve. It keeps well in the refrigerator for days.

Tuscan Pasta Salad
with Artichokes and Sun Dried Tomatoes

If you would like to serve a healthy main course salad that will have everyone asking for the recipe, this is the one. I prepared it for a Mediterranean cooking class and it received rave reviews.

❖ In a large saucepan, cook pasta in salted water according to package directions until al dente. Chill under cold running water. Drain and set aside. In a large bowl, combine pasta, artichoke hearts, tomatoes, olives, ham, cheese, and spinach leaves. Set pine nuts aside. In a small jar, combine olive oil, garlic, basil, and vinegar. Pour into salad bowl and toss gently. Top individual servings with pine nuts if desired.

---

*Roasted red peppers can be substituted for the sun dried tomatoes.

**To toast pine nuts, cook in a dry frying pan over medium heat for 1 to 2 minutes or until lightly golden. Watch carefully to prevent burning.

Serves 8

½ pound penne pasta (small tube shape)
1 can (14 ounces) artichoke hearts, drained and cut into quarters
½ cup oil-packed sun-dried tomatoes*, chopped
1 cup black olives, cut in half
½ pound lean ham or prosciutto, sliced
4 ounces (½ cup crumbled) tomato-basil seasoned feta cheese
6 ounces (about 8 cups) fresh small spinach leaves, washed and drained
¼ cup toasted pine nuts**, optional

Dressing:
¼ cup olive oil
1 teaspoon minced garlic
¼ cup chopped fresh basil
3 tablespoons balsamic vinegar

Nutritional information per serving:

Calories	290
Fat, gm.	14
Protein, gm.	13
Carbs, gm.	30
Cholesterol, mg.	25
Fiber, gm.	3.6

CHAPTER 3

Eggs and Breakfast

Artichoke and Red Pepper Pie
Bacon and Egg Pizza
Cheesy Sausage Bake
Crustless Mexican Quiche
Italian Egg Puff
Mushroom and Artichoke Frittata Squares
Orange Marmalade French Toast
Sausage and Spinach Breakfast Casserole
Scotch Eggs
Strawberry Breakfast Salsa
Swedish Pancakes
Swiss Sweet Onion Pie
Vegetable Frittata

Eggs and Breakfast Cooking Tips

Eggs are one of nature's most nourishing foods. They have the highest quality of natural protein. They are also a source of vitamin A, B, D, E, iron, selenium, and the phytochemical lutein.

For years, eggs were on the list of forbidden foods because it was believed that cholesterol in the diet increased blood cholesterol levels. We now know that for most people, saturated fat has much more of an effect. Eggs, though high in cholesterol, are low in saturated fat.

One egg contains 7 grams of protein, 4 grams of fat, and 75 calories.

Keep eggs refrigerated at or below 40°F in the original carton in the coldest section of the refrigerator, not in the door.

Processed liquid egg substitutes are available in liquid or frozen forms. They are cholesterol-free and are usually made from a base of egg white with added gums, emulsifiers, milk solids, and color. They can often be used as a substitute for eggs in cooking and baking.

Egg substitutes cook up like whole eggs and can be used for scrambling and in omelets. Not all brands work well in baking.

The color of chicken eggs does not affect the quality or flavor of the eggs. They just come from different varieties of chickens.

Ordinary eggs need to be thoroughly cooked to prevent possible salmonella contamination. Raw or undercooked eggs should not be consumed; however, pasteurized fresh eggs in the shell are now available in some grocery stores. They would be safe to use without cooking. Egg substitutes have also been pasteurized and can be used when raw eggs are called for in a recipe.

The green ring that sometimes forms around the yolk in a hard-boiled egg is due to a chemical reaction between the sulfur and the iron in the egg. It is more likely to form in older eggs with extended heat. It is perfectly safe to eat although it is not very attractive.

Artichoke and Red Pepper Pie

This makes a delicious brunch or meatless supper meal if you enjoy artichokes.

❖ Preheat oven to 350°F, or 325°F if using a glass pan. Butter a deep-dish pie pan. In a medium skillet, heat oil. Add pepper and cook until tender. Add artichokes, Italian seasoning, salt, and pepper. Stir to mix. Spoon into pie pan. In a medium bowl, combine eggs, half-and-half, flour, and ¾ cup of the cheese. Beat well. Pour over vegetables. Sprinkle remaining cheese on top. Bake for 40 to 50 minutes or until set in the middle. A knife inserted in the middle should come out clean. Sprinkle parsley on top to garnish.

Serves 6

1 tablespoon canola oil
1 medium red pepper, thinly sliced
2 cans (14 ounces each) quartered artichokes, drained
1 teaspoon Italian seasoning
1 teaspoon salt
½ teaspoon black pepper
5 large eggs
½ cup fat-free half-and-half
2 tablespoons flour
1¼ cups (5 ounces) grated Fontina or Swiss cheese, divided
2 tablespoons finely chopped parsley for garnish

Nutritional information per serving:

Calories	235
Fat, gm.	13
Protein, gm.	14
Carbs, gm.	15
Cholesterol, mg.	175
Fiber, gm.	5.5

Bacon and Egg Pizza

Serves 6

1 pizza crust (e.g., Pillsbury refrigerated
  pizza roll)
6 slices bacon, diced
1 cup finely chopped onion
¼ pound sliced mushrooms
1 medium red pepper, thinly sliced
1 cup shredded mozzarella cheese
4 large eggs
¼ cup water
½ teaspoon salt
¼ teaspoon pepper

Nutritional information per serving:

Calories	265
Fat, gm.	12
Protein, gm.	14
Carbs, gm.	26
Cholesterol, mg.	100
Fiber, gm.	1.0

This will convert anyone into a breakfast eater. Kids and adults will love this special breakfast or brunch treat.

❖ Preheat oven to 400°F. Open pizza crust container and spread dough in a 10" × 15" baking pan. Form a ½-inch raised crust around the edges. Bake for 5 to 8 minutes or just until crust is beginning to brown. Remove from oven and set aside. Reduce oven temperature to 350°F. In a small skillet, cook bacon over medium heat until crisp. Drain excess fat and discard. Add onion to skillet and cook until translucent. Add mushrooms and pepper and cook until tender. Spoon bacon and vegetables on top of pizza crust. Sprinkle with cheese. In a small bowl, combine eggs and water. Beat well. Add salt and pepper. Pour over crust. Bake 15 to 20 minutes or until eggs have set.

***

Note: *Any combination of cooked vegetables can be substituted for the onions, mushrooms, and pepper.*

Cheesy Sausage Bake

This is a great dish to put together ahead of time. Assemble all ingredients, cover baking dish, and refrigerate overnight or until ready to bake. Serve this for breakfast, brunch, or a light supper.

❖ Preheat oven to 350°F or 325°F if using a glass or nonstick pan. Butter a 9" × 13" baking dish. In a medium skillet, cook sausage over medium-high heat until brown. Drain and discard any excess fat. Add mushrooms and cook until tender. Sprinkle with pepper. Set aside. In a large bowl, combine cream cheese and ricotta cheese. Beat well. Add flour, baking powder, and salt. Stir to mix. Add eggs, 2 at a time, and beat until fully incorporated. Add sausage and mushroom mixture and 2 cups of the cheese. Stir to mix. Spoon into baking pan. Sprinkle remaining cheese on top. Bake for 45 to 55 minutes or until set in the middle. Cool for 10 minutes before cutting. Serve with salsa on the side.

─────

Note: *For a smaller group, cut the recipe in half and bake it in a 9" × 9" baking dish.*

Serves 10

½ pound low-fat bulk turkey sausage, crumbled
1 pound sliced mushrooms
¼ teaspoon black pepper
4 ounces fat-free cream cheese
2 cups part skim ricotta cheese
½ cup flour
1 tablespoon baking powder
1 teaspoon salt
10 large eggs
3 cups shredded Monterey jack cheese, divided
1 cup salsa

Nutritional information per serving:

Calories	335
Fat, gm.	21
Protein, gm.	25
Carbs, gm.	12
Cholesterol, mg.	240
Fiber, gm.	0.7

Serves 6

5 large eggs
½ teaspoon baking powder
¼ cup flour
¼ teaspoon salt
¼ teaspoon white pepper
1 cup low-fat small-curd cottage cheese
1½ cups (6 ounces) shredded Monterey jack cheese, divided
2 tablespoons butter or margarine, melted
1 can (4 ounces) diced green chilies
¼ teaspoon crushed red pepper
½ cup sliced black olives
1 medium tomato, seeded and chopped
½ cup salsa
¼ cup fat-free sour cream

Nutritional information per serving:

Calories	270
Fat, gm.	18
Protein, gm.	17
Carbs, gm.	10
Cholesterol, mg.	190
Fiber, gm.	0.5

Crustless Mexican Quiche

Save all the calories of a pie crust and serve this great-tasting and very attractive quiche. Kick up the heat with the crushed red pepper.

❖ Preheat oven to 350°F. Butter an 8-inch pie pan. In a large bowl, beat eggs until light and lemon colored. Add baking powder, flour, salt, pepper, and cottage cheese. Beat well. Stir in half of the cheese, butter, crushed red peppers, and green chilies. Spoon into baking pan. Sprinkle with remaining shredded cheese and arrange black olives on top. Bake for 45 to 55 minutes or until set in the middle and lightly brown. Remove from oven and top with chopped tomato. Serve on individual plates and top with salsa and a dollop of sour cream.

Italian Egg Puff

This is a crustless quiche that is healthy and tasty too!

❖ Preheat oven to 325°F. Grease a 9-inch deep-dish pie pan. In a medium skillet, heat oil. Add pepper and mushrooms. Cook until tender. Remove from heat and set aside. In a large bowl, combine egg substitute, ricotta cheese, milk, Italian seasoning, salt, and pepper. Add reserved pepper and mushrooms. Stir until mixed. Pour into baking pan. Bake for 35 to 40 minutes or until knife inserted in the middle comes out clean. Sprinkle with mozzarella cheese. Return to oven and heat until cheese is melted or place under broiler to brown cheese. Let stand 5 minutes before serving.

Serves 6

1 tablespoon canola oil
1 large red pepper, diced
¼ pound sliced fresh mushrooms
1½ cups egg substitute, or 6 eggs
¾ cup fat-free ricotta cheese
⅓ cup fat-free milk
1 teaspoon Italian seasoning
¼ teaspoon salt
¼ teaspoon pepper
1 cup shredded mozzarella cheese

Nutritional information per serving:

Calories	210
Fat, gm.	13
Protein, gm.	16
Carbs, gm.	7
Cholesterol, mg.	20
Fiber, gm.	0.6

Mushroom and Artichoke Frittata Squares

Serves 8

1 tablespoon olive oil
1 small onion, finely chopped
½ medium red pepper, finely chopped
½ pound fresh mushrooms, finely chopped
1 teaspoon minced garlic
1 teaspoon Italian seasoning
Dash red pepper flakes
1 can (14 ounces) artichoke hearts,
   drained and chopped
3 eggs, lightly beaten
½ cup shredded Cheddar cheese
6 tablespoons bread crumbs, divided
¼ cup shredded Parmesan cheese

Nutritional information per serving:

Calories	130
Fat, gm.	6
Protein, gm.	7
Carbs, gm.	12
Cholesterol, mg.	75
Fiber, gm.	3.7

This is a versatile recipe that can be served for brunch or it can be cut into small pieces and served as an appetizer or snack.

1. Preheat oven to 325°F. Butter a 7" × 11" baking pan. In a large skillet, heat oil. Add onion and cook over medium heat until translucent. Add pepper, mushrooms, garlic, Italian seasoning, and pepper flakes. Cook until vegetables are tender. Add artichokes, eggs, Cheddar cheese, and 4 tablespoons bread crumbs. Stir to mix. Pour into baking pan. Sprinkle with remaining 2 tablespoons bread crumbs and Parmesan cheese. Bake for 35 to 40 minutes or until middle is set and top is lightly browned.

2. This can be served with salsa and sour cream on the side.

Orange Marmalade French Toast

I am not usually a fan of French toast, but this one made me a convert. You don't even need syrup. For an easy morning, put it together the night before and cook it in just a few minutes.

1. Spread marmalade on one side of 4 pieces of bread. Top each piece of bread with another piece of bread to make a sandwich. Place sandwiches in a 9" × 13" pan. Set aside. In a small bowl, combine eggs, milk, Splenda, cinnamon, nutmeg, and salt. Whisk to mix. Pour mixture on top of bread in the pan. Let stand 5 minutes and turn each bread sandwich over. Let stand 20 minutes or until bread has absorbed the milk mixture. This can be made the night before. Cover the pan and refrigerate until ready to bake.

2. This French toast can be either baked or cooked in a skillet.

3. To Bake: Preheat oven to 400°F. Coat a 7½" × 10½" baking pan with butter spray. Place 2 of the sandwiches in the pan. Bake for 10 minutes or until the bottom side is brown. Turn sandwich and continue baking 5 to 10 minutes or until the other side is brown. Repeat with remaining sandwiches. If you prefer, cook all sandwiches together on a large nonstick baking sheet.

4. To Cook in a Skillet: Spray a nonstick skillet with butter spray. When pan is hot, place sandwiches in skillet and cook over medium heat. Cook until brown on both sides of each sandwich. Add additional butter spray as needed.

5. Serve with powdered sugar or your favorite syrup.

Serves 4

¼ cup orange marmalade
8 slices bread
4 eggs
1 cup fat-free milk
1 tablespoon granular Splenda or sugar
½ teaspoon cinnamon
¼ teaspoon nutmeg
Dash salt
Butter spray

Nutritional information per serving:

Calories	265
Fat, gm.	6
Protein, gm.	11
Carbs, gm.	42
Cholesterol, mg.	180
Fiber, gm.	1.4

Sausage and Spinach Breakfast Casserole

Serves 10

3 cups seasoned croutons
1 pound low-fat turkey sausage
1 medium red pepper, thinly sliced
2½ cups fat-free milk
1 tablespoon dry mustard
1 teaspoon salt
½ teaspoon black pepper
4 large eggs
1 package (10 ounces) frozen chopped
  spinach, thawed and squeezed dry
2 cups shredded Monterey jack cheese,
  divided

Nutritional information per serving:

Calories	265
Fat, gm.	15
Protein, gm.	18
Carbs, gm.	14
Cholesterol, mg.	120
Fiber, gm.	1.7

Impress your family or guests with a very attractive, colorful morning treat that tastes as good as it looks! It really is the most eye-appealing brunch-type recipe in this book. You can bake it immediately after you put it together, or keep it in the refrigerator to bake when you need it.

1. Butter a 9" × 13" baking dish. Spread croutons on bottom of the pan. In a medium skillet, cook sausage over medium heat until brown. Break up sausage into small pieces as it cooks. Drain and discard any fat. Add red pepper and cook until tender. Spread crumbled sausage and pepper over croutons. In a medium bowl, combine milk, dry mustard, salt, pepper, eggs, spinach, and three-quarters of the cheese. Stir to mix. Pour into casserole. Sprinkle with remaining cheese. Cover and refrigerate overnight or until ready to bake.

2. Preheat oven to 325°F. Bake, uncovered, 45 to 55 minutes or until set in the middle and brown on the top.

3. If desired, serve with salsa on the side.

4. For a smaller group, cut this recipe in half and bake it in an 8" × 8" or a 9" × 9" baking pan. If you like leftovers, make the whole recipe. It warms up beautifully in the microwave.

Scotch Eggs

This is a quick way to transform an ordinary hard-boiled egg into an elegant breakfast meal. Remember this recipe at Easter time and use it with your leftover Easter eggs.

1. Preheat oven to 350°F. Butter a 7" × 11" baking pan. Divide sausage into 6 equal portions. Using your hands, wrap 2 ounces of sausage around each egg. Set aside. Place bread crumbs in a small bowl. In another small bowl, combine egg, water, and mustard. Stir to mix. Take each sausage-wrapped egg and roll in beaten egg mixture and then roll in bread crumbs. Place on baking pan. Bake for 30 minutes or until brown on all sides. Turn every 10 minutes. Cut in half lengthwise and serve with sauce if desired.

2. To prepare sauce: Melt butter in small, heavy saucepan. Add flour and cook 1 minute. Add milk and cook, stirring constantly, until mixture comes to a boil. Reduce heat and boil gently for 2 minutes. Add mustard and salt and pepper to taste.

Serves 6

12 ounces low-fat bulk turkey sausage
6 hard-boiled eggs, peeled
1 cup dry bread crumbs
1 egg, lightly beaten
1 tablespoon water
1 teaspoon Dijon mustard

Sauce (optional):
2 tablespoons butter
2 tablespoons flour
1 cup fat-free milk
1 tablespoon Dijon mustard
Salt and pepper to taste

Nutritional information per serving (without sauce):

Calories	175
Fat, gm.	10
Protein, gm.	15
Carbs, gm.	6
Cholesterol, mg.	250
Fiber, gm.	0.3

Strawberry Breakfast Salsa

Serves 4

½ *cup sugar-free apricot preserves*
2 *tablespoons water*
½ *teaspoon cinnamon*
¼ *teaspoon allspice*
1 *quart fresh strawberries, sliced*

Nutritional information per serving:

Calories	65
Fat, gm.	0
Protein, gm.	1
Carbs, gm.	15
Cholesterol, mg.	0
Fiber, gm.	3.4

This is a recipe for when simple is best. I am happy that strawberries are so low in calories, because when I make this salsa, I can't stop eating it. What a treat to enjoy for breakfast on yogurt or oatmeal. It can also transform ice cream or plain cake into a great dessert.

1. In a small saucepan, combine apricot preserves, water, cinnamon, and allspice. Stir over medium heat until mixture is blended. Cool to room temperature. Add strawberries and stir gently. Cover and refrigerate until ready to serve.

2. Serve with vanilla yogurt, ice cream, or as a sauce on angel food cake.

Swedish Pancakes

These traditional pancakes are often on the menu in restaurants that specialize in breakfast meals. You can make your own very easily with this recipe.

1. In a medium bowl, combine flour, salt, sugar, and baking powder. Stir to mix well. In a small bowl, combine egg, butter, milk, and vanilla. Combine the egg mixture with the flour mixture. Stir gently. Add water as needed. The batter should be very thin. Heat a nonstick skillet or griddle. Spray lightly with butter spray. Pour mixture into hot skillet and cook over medium heat until brown on both sides.

2. The secret to the light, thin nature of this pancake is adding the right amount of water to keep the batter thin.

Note: *The traditional way to serve Swedish pancakes is with lingonberries.*

Serves 4

¾ cup flour
½ teaspoon salt
2 tablespoons sugar
1 teaspoon baking powder
1 large egg, lightly beaten
1½ tablespoons butter or margarine,
  melted
½ cup milk
½ teaspoon vanilla
½ cup water, if needed
Butter spray

Nutritional information per serving:

Calories	175
Fat, gm.	6
Protein, gm.	4
Carbs, gm.	26
Cholesterol, mg.	60
Fiber, gm.	0

Swiss Sweet Onion Pie

Serves 6

1 9-inch pie shell
1 tablespoon canola oil
2 cups thinly sliced sweet onions
4 eggs
2 cups shredded Swiss cheese
1 tablespoon cornstarch
1½ cups fat-free half-and-half
1 teaspoon salt
¼ teaspoon white pepper
¼ teaspoon black pepper
¼ teaspoon nutmeg

Nutritional information per serving:

Calories	385
Fat, gm.	23
Protein, gm.	19
Carbs, gm.	26
Cholesterol, mg.	155
Fiber, gm.	1.4

There is something special about this recipe. It gets rave reviews every time I serve it. The sweet onions and Swiss cheese give this pie a wonderful flavor and texture. The calories and fat have been reduced significantly from an original recipe that used heavy cream. Serve it for brunch or lunch or as a supper side dish.

❖ Preheat oven to 350°F. Place refrigerated prepared pie crust into 9-inch pie pan. Set aside. In a medium skillet, heat oil. Add onions and cook until lightly brown. Remove from heat and set aside. In a medium bowl, beat eggs. Brush a small amount of egg on bottom of pie shell. Spoon onions into the pie shell. Mix the cheese and cornstarch together and spoon over the onions in bottom of the pie shell. Add the half-and-half, salt, white pepper, black pepper, and nutmeg to the bowl of eggs. Beat well. Pour over the cheese and onions. Sprinkle with additional nutmeg if desired. Bake for 40 to 45 minutes or until set in the middle.

Vegetable Frittata

Using frozen vegetables and hash brown potatoes, this is a fast and easy recipe. Serve it for breakfast or for a quick supper.

1. Preheat broiler. In a medium bowl, combine eggs, water, mustard, salt, and pepper. Beat to mix and set aside. In a medium saucepan, cook vegetables just until tender-crisp. Drain and set aside. In a 10-inch ovenproof nonstick skillet, heat oil. Add hash brown potatoes and cook over medium heat until lightly brown. Add vegetables and egg mixture. Cover and cook over medium heat until almost set, without stirring. Top with cheese and place under broiler until eggs are cooked and cheese is melted.

2. Note: Protect handle of skillet by wrapping it in aluminum foil before placing under the broiler.

Serves 4

6 large eggs
¼ cup water
2 teaspoons Dijon mustard
½ teaspoon salt
½ teaspoon pepper
3 cups frozen mixed vegetables, cut into bite-sized pieces
1 tablespoon canola oil
2 cups frozen hash brown potatoes
1 cup shredded low-fat Cheddar cheese

Nutritional information per serving:

Calories	350
Fat, gm.	15
Protein, gm.	22
Carbs, gm.	32
Cholesterol, mg.	290
Fiber, gm.	3.0

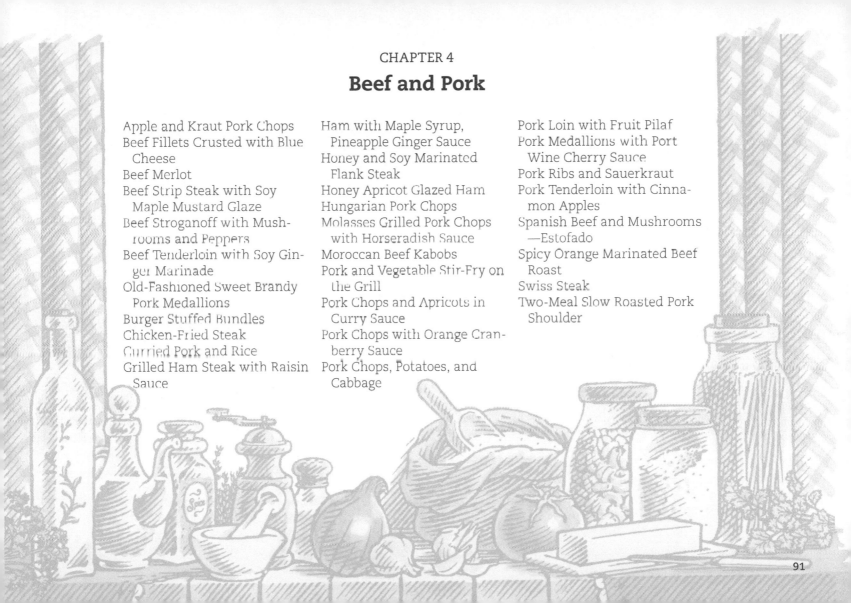

CHAPTER 4
Beef and Pork

Apple and Kraut Pork Chops
Beef Fillets Crusted with Blue
  Cheese
Beef Merlot
Beef Strip Steak with Soy
  Maple Mustard Glaze
Beef Stroganoff with Mush-
  rooms and Peppers
Beef Tenderloin with Soy Gin-
  ger Marinade
Old-Fashioned Sweet Brandy
  Pork Medallions
Burger Stuffed Bundles
Chicken-Fried Steak
Curried Pork and Rice
Grilled Ham Steak with Raisin
  Sauce

Ham with Maple Syrup,
  Pineapple Ginger Sauce
Honey and Soy Marinated
  Flank Steak
Honey Apricot Glazed Ham
Hungarian Pork Chops
Molasses Grilled Pork Chops
  with Horseradish Sauce
Moroccan Beef Kabobs
Pork and Vegetable Stir-Fry on
  the Grill
Pork Chops and Apricots in
  Curry Sauce
Pork Chops with Orange Cran-
  berry Sauce
Pork Chops, Potatoes, and
  Cabbage

Pork Loin with Fruit Pilaf
Pork Medallions with Port
  Wine Cherry Sauce
Pork Ribs and Sauerkraut
Pork Tenderloin with Cinna-
  mon Apples
Spanish Beef and Mushrooms
  —Estofado
Spicy Orange Marinated Beef
  Roast
Swiss Steak
Two-Meal Slow Roasted Pork
  Shoulder

Beef and Pork Cooking Tips

When trying to brown pieces of meat, avoid overcrowding the pan. If there is too much meat in the pan, the liquid released from the meat causes the food to steam instead of brown. Blot the raw meat dry with a paper towel, and place only as much meat in the pan as will fit without touching or stacking up the sides of the skillet.

When browning meat, toss meat in a flour-and-seasoning mixture to create a dry surface. That helps the meat brown better when frying or sautéing.

To brown meat evenly, check your pans. Meat cannot brown evenly in a warped skillet or in a thin, inexpensive pan. Make sure the pan is properly sized to the burner. If the skillet is too big for the burner, only the center will fully heat.

A Dutch oven is a large, heavy pan that is ovenproof. It also has a tight cover. It is used in the slow, moist cooking of meat and vegetable–type meals.

When a recipe suggests a large skillet, it is a skillet 11 to 12 inches in diameter. A medium skillet is 10 inches in diameter.

When meat has been marinated in a marinade, do not use the marinade as a sauce without bringing it to a full boil for 5 minutes in a saucepan. If the marinade mixture is going to serve as both a marinade and a sauce to pass, it is best to set aside some of the marinade before combining it with the meat. Use the reserved marinade as your sauce.

When pounding meat for cutlets or for tenderizing, use a smooth meat mallet or a large rubber mallet. Sprinkle meat on both sides with a few drops of water. Place the meat between two pieces of plastic wrap. Pound the meat to the desired thickness. The water prevents the meat from sticking to the plastic wrap.

To remove any grease that forms after frying meat in a skillet, take a piece of paper towel or a piece of bread. Tilt the skillet and soak up the grease on the towel or bread.

The postcooking resting time is very important if you want your meat to be tender and moist. While cooking, the moisture from the meat is drawn to the outer surface of the meat. If you cut the meat right off the grill or right out of the oven, those juices will run out onto your platter. As the meat surface cools, the meat juices are reabsorbed throughout the meat.

The temperature used in cooking meat, fish, pasta, and various sauces is important. Boiling, poaching, and simmering are all forms of moist-heat cooking. Boiling means there are big moving bubbles in the liquid, and it occurs at 212°F or above. It is used in cooking starchy foods like pasta and potatoes. Simmering occurs at 185°F to 205°F and only very small bubbles are created. This gentle cooking prevents meat from becoming tough and stringy and keeps sauces from breaking down. Poaching is the lowest temperature of moist cooking, with no forming of bubbles, and a temperature of 160°F to 180°F. This is used for gentle cooking of fish or eggs.

Apple and Kraut Pork Chops

No cookbook is complete without a recipe with sauerkraut in it. The lowly fermented cabbage has recently been found to have healthful phytochemicals, and it is a calorie bargain. That makes me happy, because I love it!

❖ In a large skillet, heat oil. Add pork chops and sprinkle with salt and pepper. Cook over medium heat until each chop is brown on both sides. Add sauerkraut and caraway seeds to skillet. Cover pan and simmer for 10 to 20 minutes or until pork is done. While pork is simmering, combine applesauce, cinnamon, and brown sugar in a small saucepan. Heat gently over low heat. When ready to serve, place sauerkraut and pork on plate or platter and top with warm applesauce, or serve applesauce on the side.

Serves 4

1 tablespoon canola oil
1½ pounds pork loin cut into 4 chops
Salt and pepper
2 cups sauerkraut, undrained
1 teaspoon caraway seeds, optional
1 cup unsweetened applesauce
⅛ teaspoon cinnamon
1 tablespoon brown sugar

Nutritional information per serving:

Calories	365
Fat, gm.	20
Protein, gm.	27
Carbs, gm.	20
Cholesterol, mg.	86
Fiber, gm.	4.0

Serves 4

Sauce:
2 tablespoons butter or margarine, divided
3 cloves garlic, minced
1 large shallot, minced
1 tablespoon flour
½ tablespoon tomato paste
1 can (10 ounces) beef consommé, undiluted
½ cup dry red wine
1 teaspoon dried thyme

Topping:
½ cup crumbled blue cheese
¼ cup dry bread crumbs or panko
1 tablespoon finely chopped fresh parsley

Steak:
1 tablespoon canola oil
4 beef tenderloin steaks (6 ounces each)
Salt and pepper to taste

Nutritional information per serving:

Calories	530
Fat, gm.	30
Protein, gm.	55
Carbs, gm.	9
Cholesterol, mg.	200
Fiber, gm.	0.6

Beef Fillets Crusted with Blue Cheese

Tender steaks are sautéed on the stovetop, finished under the broiler with blue cheese, and dressed with a rich wine sauce. Both the sauce and the cheese topping can be prepared a day ahead of time and stored separately in the refrigerator.

1. Sauce: In a medium saucepan, heat 1 tablespoon butter. Add garlic and shallot. Cook over medium heat for 2 minutes. Add flour and continue to cook for 2 minutes, stirring constantly. Stir in tomato paste. Add consommé and bring to a boil, stirring constantly. Add wine and thyme. Reduce heat and simmer uncovered until volume has been reduced by about half and sauce is thickened. Remove from heat and set aside.

2. Topping: In a small bowl, combine blue cheese, bread crumbs, and parsley. Mix well and set aside.

3. Steak: Preheat broiler. Heat oil in heavy skillet over medium-high heat. Sprinkle meat with salt and pepper and place in hot oil. Sear each steak for 2 to 3 minutes on each side to form a nice crust. Reduce heat to medium and continue to cook steaks, turning occasionally, to desired degree of doneness. Transfer steaks to a shallow rimmed baking sheet. (Reserve skillet.) Press equal portions of the cheese mixture onto the top of each steak. Place under broiler for 2 to 3 minutes or until cheese mixture browns. Watch carefully to prevent burning. Transfer steak to serving platter. Pour the sauce into the reserved skillet and bring to a boil, scraping up the browned bits in the skillet. Boil for about 2 minutes. Remove from heat and whisk in 1 tablespoon of butter. Adjust seasoning with salt and pepper. Spoon sauce over the steaks.

Beef Merlot

Put this together in minutes, but the longer you cook it, the better it tastes. Simmer it in an oven for 1 to 2 hours, or cook it in a slow cooker all day.

❖ Preheat oven to 325°F. In a large, ovenproof skillet or Dutch oven, heat oil. Add beef and cook until brown. Sprinkle with salt and pepper. Add all remaining ingredients except the sugar. Stir to mix. Cover and bake for about 2 hours or until meat is tender. Check occasionally and add additional water if it gets too dry. Add sugar if desired to take away the slight bitter taste of the wine. Serve on cooked noodles.

———

*Cream of mushroom soup with roasted garlic is good in this recipe.

———

Note: This recipe works well in a slow cooker.

Serves 6

1 tablespoon canola oil
1½ pounds lean beef, cut into 1-inch cubes
Salt and pepper
2 cups baby carrots
2 medium onions, peeled and quartered
½ pound sliced mushrooms
1 teaspoon ground thyme
1 can (10 ounces) cream of mushroom soup*
1 cup merlot or other dry red wine
1 teaspoon sugar, optional

Nutritional information per serving (without the noodles):

Calories	275
Fat, gm.	12
Protein, gm.	27
Carbs, gm.	14
Cholesterol, mg.	65
Fiber, gm.	1.3

Serves 4

4 strip steaks or any tender lean beef
  steak (8 ounces each)

Sauce:
¼ cup soy sauce
2 tablespoons Dijon mustard
1 tablespoon lemon juice
1 tablespoon maple syrup
⅛ teaspoon dried thyme
½ teaspoon cornstarch

Nutritional information per serving:

Calories	500
Fat, gm.	25
Protein, gm.	65
Carbs, gm.	4
Cholesterol, mg.	185
Fiber, gm.	0.4

Beef Strip Steak with Soy Maple Mustard Glaze

You will love this recipe because it can be used with steaks cooked on an outdoor grill or on the stove in a skillet. The sauce is simple but it makes the steak so special.

❖ Heat grill to medium heat. Place steak on a plate or pan. Combine all sauce ingredients in a small saucepan. Cook over medium heat, stirring constantly, until mixture comes to a boil. Remove from heat. Brush sauce on both sides of each steak. Grill until desired consistency. Watch carefully to prevent burning. Pass extra sauce on the side.

———

Note: *The steaks can also be cooked on a stove in a skillet. Sear each piece of meat on both sides over medium-high heat. Reduce temperature and add sauce. Cook until steak reaches desired doneness. Watch carefully to prevent burning.*

Beef Stroganoff with Mushrooms and Peppers

The addition of mushrooms and peppers makes this different from the usual Stroganoff. To make this quicker, splurge on beef tenderloin or beef strip steak and only simmer the meat 10 to 15 minutes to blend the flavors.

1. Preheat oven to 325°F. Slice beef across the grain into thin strips. In a Dutch oven or a heavy ovenproof pan, heat 1 tablespoon oil. Add meat and cook over medium-high heat until brown on all sides. Sprinkle with salt and pepper. Add onion and cook until lightly brown. Add garlic and paprika. Cook for 1 minute, stirring constantly. In a shaker, combine flour with ½ cup of broth. Pour into skillet along with remaining broth and mustard. Cook, stirring constantly, until mixture comes to a boil. Cover pan and bake for 1 to 1½ hours or until beef is very tender. Check occasionally and add additional broth or water if it gets too dry. While meat is baking, heat 1 tablespoon oil in large skillet. Add pepper and mushrooms. Cook until tender. When meat is done, combine with vegetables and sour cream. Stir to mix. Adjust seasoning with extra salt and pepper if desired. Garnish with chopped parsley.

2. Serve with cooked noodles or mashed potatoes.

Serves 4

1 pound beef top round, cut into 1-inch strips
2 tablespoons canola oil, divided
Salt and pepper
1 large onion, thinly sliced
2 teaspoons minced garlic
1 teaspoon paprika
1 tablespoon flour
2 cups fat-free beef broth, divided
1 tablespoon honey mustard
1 large red pepper, thinly sliced
½ pound sliced mushrooms
½ cup fat-free sour cream
Chopped parsley for garnish, optional

Nutritional information per serving (without the noodles):

Calories	335
Fat, gm.	17
Protein, gm.	32
Carbs, gm.	13
Cholesterol, mg.	75
Fiber, gm.	1.8

Beef Tenderloin with Soy Ginger Marinade

Serves 4

*1½ pounds beef tenderloin,
  cut into 4 steaks*

Marinade:
*¼ cup soy sauce
½ teaspoon ginger
1 teaspoon minced garlic
¼ cup finely chopped onion
2 tablespoons steak sauce
½ cup red wine
½ cup canola oil
Dash hot pepper sauce*

Nutritional information per serving:

Calories	460
Fat, gm.	16
Protein, gm.	49
Carbs, gm.	3
Cholesterol, mg.	140
Fiber, gm.	0

The combination of the soy sauce, ginger, and red wine gives the steak an extraordinary flavor.

❖ Place tenderloin steaks in a large resealable plastic bag. Set aside. In a small bowl or jar, combine all marinade ingredients. Mix well and pour into bag with the meat. Marinate for 1 to 3 hours. Remove from marinade and grill or pan fry to desired doneness.

_____

Note: *Beef tenderloin is the very best meat to use for this recipe, but I also tested it with less tender cuts of meat such as sirloin and eye of the round. The meat definitely was not as tender, but it was still very good.*

Old-Fashioned Sweet Brandy Pork Medallions

This is a fabulous recipe that everyone loves. Make it once and it is sure to become a family favorite.

1. In a small saucepan, combine brandy and brown sugar. Cook over medium heat just until sugar melts. Remove from heat and cool to room temperature. Add orange juice, soy sauce, oil, ginger, and pepper. Pour marinade into large resealable plastic bag. Trim white membrane and any fat from pork. Place pork into bag with the marinade. Seal and marinate for 30 minutes or several hours. (The meat may also be marinated overnight.)

2. Preheat grill. Spray grate with cooking spray. Remove meat from marinade. Place meat on grill. Cover grill and cook over medium heat until brown on the outside and slightly pink in the inside. Remove from grill and let stand for 10 minutes before slicing.

Serves 4

¼ cup brandy
¼ cup brown sugar
¼ cup orange juice
¼ cup soy sauce
1 tablespoon canola oil
½ teaspoon ground ginger
¼ teaspoon pepper
1¼ pounds pork tenderloin

Nutritional information per serving:

Calories	245
Fat, gm.	6
Protein, gm.	44
Carbs, gm.	3
Cholesterol, mg.	90
Fiber, gm.	0.2

Burger Stuffed Bundles

Serves 4

1 cup Stove Top stuffing mix
1 pound lean ground beef
2 tablespoons fat-free milk
1 egg, lightly beaten
½ teaspoon salt
¼ teaspoon pepper

Sauce:
1 can (10 ounces) cream of mushroom
   soup
1 tablespoon catsup
1 teaspoon Worcestershire sauce
½ cup fat-free milk

Nutritional information per serving:

Calories	300
Fat, gm.	12
Protein, gm.	34
Carbs, gm.	15
Cholesterol, mg.	125
Fiber, gm.	0.2

This is a good dish to prepare ahead of time and refrigerate until ready to bake. The sauce is so good you will want to serve it on mashed potatoes or cooked noodles.

❖ Preheat oven to 350°F. Grease a 2-quart baking pan or casserole dish. Prepare stuffing mix according to package directions. In a large bowl, combine stuffing, ground beef, 2 tablespoons milk, egg, salt, and pepper. Stir to mix well. Form meat mixture into meatballs. Choose the size that you prefer. Place in baking dish. In a small bowl, combine all sauce ingredients. Stir to mix well. Pour over meatballs. Cover and bake for 45 to 60 minutes or until meat is thoroughly cooked.

Chicken-Fried Steak

Now why would chicken-fried steak be in the beef and pork section? I really can't explain it, but traditionally, chicken-fried steak is made from beef cube steak.

❖ Cut meat into 4 pieces. Combine ¼ cup milk and egg in a shallow bowl. Set aside. Combine flour, salt, and pepper in another large, shallow bowl. Dip cutlets into milk mixture, and then into the flour, shaking off excess. (Reserve remaining flour for making gravy.) In a large nonstick skillet, heat oil over medium heat. Brown each cutlet on both sides. Transfer to serving platter and keep warm. Combine 2 tablespoons of the reserved flour and broth in a shaker or jar with a lid. Shake to mix well. Pour into skillet and add ¼ cup milk. Bring to a boil, stirring constantly to deglaze the pan. Cook until gravy is thickened. Add additional milk or water if gravy gets too thick. Season with salt and pepper to taste. Pour gravy over steaks and serve.

Serves 4

1 pound beef cube steak
½ cup milk, divided
1 egg, lightly beaten
1 cup flour
½ teaspoon salt
¼ teaspoon pepper
1 tablespoon canola oil
1 cup fat-free beef or chicken broth
Salt and pepper to taste

Nutritional information per serving:

Calories	410
Fat, gm.	20
Protein, gm.	31
Carbs, gm.	26
Cholesterol, mg.	120
Fiber, gm.	0

Curried Pork and Rice

Serves 6

1 tablespoon canola oil
1 pound boneless pork loin,
  cut into 1-inch cubes
1 large onion, chopped
2 teaspoons curry powder
2 cups fat-free chicken broth
3 large carrots, peeled and sliced
¾ cup coconut milk
1 cup basmati rice or long-grain rice
1 can (15 ounces) garbanzo beans,
  drained
1 package (10 ounces) frozen chopped
  spinach, thawed and squeezed dry

Nutritional information per serving:

Calories	450
Fat, gm.	18
Protein, gm.	23
Carbs, gm.	50
Cholesterol, mg.	35
Fiber, gm.	6.7

This is an unusual combination of ingredients that make a colorful, very tasty meal.

❖ Heat oil in a large, deep skillet. Add meat and cook over medium-high heat until brown on all sides. Add onion and curry powder. Cook until onion is translucent. Add chicken broth to deglaze the pan. Add carrots, coconut milk, and rice. Bring to a boil. Reduce heat, cover pan, and boil gently for 20 minutes or until rice is tender. Add beans and spinach. Stir to mix and heat through.

Grilled Ham Steak with Raisin Sauce

This is a simple sauce that really dresses up a plain slice of ham. The raisins are great, but the sauce would also be good with any other dried fruits such as cranberries, cherries, or any combination of diced dried fruit.

❖ Preheat grill. Grill ham over medium heat until lightly browned. (Ham can also be cooked in a skillet on the stove.) In a medium saucepan, combine all sauce ingredients. Bring to a boil, reduce heat, and simmer for 10 minutes or until sauce is the consistency of syrup. Place ham on a serving platter and top with sauce.

Serves 6

2 pounds lean ham steak

Sauce:
1 cup golden raisins
½ cup currant jelly
1 tablespoon brown sugar
2 tablespoons cider vinegar
¼ cup water
1 teaspoon cornstarch
1 tablespoon Worcestershire sauce
¼ teaspoon cinnamon
⅛ teaspoon cloves
⅛ teaspoon ginger

Nutritional information per serving:

Calories	335
Fat, gm.	6
Protein, gm.	30
Carbs, gm.	40
Cholesterol, mg.	70
Fiber, gm.	1.3

Ham with Maple Syrup, Pineapple Ginger Sauce

Serves 12

5 pounds extra-lean ham

Sauce:
⅔ cup maple syrup
⅔ cup brown sugar
⅓ cup Dijon mustard
¼ teaspoon ginger
1½ tablespoons cornstarch
⅔ cup pineapple chunks in juice
⅓ cup golden raisins

Nutritional information per serving:

Calories	335
Fat, gm.	9
Protein, gm.	37
Carbs, gm.	26
Cholesterol, mg.	90
Fiber, gm.	0.5

Lean ham is a healthful choice for meat and has only 150 calories for a 4-ounce serving. This recipe makes a ham dinner special, with the addition of a sweet ginger sauce to use in basting the ham while it is baking and to serve on the side.

1. Preheat oven to 350°F. Choose a lean ham or ham slices suitable in amount for your meal. Place in baking pan. Bake until ham reaches an internal temperature of 140°F when tested in the center with a meat thermometer. While baking, baste occasionally with sauce.

2. To prepare sauce, combine maple syrup, brown sugar, mustard, ginger, and cornstarch in a medium saucepan. Stir to mix. Cook over medium-high heat, stirring constantly, until mixture comes to a rolling boil. Remove from heat. Use this mixture to baste the ham occasionally as it bakes. When ham is done, remove from the oven and place on serving platter. Add pineapple and raisins to the remaining sauce. Heat through and pass in a side dish with the ham.

Honey and Soy Marinated Flank Steak

If you have never grilled a flank steak, try this fantastic recipe. Marinating the steak in this flavorful marinade helps tenderize the meat. It is best to grill or broil with hot heat and serve the meat medium to medium-rare in the middle.

1. Place flank steak in a large resealable plastic bag. In a pint jar, combine all marinade ingredients. Shake to mix. Pour into bag with the meat. Marinate several hours or, preferably, overnight. Turn occasionally.

2. When ready to prepare, heat grill or broiler. Remove steak from marinade and grill over hot heat or broil in the oven about 5 to 10 minutes per side or until meat is brown on the outside and pink in the middle. Sprinkle with salt and pepper. Let rest 10 minutes before serving. Slice meat in thin slices, on the diagonal and across the grain.

Serves 6

2 pounds flank steak

Marinade:
¼ cup soy sauce
¼ cup honey
½ cup beer
½ cup canola oil
3 tablespoons white vinegar
1 teaspoon ground ginger
½ teaspoon garlic powder
1 small onion, finely chopped
Salt and pepper to taste

Nutritional information per serving:

Calories	265
Fat, gm.	15
Protein, gm.	30
Carbs, gm.	3
Cholesterol, mg.	75
Fiber, gm.	0

Honey Apricot Glazed Ham

Serves 8

3 pounds lean boneless ham
½ cup brandy
1 cup dried apricot halves, quartered
½ cup golden raisins
⅛ teaspoon nutmeg
⅛ teaspoon cloves
⅛ teaspoon ginger
¼ cup frozen orange juice concentrate
¼ cup apricot preserves

Nutritional information per serving:

Calories	325
Fat, gm.	8
Protein, gm.	34
Carbs, gm.	28
Cholesterol, mg.	80
Fiber, gm.	2

This aromatic sauce makes ham so special.

❖ Preheat oven to 325°F. Grease a small baking pan. Place ham in pan. In a small saucepan, combine all remaining ingredients. Bring to a boil. Pour mixture over ham. Cover loosely with foil. Bake for 40 to 60 minutes and baste occasionally during baking period. Add water to bottom of the pan if it gets too dry.

Hungarian Pork Chops

The creamy yogurt sauce is enhanced with paprika and a touch of lemon. It is quite easy. Pound the meat, sauté it, and add the sauce ingredients to the same pan.

❖ Place boneless pork loin chops in between sheets of heavy plastic wrap and pound with a rolling pin or smooth side of meat mallet. (To keep meat from sticking to the plastic, sprinkle top and bottom of each piece of meat with water.) Mix the flour, salt, and pepper together in a large plastic bag. Add pork and toss until each piece is coated. Heat 2 tablespoons oil in large nonstick skillet. Add pork and cook over medium-high heat until brown on each side. Remove pork from the pan and set aside. Add shallots or onion to the pan with the paprika and caraway seeds. Cook for 1 minute. Add wine and 1 cup of the broth to the pan to deglaze it. Cook until mixture boils, stirring to loosen browned meat pieces from the bottom of the pan. Mix remaining broth and cornstarch together. Add to the pan and bring to a boil until mixture thickens. Return pork to the pan and heat through. When ready to serve, place pork on serving plate. Add yogurt, lemon juice, and cayenne pepper to the sauce. Add additional broth or wine if needed to thin sauce. Add salt and pepper to taste. Spoon sauce over pork.

Serves 4

4 (6 ounces each) boneless pork loin chops
½ cup flour
½ teaspoon salt
½ teaspoon pepper
3 tablespoons canola oil, divided
2 large shallots or 1 medium onion, chopped
2 tablespoons paprika
1 tablespoon caraway seeds, optional
½ cup dry white wine
2 cups fat-free chicken broth, divided
2 tablespoons cornstarch
1 cup low-fat plain yogurt
1 tablespoon lemon juice
Dash cayenne pepper
Salt and pepper to taste

Nutritional information per serving:

Calories	480
Fat, gm.	28
Protein, gm.	32
Carbs, gm.	22
Cholesterol, mg.	85
Fiber, gm.	0.9

Molasses Grilled Pork Chops with Horseradish Sauce

Serves 4

4 (6 ounces each) boneless
   pork loin chops
½ cup soy sauce
¼ cup molasses
1 teaspoon minced garlic

Sauce:
¼ cup low-fat mayonnaise
¼ cup fat-free sour cream
1 tablespoon prepared horseradish
1 tablespoon finely chopped onion
Salt and pepper to taste

Nutritional information per serving:

Calories	325
Fat, gm.	21
Protein, gm.	28
Carbs, gm.	6
Cholesterol, mg.	85
Fiber, gm.	0.4

Try this combination of sweet molasses and soy sauce to marinate pork. Grill the chops to a golden brown, and then pass the horseradish sauce.

1.   Place pork chops in a large resealable plastic bag. Combine soy sauce, molasses, and garlic. Pour into bag. Seal bag and turn to coat meat. Refrigerate 2 to 12 hours, turning occasionally.

2.   When ready to prepare, heat grill. Spray with cooking spray. Remove pork chops from marinade, discarding marinade. Place chops on grill. Cover and grill about 5 minutes on each side or until meat is done. (Pork can be slightly pink in the middle and still be safe to eat.) Prepare sauce by combining all remaining ingredients in a small bowl. Serve with the pork chops.

Moroccan Beef Kabobs

Season your kabobs with something a little different. The flavor combination of cilantro, cumin, cinnamon, and paprika is wonderful on the beef and vegetables.

1. Preheat oven broiler. In a small saucepan, cook potatoes in boiling salted water just until tender. Drain. Place potatoes, beef, onion, and peppers in a large resealable plastic bag. In a small custard cup, combine seasoning ingredients. Add seasoning mixture to bag with the meat and vegetables. Mix gently to coat. Remove meat and vegetables from the bag and alternately thread beef and vegetables pieces onto four metal skewers. Place on broiler pan about 3 inches from the heat. Broil for 5 to 10 minutes or until meat reaches desired doneness.

2. Serve on a bed of couscous or rice.

If very small potatoes are not available, cut potatoes in half.

Serves 4

8 small red potatoes*
1 pound beef tenderloin, cut into 2-inch cubes
1 large onion, cut into 2-inch cubes
1 large red pepper, cut into 2-inch cubes
1 large green pepper, cut into 2-inch cubes

Seasoning:
¼ cup chopped cilantro
1 teaspoon minced garlic
2 teaspoons cumin
¼ teaspoon cinnamon
1 teaspoon paprika
Dash ground red pepper
¼ cup olive oil

Nutritional information per serving:

Calories	400
Fat, gm.	26
Protein, gm.	22
Carbs, gm.	20
Cholesterol, mg.	80
Fiber, gm.	2.4

Pork and Vegetable Stir-Fry on the Grill

Serves 4

1 pound pork tenderloin, trimmed and
* cut into thin slices*
⅓ cup soy sauce
2 tablespoons honey
1 teaspoon minced garlic
½ teaspoon minced fresh ginger
¼ teaspoon dried crushed red pepper
¼ teaspoon black pepper

Vegetables:
4 cups of an assortment of fresh
* or frozen vegetables of your choice*
Olive oil spray
1 tablespoon olive or canola oil
¼ cup dry-roasted peanuts

Nutritional information per serving:

Calories	320
Fat, gm.	12
Protein, gm.	30
Carbs, gm.	23
Cholesterol, mg.	75
Fiber, gm.	5.5

Combine fresh or frozen garden vegetables and pork tenderloin for a wonderful outdoor meal on the grill.

1. Place pork slices in a large resealable plastic bag. In a small jar, combine soy sauce, honey, garlic, ginger, red pepper, and black pepper. Mix well. Pour into bag with meat. Refrigerate meat until ready to prepare the meal. Assemble a variety of fresh vegetables on a large platter or thaw a bag of mixed frozen vegetables.

2. When ready to prepare the meal, heat grill to medium-hot. Spray a large grill basket with oil spray. Add vegetables and cook until all vegetables are tender.

3. While vegetables are cooking, heat iron skillet on the other half of the grill. Add oil to the pan. Using a slotted spoon or tongs, remove pieces of meat from the marinade. Cook over hot heat, stirring frequently, until meat is well browned. Add hot vegetables and remaining marinade to the skillet. Cook for a few minutes longer until the mixture is completely heated through. Serve directly from the skillet or pour into serving bowl.

4. Top with peanuts right before serving.

Pork Chops and Apricots in Curry Sauce

Dress up your pork chops with apricots and a great sauce.

1. Preheat oven to 350°F. Grease a 7" × 11" baking pan. Place pork chops in pan. Sprinkle with salt and pepper. Drain apricots, reserving ½ cup juice. Place 2 apricot halves on each chop, skin-side up. Set aside. Heat oil in medium skillet. Add onion and cook over medium heat until translucent. Add mushrooms and cook until tender. Spoon mixture into pan with the pork chops. In a small bowl, combine curry powder, soup, wine, and reserved apricot juice. Stir to mix and pour over chops. Bake, uncovered, for 40 to 60 minutes or until meat is tender. Check occasionally and add water if it gets too dry.

2. Serve with cooked noodles or mashed potatoes.

Serves 4

4 individual pork loin chops (about 1½ pounds)
Salt and pepper
1 can (15 ounces) apricot halves
1 tablespoon canola oil
1 medium onion, chopped
½ pound sliced mushrooms
1 tablespoon curry powder
1 can (10 ounces) cream of mushroom soup
½ cup dry white wine

Nutritional information per serving:

Calories	420
Fat, gm.	26
Protein, gm.	30
Carbs, gm.	17
Cholesterol, mg.	85
Fiber, gm.	3.3

Pork Chops with Orange Cranberry Sauce

Serves 4

¼ cup orange juice
1 can (15 ounces) cranberry sauce
¼ cup soy sauce
1 tablespoon honey
½ teaspoon ginger
1 teaspoon cornstarch
1 tablespoon canola oil
4 pork loin chops, about 1 pound
Salt and pepper to taste

Nutritional information per serving:

Calories	395
Fat, gm.	14
Protein, gm.	18
Carbs, gm.	49
Cholesterol, mg.	60
Fiber, gm.	1.3

The combination of cranberry, soy sauce, honey, and ginger creates a wonderful sauce for pork.

❖ In a small saucepan, combine orange juice, cranberry sauce, soy sauce, honey, ginger, and cornstarch. Cook over medium heat, stirring constantly, until mixture comes to a full boil. Remove from heat and set aside. In a large skillet, heat oil. Add pork to pan and sprinkle with salt and pepper. Cook over medium-high heat, until each piece is golden brown on both sides. Add cranberry mixture and simmer, turning chops occasionally, 10 to 15 minutes or until chops are completely cooked through. If mixture gets too thick, add water to thin to desired consistency.

Pork Chops, Potatoes, and Cabbage

In this recipe the pork chops are exceptionally moist and tender.

❖ In a large skillet*, heat oil. Add pork chops and cook over medium-high heat until each piece of meat is brown on both sides. Sprinkle with salt and pepper. Remove from pan and set aside. Add onion and cook until translucent. Add water to deglaze the pan. Return pork chops to the pan. Cover pork with sliced potatoes. Sprinkle potatoes with salt and pepper. Spoon soup over the potatoes. Place cabbage in corners of the skillet. Bring to a boil. Reduce heat, cover pan, and simmer for 1 to 1½ hours or until potatoes and cabbage are done. Check occasionally and add water if it gets too dry.

Note: This can also be baked in the oven at 300°F instead of cooking it on the stove. Check occasionally and add water if necessary.

*It is important to use a large enough skillet for this recipe. It should be a deep 11- or 12-inch skillet that has a cover. A Dutch oven would also work well.

Serves 4

1 tablespoon canola oil
4 (6 ounces each) boneless pork loin
   chops
Salt and pepper
1 large onion, sliced
1 cup water
3 large potatoes, peeled and sliced
Salt and pepper
1 can (10 ounces) cream of mushroom
   soup
1 small head of cabbage, quartered

Nutritional information per serving:

Calories	425
Fat, gm.	23
Protein, gm.	30
Carbs, gm.	25
Cholesterol, mg.	80
Fiber, gm.	1.6

Pork Loin with Fruit Pilaf

Serves 4

1 tablespoon canola oil
1½ pounds pork loin, cut into 4 chops
Salt and pepper
¾ cup basmati rice or white rice
½ cup chopped onion
1½ cups fat-free chicken broth
¼ teaspoon thyme
¼ teaspoon cinnamon
¼ teaspoon ginger
1 can (15 ounces) fruit cocktail, drained
½ cup chopped green onions
1 teaspoon lemon zest, optional

Nutritional information per serving:

Calories	475
Fat, gm.	20
Protein, gm.	30
Carbs, gm.	44
Cholesterol, mg.	85
Fiber, gm.	2.0

Serve a complete meal in one pan with beautifully browned pork loin chops served on a bed of rice and fruit.

❖ In a large skillet, heat oil. Add pork loin chops, sprinkle with salt and pepper, and cook over medium heat until each piece of meat is brown on both sides. The meat does not have to be completely done at this point. Remove meat from pan and set aside. Add rice and onion to skillet. Cook, stirring occasionally, until rice is golden brown. Add broth, thyme, cinnamon, and ginger. Stir to mix. Place meat over the rice. Cover and bring to a boil. Reduce heat and simmer for 20 minutes or until rice is tender. Stir in fruit and green onions. Replace cover and heat through. Fluff lightly with a fork. Sprinkle with lemon zest.

_____

Note: *Dried mixed fruits or raisins can be substituted for the canned fruit cocktail.*

Pork Medallions with Port Wine Cherry Sauce

This will impress your guests. It looks and tastes like a gourmet meal, but it is deceptively simple.

❖ In a small bowl, combine wine, dried cherries, jam, and mustard. Set aside. In a medium nonstick skillet, heat oil. Add pork, sprinkle with salt and pepper, and cook over medium-high heat until each piece is brown on both sides. Do not overcook. Remove pork from pan and set aside. Add wine mixture to the skillet. Scrape bottom of the pan with a wooden spoon to loosen browned bits. Bring to a boil, reduce heat, and boil gently until mixture is reduced in half and has a syrupy consistency. Whisk in butter. Arrange pork on individual plates or a platter and top with sauce.

Serves 4

1 cup port wine
⅓ cup dried cherries
2 tablespoons sugar-free raspberry jam
1 teaspoon Dijon mustard
1 tablespoon canola oil
*1¼ pounds pork tenderloin, cut into 1-
  inch slices*
Salt and pepper
1 tablespoon butter or margarine

Nutritional information per serving:

Calories	340
Fat, gm.	13
Protein, gm.	43
Carbs, gm.	12
Cholesterol, mg	100
Fiber, gm.	0.5

Pork Ribs and Sauerkraut

Serves 4

2 pounds spareribs or country-style
  pork ribs
1 tablespoon canola oil
2 large apples, peeled, cored and sliced
1 can (32 ounces) sauerkraut
¼ cup brown sugar
1 tablespoon caraway seeds, optional
½ cup fat-free chicken broth

Nutritional information per serving:

Calories	485
Fat, gm.	30
Protein, gm.	26
Carbs, gm.	28
Cholesterol, mg.	110
Fiber, gm.	7.0

If you are in the mood for a good old-fashioned dinner, try this. Recently cancer-fighting phytochemicals have been identified in sauerkraut. Who would have thought?

1.   Preheat oven to 300°F. Place ribs in a large Dutch oven and brown over medium-high heat. Add all remaining ingredients. Cover pan and bake for 1 to 3 hours or until pork is very tender. Check occasionally and add water if it gets too dry.

2.   This can also be combined in a slow cooker and cooked for 8 to 10 hours.

Pork Tenderloin with Cinnamon Apples

There is something special about the combination of pork and apples. By using pork tenderloin, you can make this quickly, but it looks like you worked all day.

1. Place apples in a large resealable plastic bag. Add orange juice, sherry, brown sugar, and cinnamon to the bag. Set aside. (This can be prepared ahead of time and refrigerated until ready to use.)

2. Cut pork tenderloin into ½-inch-thick slices. Sprinkle with salt and pepper. In a large skillet, heat oil. Add pork and brown quickly over high heat. Remove from heat and set aside. Add apple mixture to the skillet. Bring to a boil. Reduce heat, cover pan, and boil gently for 10 minutes or until apples are tender. Return pork to the pan and heat through. Add chicken broth to thin sauce if desired. Serve pork on a platter and top with apples and sauce.

Serves 4

4 medium apples, peeled, cored, and
*   sliced*
2 tablespoons orange juice
¼ cup dry sherry
¼ cup brown sugar
¼ teaspoon cinnamon
1½ pounds pork tenderloin
Salt and pepper
1 tablespoon canola oil
¼ cup fat free chicken broth, if needed

Nutritional information per serving:

Calories	425
Fat, gm.	11
Protein, gm.	29
Carbs, gm.	52
Cholesterol, mg.	110
Fiber, gm.	2.5

Serves 6

1 tablespoon canola oil
2 pounds lean beef, cubed
Salt and pepper
1 large onion, chopped
½ cup red wine
1 can (15 ounces) seasoned stewed
   tomatoes
½ teaspoon cumin
½ teaspoon thyme
½ teaspoon basil
¼ teaspoon allspice
2 cups fat-free beef or chicken broth,
   divided
½ pound sliced mushrooms
½ cup dried apricot halves, cut in half
½ cup prunes, pitted and cut in half
2 tablespoons flour, if needed

Nutritional information per serving:

Calories	345
Fat, gm.	10
Protein, gm.	24
Carbs, gm.	40
Cholesterol, mg.	85
Fiber, gm.	3.3

Spanish Beef and Mushrooms—Estofado

There are some surprising ingredients in this recipe that give it full-bodied flavor and make it extra healthy.

1. In a Dutch oven or a large skillet that has a cover, heat oil. Add beef cubes, sprinkle with salt and pepper, and cook over medium heat until brown. Add onion and cook until translucent. Add wine, tomatoes, cumin, thyme, basil, allspice, and 1 cup of broth. Stir to mix and bring to a boil. Reduce heat, cover pan, and simmer for 45 to 60 minutes or until beef is tender. Check occasionally and add additional broth to thin if needed. Add mushrooms, apricots, and prunes. Cover pan and simmer another 20 to 30 minutes.

2. If mixture needs to be thickened, mix 2 tablespoons flour in ½ cup broth or water. Stir into pan and bring to a boil.

3. Serve with cooked noodles.

Spicy Orange Marinated Beef Roast

Use this recipe when you want a really good roast beef dinner. The flavor is wonderful!

❖ Place beef roast in large resealable plastic bag. In a large jar, combine all remaining ingredients. Shake to mix. Pour into plastic bag with meat. Close bag and refrigerate. Marinate overnight. Preheat oven to 325°F. Drain roast, reserving marinade. Place roast in baking pan. Bake for 1 to 1½ hours or until meat reaches desired temperature. Baste occasionally with reserved marinade. Let stand for 10 to 20 minutes before serving. Cut into thin slices.

Note: *Choose a tender cut of beef when using this dry roasting method of cooking.*

Serves 6

3 pounds beef top sirloin or another
  tender cut of beef
1 cup orange juice
1 cup tomato juice
¼ cup canola oil
2 cloves garlic, minced
½ teaspoon allspice
½ teaspoon chili powder
¼ teaspoon cumin
1 teaspoon salt

Nutritional information per serving:

Calories	485
Fat, gm.	30
Protein, gm.	48
Carbs, gm.	6
Cholesterol, mg.	135
Fiber, gm.	0.4

Swiss Steak

Serves 6

1 tablespoon canola oil
1 large onion, chopped
2½ pounds top round steak
¼ cup flour
Salt and pepper
2 cups shredded carrots
1 teaspoon minced garlic
1 can (29 ounces) crushed tomatoes
1½ cups water, divided

Nutritional information per serving:

Calories	400
Fat, gm.	20
Protein, gm.	42
Carbs, gm.	14
Cholesterol, mg.	110
Fiber, gm.	2.8

This is one of those recipes that is passed from generation to generation. Everyone loves a home-cooked meal that fills the house with wonderful aromas.

❖ Preheat oven to 325°F. In a large, ovenproof skillet, heat oil. Add onion and cook over medium heat until translucent. Remove onion from pan and set aside. Sprinkle steak with flour on both sides. Place meat in skillet, sprinkle with salt and pepper, and cook until brown on both sides. Add carrots, garlic, tomatoes, reserved onion, and 1 cup water. Bring to a boil. Remove from heat, cover pan, and bake for 1 hour or until meat is very tender. Check occasionally and add additional water if needed to prevent mixture from getting too dry.

Two-Meal Slow Roasted Pork Shoulder

This slowly roasted pork shoulder will feed a family of four at least twice. The second time around, it can be turned into barbecued pork for sandwiches or wraps.

❖ Preheat the oven to 350°F. Heat enough oil in a large baking pan to brown the roast. Brown it well on all sides over high heat and transfer the roast to a platter. Lower the heat and discard all but a thin film of oil from the pan. Sauté the garlic over low heat for about a minute, not allowing it to burn. Add the broth to the pan together with the thyme and rosemary. Return roast to the pan and bring the contents to a boil. Cover pan and place the pan in the oven. Bake for about 2 to 3 hours or until the meat is very tender. Remove the roast to a clean platter and let it rest for a few minutes. Skim any fat from the meat juices. Add salt and pepper to taste. Slice the roast and pass the juices along with the meat.

❖ Second time around: Reheat the leftovers in their own juices, and when thoroughly heated, remove the meat from the juices. Shred the pork by pulling it apart with two forks and transfer the shredded meat into your favorite bottled barbecue sauce.

Serves 10

2 tablespoons canola oil
4–5-pound pork shoulder roast
* or "Boston Butt" roast*
4 teaspoons minced garlic
2 cups fat-free chicken broth
2 teaspoons dried thyme
1 teaspoon crumbled dried rosemary
Salt and pepper
1 cup distilled white vinegar
1 cup cider vinegar
1–3 teaspoons crushed red pepper flakes
1–3 teaspoons hot red pepper sauce
1–2 tablespoons sugar
Salt and pepper

continued >>

Two-Meal Slow Roasted Pork Shoulder (continued)

Nutritional information per serving without the optional sauce:

Calories	335
Fat, gm.	16
Protein, gm.	47
Carbs, gm.	1
Cholesterol, mg.	140
Fiber, gm.	0.1

❖ Mix all the ingredients together, starting with lesser amounts of the pepper flakes, hot sauce, and sugar; taste and add more of the ingredients until it's just to your liking. Moisten the shredded pork with some of the sauce and pass the extra sauce at the table.

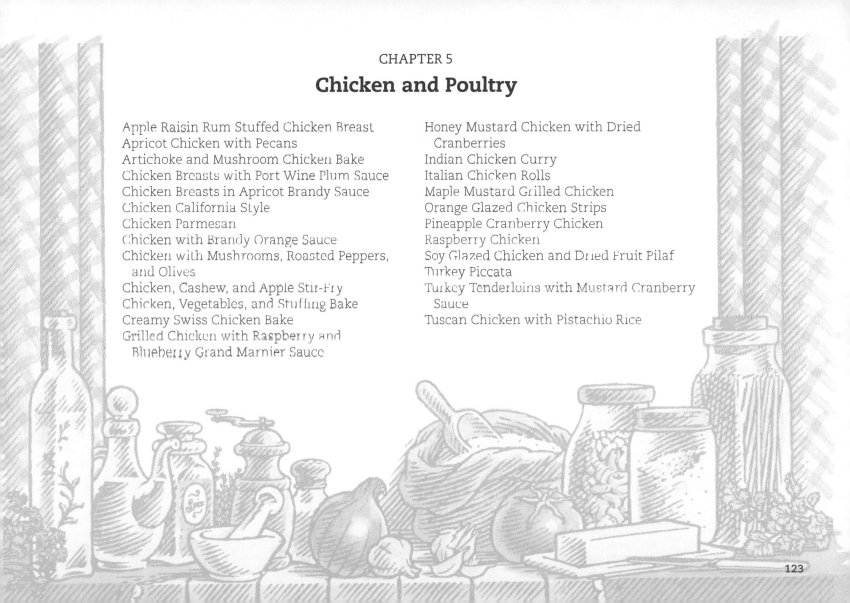

CHAPTER 5

Chicken and Poultry

Apple Raisin Rum Stuffed Chicken Breast
Apricot Chicken with Pecans
Artichoke and Mushroom Chicken Bake
Chicken Breasts with Port Wine Plum Sauce
Chicken Breasts in Apricot Brandy Sauce
Chicken California Style
Chicken Parmesan
Chicken with Brandy Orange Sauce
Chicken with Mushrooms, Roasted Peppers,
   and Olives
Chicken, Cashew, and Apple Stir-Fry
Chicken, Vegetables, and Stuffing Bake
Creamy Swiss Chicken Bake
Grilled Chicken with Raspberry and
   Blueberry Grand Marnier Sauce

Honey Mustard Chicken with Dried
   Cranberries
Indian Chicken Curry
Italian Chicken Rolls
Maple Mustard Grilled Chicken
Orange Glazed Chicken Strips
Pineapple Cranberry Chicken
Raspberry Chicken
Soy Glazed Chicken and Dried Fruit Pilaf
Turkey Piccata
Turkey Tenderloins with Mustard Cranberry
   Sauce
Tuscan Chicken with Pistachio Rice

Chicken and Poultry Cooking Tips

To pound or not to pound, that is the question. Chicken breasts come in various sizes (from 4 to 9 ounces), and each piece may be uneven in thickness. To ensure even cooking, use the smooth end of a meat pounder or mallet to pound the chicken to an even thickness.

To determine how much chicken you will need for a recipe, use these guidelines:

One 3–4-pound chicken	**3–4 cups** cut-up chicken pieces
Two whole chicken breasts	**2 cups** cut-up chicken pieces
¾ pound chicken breast	**2 cups** cut-up chicken pieces
5-ounce can chicken breast	**1 cup** cut-up chicken pieces

Keep safety in mind when handling uncooked chicken and poultry. Use a separate cutting board for uncooked chicken. Wash all knives, utensils, cutting boards, and countertops that have come into contact with raw chicken with hot, soapy water.

Chicken needs to be cooked until it is completely done, but avoid overcooking. If chicken is overcooked, it loses moisture and becomes dry and tough. This is especially true of breast meat because it contains little fat. Cook chicken just until its juices run clear and it is no longer pink in the middle.

To ensure doneness, cook poultry to 170°F for breasts and 180°F for other parts of a whole bird.

Occasionally, you may see traces of pink in the meat near the bones in cooked chicken. This is probably traces of bone pigment that has leached out during cooking. It is not uncooked meat. This occurs more often when chicken is frozen and then defrosted and cooked. While it may be aesthetically unpleasant, the meat is perfectly safe if the chicken is otherwise fully cooked.

When cutting up chicken for a recipe, it may work better to slice it thinly instead of cutting it into large cubes.

There are no hormones used in the production of chickens. The use of hormones has been banned by the U.S. Food and Drug Administration (FDA).

Free-range chickens, which are allowed to roam freely and forage for food rather than being confined to chicken coops, are no more nutritious than traditionally raised chickens. Some studies report that free-range chickens are more likely to be contaminated from bacteria found in soil.

Apple Raisin Rum Stuffed Chicken Breasts

It smells like apple pie when you are baking this marvelous chicken dish.

1. Preheat oven to 350°F. Grease a 7" × 11" baking pan. In a small custard cup, combine raisins and rum. Heat in the microwave for 1 minute. Set aside. Lightly pound each chicken breast to flatten to even thickness. Sprinkle each side with salt and pepper. Set aside. In a small bowl, combine brown sugar, cinnamon, curry powder, apple, and reserved raisins and rum. Stir to mix. Place a small mound (about 2 tablespoons) on each chicken breast. Roll each breast and secure with toothpicks. Place each stuffed breast seam-side down in baking pan. Spoon remaining apple mixture on top of and around chicken in the pan. Sprinkle each breast with paprika. Cover with foil and bake for 40 to 45 minutes or until chicken is thoroughly cooked. Uncover and top breasts with melted butter. Place under the oven broiler for 5 minutes or until lightly brown on top.

2. When serving the chicken, spoon the extra sauce on top. It's great!

Serves 4

¼ cup raisins
2 tablespoons rum
4 boned and skinned chicken breast halves
Salt and pepper
2 tablespoons brown sugar
¼ teaspoon cinnamon
½ teaspoon curry powder
1 large apple, cored, peeled, and finely chopped
Dash paprika
2 tablespoons butter or margarine, melted

Nutritional information per serving:

Calories	210
Fat, gm.	7
Protein, gm.	20
Carbs, gm.	17
Cholesterol, mg.	65
Fiber, gm.	1.4

Apricot Chicken with Pecans

Serves 4

½ cup flour
½ teaspoon paprika
½ teaspoon salt
½ teaspoon pepper
4 boned and skinned chicken breast
  halves
1 tablespoon canola oil

Sauce:
⅓ cup honey mustard
⅓ cup sugar-free apricot preserves
2 tablespoons balsamic vinegar
½ teaspoon curry powder
½ cup chopped pecans
½ cup chicken broth, if needed

Nutritional information per serving:

Calories	285
Fat, gm.	12
Protein, gm.	25
Carbs, gm.	19
Cholesterol, mg.	50
Fiber, gm.	1.1

Create a wonderful chicken meal with the flavors of mustard and curry and the sweetness of apricot preserves and pecans.

❖ Preheat oven to 350°F. Grease a 7" × 11" baking pan. In a shallow bowl, combine flour, paprika, salt, and pepper. Lightly pound chicken to an even thickness. Dredge each piece of chicken in flour mixture. Heat oil in large nonstick skillet. Add chicken and cook over medium heat until each piece is browned on both sides. Place chicken in baking pan. In a small bowl, combine mustard, apricot preserves, vinegar, curry powder, and pecans. Spoon over chicken. Bake for 15 to 20 minutes or just until chicken is cooked through. Add a small amount of chicken broth or water to bottom of the pan if it gets too dry. Do not overcook.

_____

Note: *The chicken can be combined with the sauce in the skillet and cooked on the stove instead of in the oven. If you use this method, watch carefully to prevent it from burning.*

Artichoke and Mushroom Chicken Bake

The flavors of the artichoke hearts, mushrooms, and sherry make this a dish you will really enjoy. If you have leftovers, it is even better the second day.

❖ Preheat oven to 350°F. Butter a 7" × 11" baking pan. Pound chicken lightly to flatten to an even thickness. Heat 1 tablespoon oil in a large skillet. Place chicken in skillet and sprinkle with salt and pepper. Cook over medium heat until each piece is browned on both sides. Chicken does not have to be thoroughly cooked at this point. Place chicken in baking pan. Sprinkle with paprika. Add 1 tablespoon oil and mushrooms to skillet and cook until tender. Mix flour in ½ cup of the broth in a shaker. Pour into skillet along with remaining broth. Bring to a boil, stirring constantly, and cook 1 to 2 minutes or until thickened. Add sherry and artichoke hearts. Stir to mix. Pour over chicken. Bake for 20 to 30 minutes or until chicken is completely done. Add water or additional broth to thin sauce if desired.

Serves 4

4 boned and skinned chicken breast halves
2 tablespoons canola oil, divided
Salt and pepper
Dash paprika
½ pound sliced mushrooms
2 tablespoons flour
2 cups fat-free chicken broth, divided
¼ cup sherry
1 can (14 ounces) quartered artichoke hearts, drained

Nutritional information per serving:

Calories	250
Fat, gm.	8
Protein, gm.	26
Carbs, gm.	18
Cholesterol, mg.	50
Fiber, gm.	6.0

Chicken Breast with Port Wine Plum Sauce

Serves 4

4 boned and skinned chicken breasts*
¼ cup flour
1 teaspoon salt
½ teaspoon pepper
1 tablespoon canola oil

Sauce:
4 medium fresh or canned plums, pitted
  and thinly sliced
½ cup port wine or grape juice
1 teaspoon sugar

Nutritional information per serving:

Calories	230
Fat, gm.	5
Protein, gm.	27
Carbs, gm.	18
Cholesterol, mg.	65
Fiber, gm.	0.8

This is a good way to add a serving of fruit to your main course and make it extra attractive too.

❖ Place chicken breasts in a large plastic bag. Combine flour, salt, and pepper. Place flour mixture into bag with chicken. Shake to coat well. In a large nonstick skillet, heat oil. Add chicken and cook over medium heat until browned on all sides and completely done in the middle. While meat is cooking, combine plums, port wine, and sugar in a small saucepan. Bring to a boil. Reduce heat, cover, and cook for 3 minutes or until plums are tender. Uncover pan and cook until sauce is slightly reduced. Place chicken on individual plates and top with plum sauce.

You may want to pound the chicken breast to ½-inch thickness before cooking. Some people like the chicken thick and plump, while others like it thin.

Chicken Breasts in Apricot Brandy Sauce

Sometimes, simple is best.

1. Lightly pound chicken breasts to an even thickness. In a large skillet, heat oil. Add chicken breasts, sprinkle with salt and pepper, and cook over medium heat until brown. Mix sauce ingredients together and pour into pan. Bring to a boil, stirring constantly. Boil gently for 5 to 10 minutes or until sauce thickens slightly and chicken is completely done.

2. Served with cooked rice or noodles.

_____

Note: *The chicken can also be grilled. Brush some of the sauce on the chicken while grilling and serve remaining sauce over cooked chicken.*

Serves 4

4 boned and skinned chicken breast
  halves
1 tablespoon canola oil
Salt and pepper

Sauce:
½ cup apricot preserves
¼ cup brandy

Nutritional information per serving:

Calories	230
Fat, gm.	5
Protein, gm.	20
Carbs, gm.	25
Cholesterol, mg.	50
Fiber, gm.	0.5

Chicken California Style

Serves 4

4 boned and skinned chicken breast
  halves
1 tablespoon canola oil
Salt and pepper
2 cups fat-free chicken broth
2 tablespoons cornstarch
1 tablespoon balsamic vinegar
1 tablespoon coarsely ground mustard
1 tablespoon Dijon mustard
1 can (14 ounces) quartered and drained
  artichoke hearts
½ cup sliced black olives or Kalamata
  olives
1 medium tomato, seeded and diced

Nutritional information per serving:

Calories	215
Fat, gm.	7
Protein, gm.	24
Carbs, gm.	13
Cholesterol, mg.	50
Fiber, gm.	4.7

Think of the yellow flowering mustard plants in the fields of Napa Valley when you enjoy this dish.

1. Lightly pound chicken to an even thickness. In a large, heavy skillet, heat oil. Add chicken and cook over medium-high heat. In a small bowl or jar, mix broth with cornstarch. Add to skillet and bring to a boil, stirring constantly. Reduce heat and simmer 5 to 10 minutes or until chicken is thoroughly cooked. Add vinegar, mustards, and artichoke hearts. Heat through. Taste and adjust seasoning with extra mustard or salt and pepper if desired. When ready to serve, top with olives and tomato.

2. Serve with noodles or mashed potatoes.

Chicken Parmesan

I like this best served in individual serving dishes. This is a meal that could easily be made for 1 or 2 persons. I often fix it for myself for supper when I am home alone.

❖ Preheat oven to 350°F. Grease 4 individual baking dishes or a 9" × 11" baking pan. Place each chicken breast between pieces of heavy plastic. Pound to flatten to an even thickness of about ½ inch. Place egg in a shallow bowl. Set aside. Combine bread crumbs and Parmesan cheese in another shallow bowl. Dip chicken pieces in egg and then in bread crumb mixture to coat each side. Sprinkle with salt and pepper. Heat oil in a large nonstick skillet. Add chicken and cook over medium-high heat until each piece is brown on both sides. Place in baking pan(s). Top with half of the cheese. Spoon sauce over cheese and sprinkle remaining cheese on top. Bake for 30 minutes or until chicken is thoroughly cooked and cheese has melted.

Serves 4

4 boned and skinned chicken breast
   halves
1 egg, lightly beaten
⅓ cup bread crumbs
2 tablespoons grated Parmesan cheese
Salt and pepper
1 tablespoon canola oil
6 ounces (1½ cups) shredded mozzarella
   cheese, divided
2 cups tomato pasta sauce, divided

Nutritional information per serving:

Calories	415
Fat, gm.	20
Protein, gm.	36
Carbs, gm.	23
Cholesterol, mg.	135
Fiber, gm.	2.5

Serves 4

1 tablespoon canola oil
4 skinless, boneless chicken breasts, cut
   into ½-inch slices
Salt and pepper
2 large leeks, white part only,
   thinly sliced
1 medium red pepper, thinly sliced
2 small zucchini, thinly sliced
½ teaspoon tarragon
1 tablespoon cornstarch
1 cup fat-free chicken broth
¼ cup brandy
½ cup fat-free sour cream
1 cup mandarin oranges or fresh orange
   sections
2 tablespoons orange zest for garnish

Nutritional information per serving:

Calories	300
Fat, gm.	6
Protein, gm.	43
Carbs, gm.	17
Cholesterol, mg.	100
Fiber, gm.	1.7

Chicken with Brandy Orange Sauce

This is an absolutely beautiful dish to serve your family or guests.

1. In a large, heavy skillet, heat oil. Add chicken slices and cook over medium-high heat until browned. Sprinkle with salt and pepper. Remove chicken from pan and set aside. Add leeks, pepper, zucchini, and tarragon to the skillet. Cook until tender. Mix cornstarch in chicken broth. Pour into pan. Bring to a boil, stirring constantly. Reduce heat and stir in reserved chicken breasts and brandy. Simmer until chicken is completely done. When ready to serve, add sour cream and heat through. Top with orange slices and garnish with orange zest.

2. Serve with cooked spaghetti, noodles, or rice.

Chicken with Mushrooms, Roasted Peppers, and Olives

I like the colorful red peppers and the green olives in this dish. It tastes as good as it looks!

1. In a large saucepan, cook pasta in boiling salted water. Cook until al dente. Drain and rinse under cold water. Set aside. Reheat pasta under hot running water when ready to serve.

2. In a heavy skillet, heat oil. Add chicken, sprinkle with salt and pepper, and cook over medium-high heat until browned. Remove chicken from the pan and set aside. (Chicken does not have to be completely cooked at this point.) Add onion to skillet and cook until translucent. Add mushrooms, garlic, and peppers. Cook until mushrooms are tender. Combine cornstarch with broth and add to the pan. Cook, stirring constantly, until mixture comes to a boil. Add wine and half-and-half. Return chicken to the pan. Cover and simmer for 10 minutes or until chicken is completely done. When ready to serve, add olives. Serve chicken and sauce over pasta. Garnish with parsley.

Serves 4

6 ounces (about 3 cups dry) pasta of your choice
1 tablespoon canola oil
4 boned and skinned chicken breast halves
Salt and pepper
1 medium onion, finely chopped
½ pound sliced mushrooms
2 teaspoons minced garlic
2 medium roasted red peppers, thinly sliced
1 tablespoon cornstarch
½ cup fat-free chicken broth
½ cup white wine
½ cup fat-free half and-half
½ cup sliced pitted green olives
¼ cup chopped parsley for garnish, optional

Nutritional information per serving:

Calories	375
Fat, gm.	9
Protein, gm.	30
Carbs, gm.	42
Cholesterol, mg.	90
Fiber, gm.	3.0

1 tablespoon canola oil
1 pound boned and skinned chicken
 breast, cut into bite-sized pieces
½ pound fresh mushrooms, sliced
1 large red bell pepper, cut into strips
2 medium apples, peeled, cored, sliced

Sauce Ingredients:
¾ cup apple juice
¾ cup fat-free chicken broth
¼ cup soy sauce
¼ teaspoon cinnamon
½ tablespoon ginger
¼ teaspoon ground red pepper
2 tablespoons cornstarch
Salt and pepper to taste
¼ cup cashews or roasted peanuts

Nutritional information per serving (without the rice):

Calories	310
Fat, gm.	9
Protein, gm.	30
Carbs, gm.	27
Cholesterol, mg.	65
Fiber, gm.	3.8

Chicken, Cashew, and Apple Stir-Fry

The fresh apples combined with chicken, mushrooms, and red pepper will fill your kitchen with the aromas of fall.

❖ In a large nonstick skillet, heat oil and add chicken. Cook over medium-high heat until browned. Add mushrooms and cook until tender. Add pepper and apples and cook until tender-crisp. While pepper and apples are cooking, combine sauce ingredients. Mix well. Pour into skillet. Stir constantly until mixture comes to a boil and thickens to desired consistency. Add additional chicken broth to thin or add additional cornstarch to thicken. Add salt and pepper to taste. Top with cashews right before serving. Serve over cooked rice.

Chicken, Vegetables, and Stuffing Bake

I especially like this one because you don't even have to brown the chicken or cut up vegetables.

❖ Preheat oven to 350°F. Grease a 7" × 11" baking pan or a 2-quart casserole dish. Place chicken slices in the pan and sprinkle with salt and pepper. Top with vegetables. Mix soup and sour cream together and spoon over vegetables. In a small bowl, mix stuffing mix with water. Let stand for 5 minutes to allow liquid to be absorbed into stuffing cubes. Spoon stuffing on top of chicken mixture. Bake for 35 to 45 minutes or until chicken is cooked through.

Serves 4

4 boned and skinned chicken breast
  halves, thinly sliced
Salt and pepper
1 bag (16 ounces) loose-pack frozen
  mixed vegetables
1 can (10 ounces) cream of mushroom
  soup
½ cup fat-free sour cream
6 ounces Stove Top stuffing cubes
1½ cups boiling water

Nutritional information per serving:

Calories	375
Fat, gm.	8
Protein, gm.	30
Carbs, gm.	40
Cholesterol, mg.	60
Fiber, gm.	2.9

Creamy Swiss Chicken Bake

Serves 4

4 boned and skinned chicken breast
  halves
Salt and pepper
4 ounces (1 cup) shredded Swiss cheese,
  divided
1 can (10 ounces) cream of chicken soup
½ cup fat-free milk
2 cups herb-seasoned stuffing cubes
Butter spray

Nutritional information per serving:

Calories	450
Fat, gm.	12
Protein, gm.	39
Carbs, gm.	47
Cholesterol, mg.	80
Fiber, gm.	0.1

You can assemble this the day before to make it even easier on the day you entertain.

❖ Preheat oven to 325°F. Grease a 7" × 11" baking pan. Place chicken breasts in pan. Sprinkle with salt and pepper. Cover with ½ of the cheese. Mix soup and milk together. Pour over chicken. Top with stuffing cubes. Spray with butter spray to moisten the bread cubes. Sprinkle remaining cheese on top. Cover and bake for 50 to 60 minutes or until chicken is completely done. Check occasionally and add extra water to bottom of the pan if it is getting too dry. Uncover the last 10 minutes of baking.

———

Note: *Another cheese of your choice may be substituted for the Swiss cheese.*

Grilled Chicken with Raspberry and Blueberry Grand Marnier Sauce

Make your 4th of July grilled chicken special with this red-and-blue sauce.

1. Sauce: In a small, heavy saucepan, combine raspberry jam, vinegar, and wine. Bring to a boil and cook uncovered, stirring occasionally, until reduced to about ¾ cup. Remove from heat and strain. Pour strained mixture back into saucepan. Mix cornstarch with orange juice in a small glass. Pour into pan. Bring to a full boil, stirring constantly, until mixture thickens. Remove from heat and stir in Grand Marnier. When ready to serve, gently stir in raspberries and blueberries. Serve warm sauce over grilled chicken.

2. Chicken: Heat grill to medium-high heat. Place chicken on grill. Sprinkle with salt and pepper. Grill until browned and completely done. Serve on individual dishes and top with berry sauce.

---

*Grand Marnier is one brand of orange-flavored liqueur.

Serves 4

Sauce:
¼ cup sugar-free raspberry jam
¼ cup red wine vinegar
1 cup dry white wine
1½ tablespoons cornstarch
⅓ cup orange juice
¼ cup Grand Marnier*
½ cup fresh raspberries
½ cup fresh blueberries

Grilled Chicken:
4 boned and skinned chicken breast halves
Salt and pepper to taste

Nutritional information per serving:

Calories	180
Fat, gm.	2
Protein, gm.	25
Carbs, gm.	15
Cholesterol, mg.	50
Fiber, gm.	0.3

Serves 4

Sauce:
2 tablespoons butter or margarine
2 tablespoons flour
½ cup fat-free chicken broth
½ cup fat-free half-and-half
2 tablespoons honey mustard
Dash red pepper
¾ cup dried cranberries
Salt and pepper to taste

Chicken:
4 boned and skinned chicken breast
   halves
1 tablespoon canola oil
Salt and pepper
1 medium orange, thinly sliced

Nutritional information per serving:

Calories	300
Fat, gm.	11
Protein, gm.	22
Carbs, gm.	28
Cholesterol, mg.	65
Fiber, gm.	1.7

Honey Mustard Chicken with Dried Cranberries

The honey mustard gives this sauce an interesting sweet yet hot taste. The cranberries add extra color and flavor. The sauce can be made ahead of time and refrigerated until ready to use.

1. Melt butter in a small saucepan. Add flour and cook over medium heat, stirring constantly, until mixture bubbles. Add broth and half-and-half. Cook, stirring constantly, over medium heat until mixture comes to a full boil. Add mustard, red pepper, and dried cranberries. Season with salt and pepper. Set aside until ready to serve. Sauce can be made ahead of time and refrigerated until ready to use. Reheat when needed over low heat and add additional broth if it is too thick.

2. To prepare the chicken, lightly pound chicken to an even thickness. Heat oil in a large skillet. Place chicken in skillet and sprinkle with salt and pepper. Cook over medium-high heat until each piece of chicken is browned on both sides and chicken is completely done. Arrange chicken on a platter and top with warm sauce. Garnish with orange slices.

Indian Chicken Curry

The hot curry powder makes this powerfully good.

1. Lightly pound chicken breasts to an even thickness. In a large skillet, heat oil. Add chicken and cook over medium-high heat until pieces are browned. Season with salt and pepper. Remove chicken from skillet and set aside. Add onions and cook until translucent. Combine cornstarch with broth and pour into skillet. Bring to a boil, stirring constantly. Add curry powder, cumin, raisins, and apricot preserves. Reduce heat and simmer for 10 minutes. Add additional broth or water, if necessary, to thin sauce to desired consistency. Return chicken to the skillet. Add apple and yogurt. Cook 5 to 10 minutes or just until apples are tender. Add salt and pepper to taste.

2. Serve over hot cooked rice.

Serves 4

4 boned and skinned chicken breast
  halves, cubed
1 tablespoon canola oil
Salt and pepper
2 cups chopped onions
2 tablespoons cornstarch
3 cups fat-free chicken broth
1 tablespoon hot curry powder
½ teaspoon cumin
¾ cup golden raisins
⅓ cup sugar free apricot preserves
1 large apple, peeled, cored and diced
1 cup low-fat plain yogurt
Salt and pepper to taste

Nutritional information per serving:

Calories	330
Fat, gm.	6
Protein, gm.	26
Carbs, gm.	43
Cholesterol, mg.	55
Fiber, gm.	3.6

Italian Chicken Rolls

Serves 4

4 boned and skinned chicken breast
  halves
Salt and pepper
1 cup part-skim ricotta cheese
½ cup grated Parmesan cheese
2 teaspoons olive oil
¼ teaspoon white pepper
2 cups spaghetti sauce
½ cup shredded mozzarella cheese

Nutritional information per serving:

Calories	410
Fat, gm.	20
Protein, gm.	35
Carbs, gm.	23
Cholesterol, mg.	90
Fiber, gm.	4.2

No one will believe you when you tell them this was an easy supper. These look impressive and they taste great.

❖ Preheat oven to 350°F. Grease a 7" × 11" baking pan. Lightly pound chicken breasts to an even thickness. Sprinkle with salt and pepper. Set aside. In a small bowl, combine ricotta, Parmesan cheese, oil, and white pepper. Stir to mix. Place about ¼ cup of the mixture in the middle of each chicken breast. Roll meat and place seam-side down in baking pan. Use toothpicks to secure the chicken if necessary. Pour sauce over chicken. Bake for 35 to 45 minutes or until chicken is thoroughly cooked. Remove from oven and sprinkle with mozzarella cheese. Return to oven for 5 minutes or until cheese is melted.

Maple Mustard Grilled Chicken

Cook it inside or outside, both work great.

❖ Heat grill to medium heat. Combine maple syrup, mustard, and vinegar together in a small jar. Shake to mix well. Place chicken between 2 sheets of plastic wrap and pound each piece with the smooth end of a meat mallet until chicken pieces are an even ½-inch thick. Coat chicken lightly with olive oil spray and sprinkle with salt and pepper. Place on greased grill rack. Baste with mustard sauce. Cook until chicken is completely done, basting every time chicken is turned on the grill. Remove from grill and pass extra sauce at the table.

Note: *In place of grilling, this chicken turns out great if cooked in a small amount of oil in a nonstick skillet over medium heat. Cook chicken until each piece is browned on both sides and completely done in the middle. Add the sauce and cook until it is slightly caramelized.*

Serves 4

⅓ cup maple syrup
⅓ cup Dijon mustard
2 tablespoons balsamic vinegar
4 skinless, boneless chicken breasts
Olive oil spray
¼ teaspoon seasoned salt
⅛ teaspoon pepper

Nutritional information per serving:

Calories	180
Fat, gm.	2
Protein, gm.	21
Carbs, gm.	19
Cholesterol, mg.	50
Fiber, gm.	0.6

Orange Glazed Chicken Strips

Serves 4

1 pound boneless, skinless chicken breast,
  cut into ½-inch strips

Glaze:
½ cup sugar-free orange marmalade*
¼ cup steak sauce
¼ cup honey
1 tablespoon lime juice
Dash hot pepper sauce
1 teaspoon prepared horseradish
2 cups cooked rice

Nutritional information per serving:

Calories	300
Fat, gm.	2
Protein, gm.	17
Carbs, gm.	55
Cholesterol, mg.	35
Fiber, gm.	0.9

The sauce that forms while the chicken is under the broiler is a flavor treat when served on a bed of rice.

❖ Preheat the broiler. Line a baking pan with foil. Spray foil with cooking spray. Arrange chicken in pan. In a small bowl, combine all glaze ingredients. Brush glaze on all sides of the chicken. Broil about 6 inches under broiler for 10 to 15 minutes or until chicken is brown on top and thoroughly cooked. Watch carefully to prevent burning. Serve chicken, and any sauce that forms in the pan, over a bed of rice.

———

*This is also wonderful with apricot preserves.

Pineapple Cranberry Chicken

Dress up your ordinary chicken breast with this colorful, healthful topping.

❖ In a small saucepan, combine pineapple, dried cranberries, jam, soy sauce, vinegar, pepper, and cornstarch. Bring to a boil, stirring constantly, until mixture comes to a rolling boil. Set aside. Lightly pound chicken to an even thickness. In a large skillet, heat oil. Add chicken and cook over medium-high heat until each piece is brown on both sides. Chicken does not have to be completely done at this point. Sprinkle with salt and pepper. Add pineapple sauce to skillet. Reduce heat, cover skillet, and simmer for 5 to 10 minutes or until chicken is thoroughly cooked. Place chicken in serving dish and top with sauce.

Serves 4

1 can (20 ounces) pineapple tidbits in
   juice, undrained
½ cup dried cranberries
½ cup sugar-free raspberry jam
2 tablespoons soy sauce
2 tablespoons raspberry vinegar
⅛ teaspoon black pepper
1 tablespoon cornstarch
4 boned and skinned chicken breast
   halves
1 tablespoon canola oil
Salt and pepper

Nutritional information per serving:

Calories	290
Fat, gm.	5
Protein, gm.	21
Carbs, gm.	40
Cholesterol, mg.	50
Fiber, gm.	2.1

Raspberry Chicken

Serves 4

4 boned and skinned chicken breast
   halves
1 tablespoon canola oil
Salt and pepper

Sauce:
½ cup finely chopped green onions
¼ cup fat-free chicken broth
½ cup sugar-free raspberry jam
¼ cup raspberry vinegar
½ cup fat-free sour cream
1 cup fresh raspberries

Nutritional information per serving:

Calories	200
Fat, gm.	5
Protein, gm.	22
Carbs, gm.	16
Cholesterol, mg.	55
Fiber, gm.	2.3

How can a dish be so attractive, so tasty, and so low in calories too? It really is a special way to serve chicken.

❖ Lightly pound chicken breasts to flatten to an even thickness. In a large skillet, heat oil. Add chicken and sprinkle with salt and pepper. Cook over medium heat until each piece is brown on both sides and thoroughly cooked. Remove from pan and place on serving platter. Add onions, broth, jam, and vinegar to the skillet. Bring to a boil and cook until sauce is reduced by half. Stir in sour cream and heat through. Serve sauce over chicken and top with fresh raspberries.

Soy Glazed Chicken and Dried Fruit Pilaf

A touch of sweetness; a touch of heat from the pepper flakes; and the complex flavors from the combination of cinnamon, ginger, and cumin make this just right.

❖ In a large skillet, heat oil. Add chicken, sprinkle with salt and pepper, and cook over medium-high heat until browned. Add brown sugar, soy sauce, and red pepper flakes. Cook, stirring constantly, about 2 minutes or until chicken is glazed. Take the skillet off the stove. Remove chicken from the skillet and set aside. Add broth, rice, cinnamon, ginger, and cumin to skillet. Return to the stove and bring to a boil. Reduce heat, cover skillet, and boil gently for 20 minutes or until rice is tender and liquid has been absorbed. Stir in dried fruit and reserved chicken. Heat through. Add additional **soy** sauce if desired. Sprinkle with green onions when ready to serve.

Note: *In this recipe, it is important to remove the chicken from the skillet after it has been glazed with the brown sugar and soy sauce. Set it aside until the rice is cooked.*

This recipe can be cut in half and will serve 3 to 4 people.

Serves 6

1 tablespoon canola oil
4 boned and skinned chicken breast
   halves, thinly sliced
Salt and pepper
2 tablespoons brown sugar
¼ cup soy sauce
¼ teaspoon red pepper flakes
3 cups fat-free chicken broth
1½ cups basmati rice
¼ teaspoon cinnamon
¼ teaspoon ginger
¼ teaspoon cumin
1 cup dried mixed fruit bits or golden
   raisins
½ cup chopped green onions

Nutritional information per serving:

Calories	350
Fat, gm.	3
Protein, gm.	19
Carbs, gm.	62
Cholesterol, mg.	35
Fiber, gm.	1.7

Serves 4

1½ *pounds turkey tenderloin, cut into*
  2-inch pieces
⅓ *cup flour*
1 *teaspoon salt*
½ *teaspoon pepper*
1 *teaspoon paprika*
1 *tablespoon canola oil*
1 *teaspoon minced garlic*
1 *cup fat-free chicken broth*
2 *teaspoons cornstarch*
½ *cup dry white wine*
¼ *cup fresh lemon juice*
3 *tablespoons capers*
1 *tablespoon butter or margarine*
4 *fresh lemon slices*

Nutritional information per serving:

Calories	350
Fat, gm.	17
Protein, gm.	35
Carbs, gm.	14
Cholesterol, mg.	100
Fiber, gm.	0.3

Turkey Piccata

If you are in the mood for something light, this is a good choice. It has a distinctive but mild lemon flavor. If you can't find turkey tenderloin, chicken breast works great.

❖ Place turkey pieces in a large plastic bag. Add flour, salt, pepper, and paprika. Toss to coat the turkey pieces. In a large nonstick skillet, heat oil. Add turkey and cook over medium-high heat until brown on all sides and turkey is thoroughly cooked. Add garlic and cook 1 minute. Remove turkey from the pan and set aside. Combine broth and cornstarch. Add to skillet. Bring to a boil, stirring constantly. Add all remaining ingredients and boil gently until mixture is reduced to half the amount. Return turkey to the pan and heat through. Garnish with lemon slices.

Turkey Tenderloins with Mustard Cranberry Sauce

Turkey is not just for Thanksgiving anymore. If you have never cooked with turkey tenderloin, try this.

❖ Preheat oven to 325°F. Place turkey tenderloin in a large plastic bag. Combine flour, salt, pepper, and thyme. Add mixture to the bag. Close bag and shake to coat the turkey pieces. Heat oil and butter in a large, ovenproof nonstick skillet. Remove turkey from bag and place in skillet. (Set remaining flour mixture aside.) Cook turkey over medium heat until brown on all sides. In a shaker, mix 2 tablespoons of the reserved flour mixture with ½ cup of the chicken broth. Combine with remaining broth, mustard, and cranberries. Pour into skillet. Bring to a boil while stirring constantly. Cook 1 minute or until mixture has thickened. Bake, covered, for 15 to 20 minutes or until turkey is thoroughly cooked.

Serves 6

2 pounds turkey tenderloin
½ cup flour
1 teaspoon salt
¼ teaspoon pepper
¼ teaspoon thyme
1 tablespoon canola oil
1 tablespoon butter or margarine
2 cups fat-free chicken broth, divided
1 tablespoon Dijon mustard
1 cup dried cranberries

Nutritional information per serving:

Calories	340
Fat, gm.	13
Protein, gm.	31
Carbs, gm.	25
Cholesterol, mg.	95
Fiber, gm.	1.1

Tuscan Chicken with Pistachio Rice

Serves 4

4 boned and skinned chicken breast
  halves
1 tablespoon canola oil
Salt and pepper
1 cup basmati or white rice
2 cups chicken broth
1 teaspoon Italian seasoning
¼ teaspoon cinnamon
1 package (10 ounces) frozen chopped
  spinach, thawed and drained
1 large tomato, seeded and chopped
1 tablespoon lemon juice
½ cup pistachio nuts

Nutritional information per serving:

Calories	395
Fat, gm.	10
Protein, gm.	32
Carbs, gm.	44
Cholesterol, mg.	50
Fiber, gm.	4.1

When you eat this, close your eyes and picture yourself in a small café in Italy.

❖ Lightly pound chicken to an even thickness. In a large, heavy skillet, heat oil. Add chicken, sprinkle with salt and pepper, and cook over medium-high heat until each piece is brown on both sides. Remove chicken from skillet and set aside. Add rice and stir for several minutes to lightly brown. Add chicken broth, Italian seasoning, and cinnamon. Stir to mix. Cover pan and boil gently for 20 minutes or until rice is tender. Return chicken to the skillet and add spinach, tomato, and lemon juice. Stir to mix and heat through. Spoon onto serving platter and top with pistachio nuts.

CHAPTER 6

Fish and Seafood

Apple Glazed Salmon
Bacon Wrapped Scallops in Brandy Marinade
Baked Sea Bass with Walnut Crumb Crust
Broiled Shrimp and Cheese on French Bread
Cod with Parmesan Dill Topping
Cornflake Crusted Cod
Crab Imperial
Grilled Tuna Steak with Roasted Vegetables
Honey Mustard Haddock
Lemon Tuna Spread
Orange Glazed Salmon
Pecan Crusted Sea Bass
Salmon Loaf with Creamy Dill Sauce
Shrimp and Feta with Italian Tomato Sauce
Shrimp in Tomato Cream Sauce on Linguine
Shrimp with Couscous, Roasted Red Peppers, and Pine Nuts
Smoked Salmon with Sun Dried Tomatoes on Fettuccine
Southwestern Tuna with Avocado Butter Sauce

Fish and Seafood Cooking Tips

There are some major health benefits to eating more fish. The lean fish are low in calories (100 to 150 calories in a 3-ounce serving) and high in protein. The cold-water fish with higher amounts of fat, such as salmon, mackerel, lake trout, herring, tuna, and sardines, are good sources of omega-3 fats. These fats may play a role in decreasing the risk of heart disease and cancer.

Fish is cooked through when it is opaque in color and it flakes easily with a fork.

For a cooking guideline, cook fish over a hot grill or over high heat in a skillet. Allow roughly 10 minutes of cooking time per each inch of thickness, 5 minutes on each side. Thinner fish needs less time, while fish cooked in sauce or foil requires more time. Do not overcook, so the fish remains moist and flavorful.

Tuna is the name given to a large number of similar-tasting fish that range in size from 6 pounds to 1,600 pounds. The smaller varieties of tuna are usually used for the less-expensive canned tuna.

If fish has a slight fishy smell, soak it in milk for 10 to 15 minutes. Remove from milk and dry with a paper towel. If fish has a strong fishy smell, it probably is not very fresh. Good fish should have only a very mild, sea-breeze aroma, not a strong fishy or ammonia-like smell.

Buy frozen fish or fresh fish from a reputable vendor. Fillets or steaks should look firm and moist, not dry or brown around the edges.

Tilapia is sweet and mild. It does not have a "fishy" flavor.

When cooking scallops, be careful not to overcook them. They become rubbery when cooked too long. If they are uneven in size, cut the larger ones into halves or quarters. Sea scallops are much larger than bay scallops.

If you are cooking with an electric oven and the recipe calls for broiling, be sure to leave the oven door partly open. This allows the broiler unit to stay on. If you close the door, the oven heats up and the broiler unit turns off.

Apple Glazed Salmon

I am always looking for another way to prepare salmon, and this one is a winner. The touch of sweetness from the currant jelly and the apples goes well with the salmon.

❖ Preheat oven to 350°F. Heat oil in a large nonstick skillet. Add salmon and sprinkle with salt and pepper. Cook over medium-hot heat until each fillet is brown on both sides. (Salmon does not need to be thoroughly cooked at this point.) Remove from heat. In a small bowl, combine jelly, apple, vinegar, and chives. Add horseradish to taste. Spoon sauce over salmon. Bake for 10 to 15 minutes or until salmon is cooked to desired doneness. (Fish will flake easily with a fork when it is thoroughly cooked.)

Note: *If the salmon fillets have skin on one side, cook in the skillet with the skin-side down first. Turn the salmon over and pull the skin off and discard. The skin can be removed very easily after the salmon has been cooked for just a few minutes. Also scrape off, and discard, any dark-colored flesh that remains.*

Serves 4

1 tablespoon canola oil
1½ pounds salmon fillets
Salt and pepper

Sauce:
½ cup currant jelly
1 medium apple, cored, peeled,
  and finely chopped
1 tablespoon balsamic vinegar
¼ cup finely chopped chives
1 tablespoon prepared horseradish

Nutritional information per serving:

Calories	335
Fat, gm.	9
Protein, gm.	34
Carbs, gm.	30
Cholesterol, mg.	90
Fiber, gm.	1.0

Bacon Wrapped Scallops in Brandy Marinade

Serves 4

12 ounces turkey or pork bacon
2 pounds whole sea scallops
¼ cup olive oil
½ cup brandy
2 tablespoons chopped parsley
½ teaspoon minced garlic
¼ teaspoon pepper
¼ teaspoon salt

Nutritional information per serving:

Calories	310
Fat, gm.	8
Protein, gm.	55
Carbs, gm.	5
Cholesterol, mg.	130
Fiber, gm.	0

You will get perfect scallops every time with this simple recipe. The brandy gives them a boost in flavor and the bacon keeps them moist. You can put them together ahead of time and keep them in the marinade until ready to serve.

1. Grease a 9" × 13" baking or broiler pan. Wrap 1 piece of bacon around each scallop, securing with toothpicks. Place wrapped scallops in a large plastic bag. In a small bowl, combine oil, brandy, parsley, garlic, pepper, and salt. Pour mixture over scallops. Marinate in refrigerator for several hours.

2. When ready to cook, preheat oven to 450°F. Remove scallops from marinade and discard marinade. Arrange scallops on baking pan. Bake for 15 to 20 minutes, turning occasionally, until bacon is brown and scallops are opaque. Remove toothpicks before serving.

Note: Use the amount of bacon needed to wrap around each scallop once. Since scallops vary in size, some smaller scallops will need only ½ slice of bacon to wrap around while larger scallops may need the whole slice.

In case you don't want to wrap your scallops in bacon, this recipe works well with just marinating the raw scallops and baking them until they become opaque.

Baked Sea Bass with Walnut Crumb Crust

Add flavor and texture to your favorite white fish. It looks impressive but it is so easy.

❖ Preheat oven to 350°F. Butter a 9" × 13" baking pan. Arrange fillets in pan and sprinkle lightly with salt and pepper. In a food processor, combine bread crumbs, walnuts, Parmesan cheese, butter, mustard, and horseradish. Blend until smooth. Gently press crumb mixture onto fillets. Spray lightly with olive oil spray. Bake 20 minutes or until fillets are cooked through. Place under broiler and broil about 2 minutes or until crust is golden brown. Watch carefully to prevent burning.

Serves 4

1½ pounds sea bass fillets or
* any mild white fish*
Salt and pepper
½ cup bread crumbs
½ cup chopped walnuts
¼ cup grated Parmesan cheese
2 tablespoons butter or margarine,
* melted*
2 tablespoons Dijon mustard
1 tablespoon prepared horseradish
Olive oil spray

Nutritional information per serving:

Calories	300
Fat, gm.	13
Protein, gm.	36
Carbs, gm.	11
Cholesterol, mg.	90
Fiber, gm.	1.2

Broiled Shrimp and Cheese on French Bread

Serves 4 (2 slices per serving)

½ pound frozen cooked shrimp,
  peeled and deveined
1 teaspoon lemon zest, optional
2 teaspoons minced garlic
1 teaspoon dill weed
1 cup low-fat shredded Swiss cheese
½ cup fat-free or low-fat mayonnaise
⅛ teaspoon white pepper
8 French bread slices or 4 bagels,
  cut in half

Nutritional information per serving:

Calories	250
Fat, gm.	3
Protein, gm.	24
Carbs, gm.	31
Cholesterol, mg.	120
Fiber, gm.	1.5

I make this when I don't feel like cooking yet I want something really good to eat.

1.   Thaw shrimp and cut into small pieces. In a small bowl, combine shrimp with all remaining ingredients except bread. Stir to mix. Cover and refrigerate until ready to use. Keeps up to 3 days.

2.   When ready to serve, preheat oven broiler. Cut 8 slices of French bread or cut 4 bagels in half. Top each piece of bread or each bagel half with a portion of the shrimp mixture. Spread the mixture evenly on top of the bread. Broil until cheese is melted and lightly brown. Serve warm.

Note: *Substitute other cheeses of your choice for the Swiss cheese. I like Monterey jack cheese in this recipe too.*

Cod with Parmesan Dill Topping

Fish is often served after lightly coating with flour and browning in a skillet. This recipe takes the fish one step further to make it a little more special.

1. In a large ovenproof skillet, heat oil. Combine cod and flour in a plastic bag. Toss to coat the fish. Place fish in skillet. Sprinkle with salt and pepper. Cook over medium heat until each piece is brown on both sides and fish is cooked through. Remove from heat.

2. Preheat oven broiler. In a small bowl, combine all topping ingredients except bread crumbs and butter spray. Stir to mix. Spoon topping on top of pieces of fish. Sprinkle with bread crumbs. Spray lightly with butter spray. Broil until topping is heated through and lightly brown on top.

Serves 4

1 tablespoon canola oil
1½ pounds cod fillets
½ cup flour
Salt and pepper to taste

Topping:
½ cup freshly grated Parmesan cheese
2 tablespoons butter or margarine, melted
2 tablespoons low-fat mayonnaise
¼ cup fat-free sour cream
½ teaspoon dried dill weed
¼ cup fine bread crumbs
Butter spray

Nutritional information per serving:

Calories	375
Fat, gm.	16
Protein, gm.	37
Carbs, gm.	20
Cholesterol, mg.	100
Fiber, gm.	0

Cornflake Crusted Cod

Serves 4

2 tablespoons milk
1 egg, lightly beaten
*2 cups cornflake crumbs**
¼ cup flour
1 teaspoon salt
¼ teaspoon pepper
2 tablespoons canola oil
2 pounds cod fillets, cut into 4 pieces

Nutritional information per serving:

Calories	320
Fat, gm.	9
Protein, gm.	43
Carbs, gm.	17
Cholesterol, mg.	140
Fiber, gm.	0.3

The cornflakes add a nice crunch without overwhelming the mild-flavored fish. This recipe will work with any white fish.

❖ In a small, shallow bowl, combine milk and egg. Whisk to mix well. In another shallow bowl, combine cornflake crumbs, flour, salt, and pepper. Stir to mix. In a large nonstick skillet, heat oil. Dip fish in milk mixture and then dredge in cornflake mixture. Place fish in pan and cook about 5 minutes per side or until fish is completely done. It should flake easily when tested with a fork.

———

You can purchase cornflake crumbs or make your own by crumbling cornflake cereal.

Crab Imperial

You will be surprised by the smooth, decadent taste of this recipe "makeover." This version is much lower in fat and calories than the original.

❖ In a medium saucepan, cook noodles in boiling salted water until al dente. Drain and set aside. In a medium, heavy saucepan, melt butter over medium heat. Add mushrooms and pepper. Cook until tender. Add flour and cook over medium heat, stirring constantly with a wooden spoon for 2 minutes. Add half-and-half and bring to a boil, stirring constantly. Take a small amount of the hot mixture and stir it into the egg yolks. When egg mixture has been heated by the sauce, pour the egg mixture into the pan with the remaining sauce. Add all remaining ingredients except the milk. Stir to mix and heat through. Add salt and pepper to taste. If mixture is too thick, thin with milk. Place hot noodles in a serving dish. Pour sauce on top. Garnish with chopped parsley or chopped green onions.

Serves 4

2 cups noodles
¼ cup butter or margarine
½ pound sliced mushrooms
½ cup diced red bell pepper
⅓ cup flour
2½ cups fat-free half-and-half
2 egg yolks, lightly beaten
¼ teaspoon white pepper
1 teaspoon Worcestershire sauce
1 teaspoon lemon juice
1 teaspoon Dijon mustard
12 ounces crab, canned or frozen
¼ cup grated Parmesan cheese
¼ cup dry white wine
Salt and pepper to taste
½ cup fat-free milk to thin, if needed

Nutritional information per serving:

Calories	440
Fat, gm.	17
Protein, gm.	30
Carbs, gm.	42
Cholesterol, mg.	220
Fiber, gm.	1.4

Grilled Tuna Steak with Roasted Vegetables

Serves 4

1½ pounds tuna steaks
2 tablespoons lemon juice
2 tablespoons lime juice
2 tablespoons soy sauce
2 tablespoons honey
2 tablespoons Dijon mustard
2 tablespoons olive or canola oil
2 tablespoons chopped fresh basil
½ teaspoon salt
Dash hot pepper sauce

Nutritional information per serving (for the tuna):

Calories	210
Fat, gm.	7
Protein, gm.	34
Carbs, gm.	2
Cholesterol, mg.	65
Fiber, gm.	very low

Marinate tuna in a lemon-lime, soy, and honey marinade and grill quickly over hot coals. Serve with grilled vegetables.

❖ Cut tuna into 4 pieces. Place in resealable plastic bag. In a small jar combine all remaining ingredients. Mix well and pour into bag with tuna. Reseal and refrigerate several hours. When ready to serve, heat grill to medium-high heat. Remove fish from bag. Grill over medium hot coals for 5 to 10 minutes per side or until lightly browned and fish flakes easily. Do not overcook or the fish will be dry.

_____

Note: *In place of grilling, the tuna can be fried in a small amount of oil in a non-stick skillet. Fry over medium heat. Watch carefully to prevent burning.*

_____

Serve with grilled vegetables.
Combine vegetables of your choice such as zucchini, yellow summer squash, red onions, red peppers, mushrooms, and asparagus. (If you use carrots or beans, they will have to be precooked.) Marinate vegetables in a resealable plastic bag in equal amounts of olive oil and balsamic vinegar and add fresh herbs of your choice. Refrigerate until ready to grill. Lightly spray a grilling basket. Add vegetables and grill vegetables until tender and lightly browned.

Honey Mustard Haddock

When you really want it simple, try this way to serve fish. You can choose other mustards such as Dijon if you prefer, and you can use other mild white fish.

❖ Preheat oven to 400°F. Butter a 7" × 11" baking dish. Cut fish into serving sized pieces. Arrange fillets in the baking dish. In a custard cup, combine olive oil, salt, honey mustard, and Cajun seasoning. Stir to mix. Distribute mixture on top of the fish. Bake for 15 to 25 minutes or until fish is completely done. It will flake easily when tested with a fork. Drizzle with lemon juice.

─────

Cajun seasoning is a mixture of spices that usually includes chili powder, onion powder, paprika, basil, peppers, and salt.

Serves 4

2 pounds haddock
1 tablespoon olive oil
¼ teaspoon salt
2 tablespoons honey mustard
½ teaspoon Cajun seasoning
2 tablespoons fresh lemon juice

Nutritional information per serving:

Calories	260
Fat, gm.	9
Protein, gm	43
Carbs, gm.	1
Cholesterol, mg.	100
Fiber, gm.	0.1

Lemon Tuna Spread

Serves 6

1 can (6 ounces) tuna, drained
1 tablespoon butter or margarine,
  softened
1 teaspoon grated lemon rind
1 teaspoon lemon juice
2 tablespoons extra-virgin olive oil
1 teaspoon Pinch of Herbs*
1 tablespoon minced garlic
½ teaspoon Worcestershire sauce
Dash Tabasco sauce, optional
Salt and freshly ground pepper to taste

**Nutritional information per serving
(without the bread):**

Calories	220
Fat, gm.	17
Protein, gm.	15
Carbs, gm.	0
Cholesterol, mg.	34
Fiber, gm.	0.1

Even if you are not a tuna lover, you may enjoy this tuna served on bread or bagels.

❖ Combine all ingredients except salt and pepper in food processor. Process until smooth. Add salt and pepper to taste. Spoon into a serving bowl. Refrigerate until ready to serve. Serve on French bread, cocktail rye bread, toasted French baguettes, or bagels.

———

Any combination of herbs of your choice may be used. One commercial brand is Lawry's Pinch of Herbs.

Pecan Crusted Sea Bass

Serves 4

¼ cup finely chopped pecans
½ cup dry bread crumbs
½ cup low-fat buttermilk
½ teaspoon hot pepper sauce
¼ cup flour
½ teaspoon salt
¼ teaspoon white pepper
1½ pounds sea bass fillets
1 tablespoon canola oil

Nutritional information per serving:

Calories	260
Fat, gm.	10
Protein, gm.	33
Carbs, gm.	10
Cholesterol, mg.	70
Fiber, gm.	0.5

This recipe will work with any white fish. It is so easy and good that your family and guests will think you really fussed.

❖ In a shallow bowl, combine pecans and bread crumbs. Set aside. In a shallow bowl, combine buttermilk and hot pepper sauce. In a plastic bag, combine flour, salt, and pepper. Add sea bass to the bag and shake until fish is coated. Take each fillet and dip in buttermilk. Remove and place fillet in bread crumb mixture. Turn to coat. Repeat with each fillet. Heat oil in a large nonstick skillet. Add fish and cook over medium heat until golden brown and fish flakes easily with a fork.

Salmon Loaf with Creamy Dill Sauce

This is an old recipe that was often served with a creamed-pea sauce. My husband prefers just a good dill sauce, so we compromised. I've listed the peas as an optional ingredient in the dill sauce. Make it the way you like it.

❖ Preheat oven to 350°F. Grease a 5" × 9" loaf pan. Remove and discard skin from the canned salmon. In a medium bowl, combine salmon, eggs, bread crumbs, and soup. Stir to mix. Spoon into pan. Bake for 50 to 60 minutes or until set. Meanwhile, prepare Dill Sauce. In a small heavy saucepan, melt butter. Add flour and stir to mix. Add milk and stir constantly with a whisk, until mixture comes to a rolling boil. Add dill, white pepper, and cheese. Add salt and pepper to taste. If desired, stir in peas right before serving. Heat through. Slice individual servings of salmon loaf and top with sauce.

Serves 6

1 can (15 ounces) salmon
2 eggs, lightly beaten
1½ cups dry bread crumbs
1 can (10¾ ounces) cream of celery soup

Dill Sauce:

1 tablespoon butter or margarine
2 tablespoons flour
1½ cups fat-free milk
½ teaspoon dill weed
Dash white pepper
2 tablespoons freshly grated Parmesan
   cheese
Salt and pepper, to taste
1 cup frozen peas, optional

Nutritional information per serving:

Calories	225
Fat, gm.	9
Protein, gm.	21
Carbs, gm.	14
Cholesterol, mg.	110
Fiber, gm.	0.7

Shrimp and Feta with Italian Tomato Sauce

Serves 4

*1½ pounds cooked shrimp, peeled and
   deveined*
¼ teaspoon red pepper flakes
*1 can (28 ounces) seasoned diced
   tomatoes*
¼ cup white wine
½ cup reduced-fat feta cheese, crumbled
¼ cup chopped fresh basil

Nutritional information per serving:

Calories	260
Fat, gm.	4
Protein, gm.	42
Carbs, gm.	13
Cholesterol, mg.	330
Fiber, gm.	1.6

What an easy recipe and yet it looks and tastes so special!

1.   Preheat oven to 400°F. Spoon shrimp into 9" × 13" baking pan. Combine red pepper flakes, tomatoes, and wine. Pour over shrimp. Top with cheese. Bake for 10 minutes or until heated through. Garnish with fresh basil.

2.   Serve over pasta or rice.

———

Note: *Choose the size shrimp that you like best for this recipe.*

Shrimp in Tomato Cream Sauce on Linguine

Serves 4

This is another recipe makeover. The original recipe had double the calories and double the fat. You can enjoy this wonderful Mediterranean dish without a bit of guilt.

8 ounces linguine
1 tablespoon olive oil
¾ cup chopped green onions
1 teaspoon minced garlic
3 tablespoons cornstarch
1 cup fat-free chicken broth, divided
1 can (12 ounces) fat-free evaporated milk
⅓ cup chopped oil-packed sun dried
   tomatoes
1 tablespoon tomato paste
1 teaspoon dried basil or ready prepared
¼ teaspoon white pepper
½ cup sweet vermouth or sweet white
   wine
1 pound cooked shrimp, peeled and
   deveined
Salt and pepper to taste
4 ounces crumbled fat-free tomato-basil
   feta cheese
¼ cup chopped parsley

1. Cook pasta in boiling salted water until al dente. Drain, rinse, and set aside. Rewarm pasta under hot water when ready to serve.

2. Heat oil in a large skillet. Add onions and garlic and cook 1 minute. Dissolve cornstarch in ¾ cup of broth. Pour broth into skillet. Add evaporated milk to skillet and bring to a boil, stirring constantly. Add sun-dried tomatoes, tomato paste, basil, white pepper, and vermouth to skillet. Bring to a boil and reduce heat. Cook until desired consistency. Add shrimp and heat through. Add salt and pepper to taste. Add additional broth to thin if desired. Place warm pasta on individual plates or into a large serving bowl. Top with sauce. Sprinkle with crumbled feta cheese and parsley.

——

Note: *Cooked chicken can be substituted for the shrimp in this recipe.*

Nutritional information per serving:

Calories	510
Fat, gm.	7
Protein, gm.	43
Carbs, gm.	69
Cholesterol, mg.	170
Fiber, gm.	2.3

Shrimp with Couscous, Roasted Red Peppers, and Pine Nuts

Serves 4

1¼ cups fat-free chicken broth
1 cup couscous
½ cup chopped green onions
½ cup diced roasted red peppers
¼ cup chopped parsley
¼ cup pine nuts, toasted
½ pound cooked shrimp, peeled and deveined

Dressing:
2 tablespoons extra-virgin olive oil
¼ cup rice wine vinegar
½ teaspoon minced garlic
¼ teaspoon cumin
Salt and pepper to taste

At a recipe-testing party where I served 5 entrees, this was the favorite dish. It takes just minutes to prepare.

❖ In a small saucepan, bring chicken broth to a boil. Remove from heat and add couscous. Cover pan and let stand for 5 minutes. Fluff with a fork. In a large bowl, combine couscous, onions, peppers, parsley, pine nuts, and shrimp. Set aside. In a small jar or bowl, combine all dressing ingredients. Mix well and pour over couscous mixture. Stir to blend. Serve warm or at room temperature.

Nutritional information per serving:

Calories	340
Fat, gm.	11
Protein, gm.	20
Carbs, gm.	40
Cholesterol, mg.	110
Fiber, gm.	3.4

Smoked Salmon with Sun-Dried Tomatoes on Fettuccine

This can be prepared ahead of time and refrigerated until ready to serve. Add a small amount of milk or chicken broth, when rewarming, to thin to desired consistency.

1. In a small bowl, combine sun-dried tomatoes with hot water to hydrate. Set aside.
2. In a large saucepan, cook fettuccine in boiling salted water until al dente. Drain and set aside.
3. While pasta is cooking, heat oil in medium skillet. Add leek, red pepper, and yellow pepper. Cook until tender. Add garlic and cook 1 minute. Drain reserved sun-dried tomatoes and add to skillet. Mix cornstarch, mustard powder, and white pepper in half-and-half. Add to skillet, stirring constantly, and cook until mixture comes to a boil. Reduce heat and simmer for 5 to 10 minutes. Add salmon and reserved pasta. Heat through. Add salt and pepper to taste. Serve on individual warm plates. Top with Parmesan cheese.

Note: *Before adding extra salt to the sauce, add the salmon. Do not add too much salt to the sauce, because the salmon is quite salty.*

-----

*Grilled fresh salmon can substitute for the smoked salmon if you prefer.

Serves 4

¼ cup sun-dried tomatoes, finely chopped
8 ounces fettuccine or spaghetti
1 tablespoon olive oil
1 large leek, white part only, thinly sliced
1 medium red pepper, thinly sliced
½ medium yellow pepper, thinly sliced
1 teaspoon minced garlic
2 teaspoons cornstarch
1 teaspoon dry mustard powder
⅛ teaspoon white pepper
1½ cups fat-free half-and-half
8 ounces smoked salmon*, broken into
  bite-sized pieces
Salt and pepper to taste
¾ cup freshly grated Parmesan cheese

Nutritional information per serving:

Calories	445
Fat, gm.	10
Protein, gm.	28
Carbs, gm.	60
Cholesterol, mg.	25
Fiber, gm.	2.5

Southwestern Tuna with Avocado Butter Sauce

Serves 4

1 large avocado, pitted and peeled
1 tablespoon butter or margarine, softened
1 tablespoon lime juice
⅓ cup chopped fresh cilantro
1 tablespoon olive oil
1 tablespoon canola oil
1 tablespoon chili powder
1½ teaspoons cumin
¼ teaspoon salt
¼ teaspoon garlic powder
4 (6 ounces each) tuna steaks

Nutritional information per serving:

Calories	350
Fat, gm.	20
Protein, gm.	40
Carbs, gm.	4
Cholesterol, mg.	70
Fiber, gm.	1.7

The mild avocado is a nice contrast to the spicy tuna.

❖ In a food processor, combine avocado, butter, lime juice, and cilantro. Process until smooth. Thin with 1 tablespoon of olive oil if desired. Spoon into small bowl and cover tightly with plastic wrap. Refrigerate until ready to use. In a small custard cup, combine chili powder, cumin, salt, and garlic powder. Rub spice mixture on tuna steaks. In a medium nonstick skillet, add 1 tablespoon canola oil. Heat over medium heat. Place tuna in skillet. Cook for 10 to 15 minutes or until lightly browned and cooked to desired doneness. (Some people prefer tuna medium-rare.) Serve tuna with avocado butter.

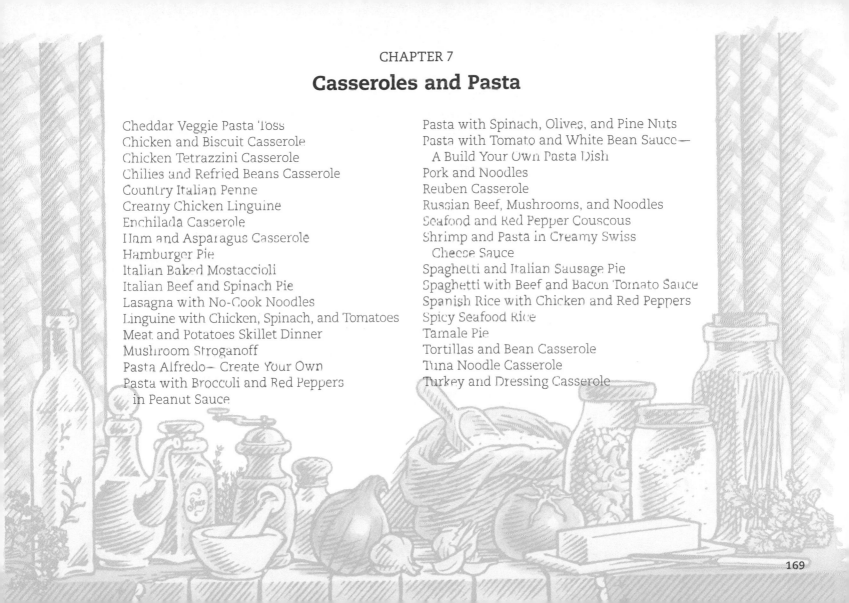

CHAPTER 7
Casseroles and Pasta

Cheddar Veggie Pasta Toss
Chicken and Biscuit Casserole
Chicken Tetrazzini Casserole
Chilies and Refried Beans Casserole
Country Italian Penne
Creamy Chicken Linguine
Enchilada Casserole
Ham and Asparagus Casserole
Hamburger Pie
Italian Baked Mostaccioli
Italian Beef and Spinach Pie
Lasagna with No-Cook Noodles
Linguine with Chicken, Spinach, and Tomatoes
Meat and Potatoes Skillet Dinner
Mushroom Stroganoff
Pasta Alfredo— Create Your Own
Pasta with Broccoli and Red Peppers
 in Peanut Sauce

Pasta with Spinach, Olives, and Pine Nuts
Pasta with Tomato and White Bean Sauce—
 A Build Your Own Pasta Dish
Pork and Noodles
Reuben Casserole
Russian Beef, Mushrooms, and Noodles
Seafood and Red Pepper Couscous
Shrimp and Pasta in Creamy Swiss
 Cheese Sauce
Spaghetti and Italian Sausage Pie
Spaghetti with Beef and Bacon Tomato Sauce
Spanish Rice with Chicken and Red Peppers
Spicy Seafood Rice
Tamale Pie
Tortillas and Bean Casserole
Tuna Noodle Casserole
Turkey and Dressing Casserole

169

Orange Glazed Salmon

When salmon is so easy and so good, enjoy it often. You will also get the health benefits of the high amount of omega-3 fats in the salmon.

1. Combine orange juice, orange marmalade, and soy sauce in a large resealable bag. Add salmon, refrigerate, and marinate for 20 minutes or until ready to serve. The salmon can be either grilled or baked.
2. To grill, preheat grill. Remove salmon from marinade and grill over medium heat until each piece is browned on both sides and cooked through.
3. To bake, preheat oven to 450°F. Line a 9" × 13" baking pan with foil. Spray with cooking spray. Remove salmon from marinade and bake for 5 minutes. Spoon marinade over salmon and return to bake for another 10 to 15 minutes or until salmon is completely done. Watch carefully to prevent burning.

Salmon fillets usually have skin on one side. The skin comes off very easily after the salmon is cooked. Although the skin is harder to remove when the fish is raw, I prefer to do that if I have time. This allows the marinade to flavor both sides of the salmon.

Note: *To make a great sauce to serve with the salmon, combine the marinade ingredients (½ cup orange juice, ¼ cup orange marmalade, and 2 tablespoons soy sauce) in a small saucepan. Bring to a boil and continue to boil gently until the mixture is reduced to a syrupy consistency.*

Serves 4

½ cup orange juice
¼ cup orange marmalade
2 tablespoons soy sauce
2 pounds salmon fillets*

Nutritional information per serving:

Calories	315
Fat, gm.	7
Protein, gm.	46
Carbs, gm.	17
Cholesterol, mg.	120
Fiber, gm.	0.2

Casseroles and Pastas Tips

Casserole dishes come in many shapes, styles, and sizes. If you don't know the size of the dish, fill it with water and measure the maximum amount it will hold. Determine the quantity in quart measurements. Use a permanent pen or marker to mark the number on the bottom of the dish or pan.

Rectangular and square pans are measured in inches. Use a ruler to measure the inside dimensions.

When a recipe calls for frozen spinach that is squeezed dry, the spinach first has to be thawed. Take a small handful of spinach and squeeze it until it is dry. Another method is to press the thawed spinach between two nested pie plates. Squeeze the two tins together, tilting the plates over the sink to drain off the liquid.

If you like your food spicy, small amounts of hot pepper sauce can be added to many casserole and pasta dishes. Pepper sauce is made from hot chili peppers such as jalapeño, cayenne, and serrano. Vinegar and seasonings are added to give each one a different flavor.

Pasta is made from special hard wheat flour called durum semolina and other cereal grains. If eggs are used in the preparation, the result is usually called noodles, although some noodles are made without eggs.

Pastas are named with Italian words that describe the shapes of the pasta. For example:

Orecchiette	=	*"little ears"*
Eliche	=	*"propellers"*
Ditali	=	*"thimbles"*
Conchiglie	=	*"conch shells"*
Linguine	=	*"little tongues"*
Vermicelle	=	*"little worms"*

The end of the Italian word often further describes the pasta. For example when the name ends in

-ricee	=	*wavy edge*
-nidi	=	*formed into nests*
-rigate	=	*ridged*
-lisce	=	*smooth surface*
-ine	=	*smaller form*
-ette	=	*smaller form*

Pasta calories add up quickly. One-half cup of cooked pasta equals about 100 calories.

Choose pasta shapes for their ability to hold and support the sauce; for example, choose tube shapes for thick sauce, and flat, long shapes for thin, smooth sauces.

When cooking pasta, use a large saucepot and bring the water to a full boil before adding the pasta. Salt the water. Add the pasta, and adjust the heat so that the water continues to boil gently during the cooking process. If the water is not boiling, the pasta does not continue to circulate and thus it tends to stick together.

It is best to cook pasta to the al dente stage. The literal translation of the Italian phrase *al dente* is "to the tooth." It is a description of a degree of doneness when cooking pasta. Al dente pasta is slightly firm when chewed, rather that being soft and mushy.

To make it easy to serve pasta for a family or company meal, cook it ahead of time. Drain it and chill it under cold running water. Place pasta in a strainer and set aside. When ready to serve, pour hot water over the pasta or put it in a pot of boiling water for 1 minute to reheat. Drain and serve.

Recipes often call for Dijon mustard. This is a special mustard made in Dijon, France. A good substitute is Dijon-style mustard. It is an American counterpart that is similar in taste.

Many recipes in this section use chopped onions. You can chop fresh onions or save time by keeping a bag of chopped onions in your freezer. One medium onion is equivalent to 1 cup chopped onions.

When onions are cut, they release a volatile sulfur vapor that brings tears to the eyes. You can cut down on the effect by chilling the onion before chopping. Fewer vapors are released at the cold temperature.

Many recipes call for fresh red peppers. These peppers are actually a variety of green pepper that has matured and changed color. They are sweeter and milder in flavor than green peppers. You can substitute green peppers if you desire, but the flavor is much more intense.

Cottage cheese and ricotta may seem to be similar products, but actually ricotta is prepared from the whey left over after making cheese. It is common in Italian recipes because it is readily available and inexpensive.

I am often asked if white or basmati rice should be rinsed with cold water before cooking. I am not a fan of rinsing rice. In my experience, the rice is more likely to become gummy if it is rinsed before cooking. It may depend on the specific rice. You can try it both ways and see which way you like better.

Wild rice is actually a seed of a marsh grass rather than rice. It is native to North America and is harvested in Minnesota, Wisconsin, and other northern states. It has to be washed and then cooked for 45 to 60 minutes in boiling water. It has a chewy texture and a nutty, earthy flavor.

Brown rice is a whole-grain rice with only the inedible husk removed. It contains the bran and the germ. It has more fiber and more nutrients than polished white rice does. It is light tan in color and has a chewy texture. It usually takes longer to cook than white rice does, unless you use a special quick-cooking brown rice.

One good method of cooking brown rice is to add boiling water to the rice in a rectangular baking pan or casserole dish. Use a little less water than the traditional ratio of 1 cup of rice to 2 cups of water. Try 1 cup of rice to 1¾ cups of water. Cover the dish tightly and bake in the oven at 375°F for 1 hour or until tender. Remove baking dish from the oven and uncover. Fluff rice with a fork and cover with a clean kitchen towel for 5 minutes.

Many recipes call for black beans or white beans. Dried beans and legumes that have been cooked are good sources of protein, fiber, and B-vitamins. They are also rich in antioxidants and may provide health benefits linked to decreased risk of heart disease and cancer.

Cheddar Veggie Pasta Toss

If you want to please a mixed group of meat-eaters and vegetarians, this is the dish to make. It is colorful and so flavorful that you will never miss the meat.

❖ Cook pasta in boiling salted water until al dente. Drain and run under cold water. Set aside. In a large skillet, heat oil. Add onion and cook until lightly browned. Add mushrooms and pepper. Cook until tender. Add garlic, tomatoes, broth, and Italian seasoning. Bring to a boil, reduce heat, and boil gently for about 10 minutes or until desired consistency. When ready to serve, add olives and broccoli. Cook 5 minutes or until broccoli is tender but not overcooked. Add reserved pasta and cheese. Heat through. Season with salt and pepper. (Add additional broth if mixture gets too thick.)

Note: Use the cheese of your choice for this recipe. If you prefer to use a low-fat cheese, the calories will be reduced to 385 and the fat to 10 grams per serving.

Serves 4

6 ounces (2 cups) penne pasta
1 tablespoon olive oil
1 cup thinly sliced red onion
8 ounces sliced mushrooms
1 medium red pepper, thinly sliced
1 teaspoon minced garlic
1 can (15 ounces) seasoned diced tomatoes
1 cup fat-free chicken or vegetable broth
2 teaspoons Italian seasoning
1 cup black olives, pitted and cut in half
2 cups broccoli florets
1 cup shredded Cheddar cheese
Salt and pepper to taste

Nutritional information per serving:

Calories	440
Fat, gm.	18
Protein, gm.	18
Carbs, gm.	51
Cholesterol, mg.	0
Fiber, gm.	6.3

Chicken and Biscuit Casserole

Serves 4

1 tablespoon canola oil
1 pound boned and skinned chicken
   breast, cubed
Salt and pepper
1 bag (16 ounces) frozen mixed
   vegetables
1 can (10 ounces) cream of chicken soup
3 cups fat-free chicken broth
1½ tablespoons cornstarch
1 cup frozen green peas
1 can (7½ ounces) refrigerated buttermilk biscuits

Nutritional information per serving:

Calories	380
Fat, gm.	9
Protein, gm.	34
Carbs, gm.	41
Cholesterol, mg.	70
Fiber, gm.	4

Make this old-time favorite easy with canned biscuits, but if you prefer, make your own biscuits. That will make this meal even more like Grandmother's supper.

❖ Preheat oven to 400°F. In a large ovenproof skillet, heat oil. Add chicken and cook over medium-high heat until brown on all sides. Sprinkle with salt and pepper. Place vegetables over the chicken. Mix soup, broth, and cornstarch together in a small bowl. Pour over chicken and vegetables. Cover pan and boil gently for 10 minutes or until vegetables are tender-crisp. Remove skillet from stovetop. Add peas. Open biscuit can, separate biscuits, and arrange on top of the chicken mixture. Place skillet in the oven and bake, uncovered, for 8 to 10 minutes or until biscuits are golden brown.

Note: *To protect the skillet handle when it is baking in the oven, wrap the handle in aluminum foil.*

Chicken Tetrazzini Casserole

This is one of those "just plain good" supper meals. The casserole is moist and mildly flavored.

❖ Preheat oven to 400°F. Butter a 7" × 11" baking pan. In a large saucepan, cook noodles in boiling salted water until al dente. Drain and rinse. Set aside. In a large skillet, melt butter. Add chicken and onion to skillet and cook over medium heat until chicken pieces are browned. Add mushrooms and garlic and cook until tender. Combine flour and 1 cup of the chicken broth in a shaker. Shake to mix. Pour into pan. Add remaining chicken broth and bring to a boil, stirring constantly. Add half-and-half and sherry. Heat through. Add salt and pepper to taste. Add olives if desired. Combine sauce with noodles. Stir to mix. If mixture is too thick, thin with extra broth. Spoon into baking pan. Sprinkle with bread crumbs and Parmesan cheese. Lightly spray with butter spray. Bake for 10 to 15 minutes or until crumbs are brown and casserole is heated through.

——

Note: *To make this recipe even quicker, use precooked chicken pieces or purchase a rotisserie chicken from the grocery store.*

——

This recipe can be easily doubled if you have a family with a big appetite.

Serves 4

4 ounces (2½ cups) medium egg noodles
2 tablespoons butter or margarine
8 ounces chicken breast, thinly sliced
1 medium onion, finely chopped
¼ pound sliced mushrooms
1 teaspoon minced garlic
3 tablespoons flour
2 cups fat-free chicken broth, divided
½ cup fat-free half-and-half
2 tablespoons dry sherry
Salt and pepper to taste
½ cup sliced green olives, optional
2 tablespoons bread crumbs
2 tablespoons grated Parmesan cheese
Butter spray

Nutritional information per serving:

Calories	338
Fat, gm.	14
Protein, gm.	18
Carbs, gm.	35
Cholesterol, mg.	70
Fiber, gm.	1.8

Serves 8

1 tablespoon canola oil
1 large onion, chopped
1 pound extra-lean ground beef
Salt and pepper
2 teaspoons cumin
1 teaspoon oregano
1 medium red bell pepper, chopped
2 cloves garlic, minced
1 can (15 ounces) seasoned fat-free
   refried beans
1 can (11 ounces) canned corn, drained
1 can (4 ounces) chopped green chilies
4 ounces low-fat shredded Cheddar cheese
¼ cup flour
1½ cups fat-free milk
3 large eggs
½ teaspoon salt
Dash hot pepper sauce

Nutritional information per serving:

Calories	340
Fat, gm.	16
Protein, gm.	23
Carbs, gm.	25
Cholesterol, mg.	115
Fiber, gm.	4.2

Chilies and Refried Bean Casserole

Everyone loves this Southwestern-flavored casserole!

❖ Preheat oven to 350°F. Grease a 9" × 13" baking pan. In a large skillet, heat oil. Add onion and cook over medium heat until translucent. Add beef, salt, pepper, cumin, and oregano and cook until meat is brown and completely done. Add red pepper and garlic. Cook until pepper is tender. Remove from heat and stir in refried beans. Spoon into baking pan. Distribute corn and green chilies over meat mixture. Sprinkle with cheese. In a small bowl, combine flour, milk, eggs, salt, and pepper sauce. Beat well. Pour into pan. Bake, uncovered, for 45 to 60 minutes or until top begins to brown and middle is set. Let stand 10 minutes before serving.

———

If desired, serve with chunky tomato salsa and a side of sour cream.

———

Note: *This can be prepared ahead of time and refrigerated until ready to bake.*

Country Italian Penne

Use Italian sausage or German bratwurst to make this hearty pasta dish.

❖ In a large skillet, cook sausage until brown and completely cooked. Drain and discard any excess fat. Add onion and cook until translucent. Add carrots and garlic and cook 2 to 3 minutes. Add tomatoes, wine, basil, red pepper flakes and Italian seasoning. Bring to a boil, reduce heat, and simmer for 30 minutes or until sauce reaches desired consistency. Add sugar if desired. Add chicken broth, if desired, to thin sauce. While sauce is simmering, cook pasta in boiling salted water until al dente. Drain well. Serve sauce over pasta and top with grated cheese.

Note: *If you have fresh basil available, substitute ¼ cup chopped fresh basil for the dried basil.*

Serves 4

½ pound low-fat Italian sausage, cut into small pieces
1 medium onion, thinly sliced
2 medium carrots, peeled and finely chopped
2 teaspoons minced garlic
1 can (28 ounces) seasoned diced tomatoes
½ cup dry red wine
1 teaspoon dried basil
1 teaspoon Italian seasoning
Dash red pepper flakes, optional
1 teaspoon sugar, optional
½ cup fat free chicken broth, optional
9 ounces (3 cups dry) penne pasta or pasta of your choice
½ cup grated Romano or Parmesan cheese

Nutritional information per serving:

Calories	440
Fat, gm.	8
Protein, gm.	30
Carbs, gm.	63
Cholesterol, mg.	60
Fiber, gm.	5.2

Serves 4

10 ounces linguine
1 tablespoon canola oil
1½ pounds boneless, skinless chicken
  breasts, thinly sliced
Salt and pepper
1 tablespoon minced garlic
1 medium red pepper, diced
1½ teaspoons Italian seasoning
2 teaspoons cornstarch
1½ cups fat-free half-and-half
3 ounces Neufchatel cheese (reduced-fat
  cream cheese)
¼ cup sherry
1 large tomato, seeded and chopped
¼ cup milk, if needed
4 ounces fat-free feta cheese

Nutritional information per serving:

Calories	640
Fat, gm.	13
Protein, gm.	60
Carbs, gm.	70
Cholesterol, mg.	115
Fiber, gm.	2.6

Creamy Chicken Linguine

This tastes and looks creamy and decadent but it is actually low in fat and calories. The original recipe had more than 50 grams of fat and 1,000 calories per serving. Enjoy this great meal without guilt.

❖ Cook linguine in boiling salted water until al dente. Rinse under cold running water. Drain well and set aside. In a large skillet, heat oil. Add chicken slices, sprinkle with salt and pepper, and cook until lightly browned. Add garlic, red pepper, and Italian seasoning. Cook until pepper is tender. Mix cornstarch in half-and-half. Add cornstarch mixture and cream cheese to skillet. Cook, stirring constantly, until mixture comes to a boil and thickens. Add sherry, tomato, and reserved linguine. Heat through. Add milk to thin if desired. Place on large serving platter and sprinkle with feta cheese.

Enchilada Casserole

If you are entertaining some fussy kids, this recipe will suit everyone. No onions. No garlic. Just great flavor and so quick!

1. Preheat oven to 350°F. Grease a 8" × 8" baking pan or a 1½-quart casserole. In a medium skillet, cook meat over medium-high heat until brown. Crumble the meat and combine with enchilada sauce. Place one-half of the meat in the baking pan. Top with one-half of the cheese and one-half of the chips. Repeat layers. Bake for 20 to 30 minutes or until heated through.

2. Serve with sour cream and extra salsa on the side.

_____

Note: *To extend this dish, spoon a layer of refried beans over the bottom of casserole.*

_____

This recipe is easy to double. Use a 2-quart casserole dish.

Serves 4

1 pound extra lean ground beef
1 can (10 ounces; 1¼ cups) enchilada sauce
1½ cups shredded Monterey jack cheese
2 cups (2 ounces) crushed tortilla chips

Nutritional information per serving:

Calories	455
Fat, gm.	26
Protein, gm.	41
Carbs, gm.	14
Cholesterol, mg.	110
Fiber, gm.	1.9

Ham and Asparagus Casserole

Serves 4

1 can (10 ounces) cream of celery soup
1 cup fat-free milk
½ cup finely chopped onion
¼ teaspoon dried marjoram
¼ teaspoon dried rosemary
½ cup shredded Cheddar cheese, divided
2 cups seasoned croutons, divided
6 ounces (1½ cups) diced ham
½ pound fresh asparagus, blanched*
2 hard-boiled eggs, sliced
1 medium tomato, sliced

Nutritional information per serving:

Calories	370
Fat, gm.	20
Protein, gm.	20
Carbs, gm.	28
Cholesterol, mg.	150
Fiber, gm.	2.9

This is a great spring casserole that would be perfect to make the week after Easter. Use your leftover ham and hard-boiled eggs and combine them with fresh asparagus.

❖ Preheat oven to 350°F. Butter a 1½-quart casserole or a 9" × 11" baking pan. In a small saucepan, combine soup, milk, onion, marjoram, and rosemary. Bring to a boil over medium heat. Reduce heat and boil gently for 5 minutes or until onion is tender. Add ¼ cup of the cheese. Remove from heat and set aside. Place 1½ cups of seasoned croutons on bottom of casserole dish. Layer ham on top. Cut asparagus into 1-inch pieces and layer on top of the ham. Pour reserved sauce into the casserole. Arrange egg slices and tomato slices on top. Crush remaining ½ cup of croutons and sprinkle on top. Sprinkle with remaining cheese. Bake for 30 minutes or until heated through. Let set a few minutes before serving.

———

*To blanch asparagus, place in boiling water for 2 minutes. Cool under cold running water. Drain well.

———

Note: *For a big crowd, double the recipe and use 1 can of cream of celery soup and 1 can of cream of mushroom soup. Double all other ingredients and bake in a 9" × 13" baking pan.*

Hamburger Pie

Put this together ahead of time and refrigerate until ready to bake. It is sure to be a hit with the whole family.

❖ Preheat oven to 350°F. Butter a deep 9-inch pie pan. Cook spaghetti in boiling salted water until al dente. Drain and rinse under cold water. Drain well. In a medium bowl, combine cooked spaghetti, egg, and Parmesan cheese. Stir to blend. Spoon into pie pan and press onto bottom and up the sides. Spread ricotta cheese on top. Set aside. In a large nonstick skillet, cook ground beef and onion over medium-high heat until meat is brown. Add Italian seasoning, fennel seeds, and tomatoes. Bring to a boil, reduce heat, and simmer for 5 to 10 minutes or until mixture reaches desired consistency. Adjust seasoning with salt and pepper. Spoon over ricotta cheese in pie plate. Bake for 30 minutes. Sprinkle with mozzarella cheese and continue to bake for 5 to 10 minutes or until cheese is melted. Let stand 10 minutes before cutting and serving.

---

*The fennel seeds give meat the flavor of Italian sausage.

Serves 4

4 ounces spaghetti, broken in half
1 egg, lightly beaten
¼ cup shredded Parmesan cheese
1 cup skim-milk ricotta cheese
¾ pound lean ground beef
1 medium onion, chopped
2 teaspoons Italian seasoning
½ teaspoon crushed fennel seeds, optional*
1 can (15 ounces) seasoned diced tomatoes
Salt and pepper to taste
½ cup shredded mozzarella cheese

Nutritional information per serving:

Calories	440
Fat, gm.	17
Protein, gm.	39
Carbs, gm.	31
Cholesterol, mg.	140
Fiber, gm.	2.3

Italian Baked Mostaccioli

Serves 4

8 ounces mostaccioli pasta*
8 ounces low-fat bulk Italian sausage
1 cup chopped onion
1 teaspoon minced garlic
1 can (15 ounces) seasoned diced
  tomatoes
1 can (8 ounces) tomato sauce
½ teaspoon dried basil
½ cup fat-free chicken broth, divided
Salt and pepper to taste
½ cup grated Parmesan cheese
½ cup shredded mozzarella cheese

Nutritional information per serving:

Calories	435
Fat, gm.	10
Protein, gm.	31
Carbs, gm.	55
Cholesterol, mg.	20
Fiber, gm.	3.8

This is a dish you can put together and serve immediately or refrigerate until ready to use. The Italian sausage gives it a hearty taste.

❖ Preheat oven to 350°F. Grease a 7" × 11" or a 10-inch round baking dish. In a large saucepan, cook mostaccioli in boiling salted water until al dente. Drain and set aside. In a large skillet, cook sausage over medium heat until brown. Crumble the sausage. Add onion and cook until translucent. Drain and discard any excess fat. Add garlic and cook 1 minute. Add diced tomatoes, tomato sauce, basil, and ¼ cup chicken broth. Bring to a boil, reduce heat, and simmer for 10 to 15 minutes. Add salt and pepper to taste. Add reserved pasta and Parmesan cheese. Stir to mix. Add additional broth if mixture needs more moisture. Spoon into baking dish. Top with mozzarella cheese. Bake for 10 to 15 minutes or until heated through and cheese is melted.

*Mostaccioli is a small, short, tube-shaped macaroni product. Other pastas such as shells, bow ties, and penne can be used.

Italian Beef and Spinach Pie

The ingredient list may seem long, but this is really quite easy to make. It may help to prepare the noodle crust ahead of time and refrigerate until ready to assemble. There is a meat sauce layer and a spinach-cheese layer on top.

1. Preheat oven to 350°F. Grease a 9-inch deep-dish pie pan. In a medium saucepan, cook noodles in boiling salted water until al dente. Rinse under cold water and drain. In a small bowl, mix noodles and egg. Press into bottom of pie pan. Set aside.
2. In a large skillet, combine ground beef, Italian sausage, and onion. Cook over medium-high heat until meat is brown and cooked through. Add mushrooms, pepper, and garlic. Cook until tender. Add tomato sauce and Italian seasoning. Simmer for 10 minutes. Add salt and pepper to taste. Set aside.
3. In a small bowl, combine spinach, ricotta, and ⅔ cup mozzarella cheese. Spread spinach mixture in pie pan over noodles. Spoon meat sauce on top. Bake for 35 to 40 minutes or until heated through. Top with ⅓ cup shredded mozzarella cheese and return to oven for 2 minutes more or until cheese is melted.
4. Serve with chopped tomato and a dollop of sour cream.

Serves 6

Crust:
3 ounces (2 cups) medium egg noodles
1 egg, lightly beaten

Tomato Meat Sauce:
½ pound extra-lean ground beef
4 ounces low-fat bulk Italian sausage
1 medium onion, finely chopped
½ pound sliced mushrooms
½ medium red pepper, thinly sliced
2 cloves garlic, minced
1 can (15 ounces) tomato sauce
2 teaspoons Italian seasoning
Salt and pepper to taste

Spinach Layer:
1 package (10 ounces) frozen chopped spinach, thawed and squeezed dry
⅔ cup fat-free ricotta cheese
⅔ cup shredded mozzarella cheese

Topping:
⅓ cup shredded mozzarella cheese
1 large tomato, seeded and chopped
¼ cup fat free sour cream

Nutritional information per serving:

Calories	330
Fat, gm.	14
Protein, gm.	27
Carbs, gm.	25
Cholesterol, mg.	90
Fiber, gm.	4

Lasagna with No-Cook Noodles

Serves 4

*¾ pound lean ground beef or Italian
  sausage*
2½ cups spaghetti sauce
1 egg, lightly beaten
1 cup skim-milk ricotta cheese
*1 cup shredded mozzarella cheese,
  divided*
1 cup shredded Parmesan cheese, divided
6 no-cook lasagna noodles

Nutritional information per serving:

Calories	565
Fat, gm.	27
Protein, gm.	49
Carbs, gm.	31
Cholesterol, mg.	190
Fiber, gm.	3.5

I usually do not like to make lasagna because it is too much work. However, after trying this recipe, I am a lasagna convert.

❖ Preheat oven to 350°F. Grease a 7" × 11" baking pan. In a medium skillet, brown meat and crumble as it cooks. Add spaghetti sauce and set aside. In a medium bowl, combine egg, ricotta, ½ cup mozzarella cheese, and ½ cup Parmesan cheese. Set aside. To assemble the lasagna, do the following: 1) Spread ⅓ cup of the meat mixture in bottom of the pan. 2) Top with a layer of uncooked noodles, breaking to fit if needed. 3) Spread one-half of the cheese mixture over noodles. 4) Layer with half of the remaining meat sauce. 5) Add another layer of noodles. 6) Spread with remaining cheese mixture. 7) Top with remaining meat sauce to cover all noodles. 8) Sprinkle with ½ cup of Parmesan cheese and ½ cup mozzarella cheese. Cover with aluminum foil. Bake for 30 minutes. Uncover and bake for another 15 minutes. Let stand 10 minutes before serving.

Linguine with Chicken, Spinach, and Tomatoes

Impress your company or your family with this colorful meal that looks so special yet is so easy to make.

❖ In a large skillet, cook bacon until crisp. Add onion and cook until translucent. Remove bacon and onion from pan and set aside. Add chicken to the skillet, sprinkle with salt and pepper, and cook over medium-high heat until brown and cooked through. Add garlic and cook 1 minute. Add reserved bacon and onion, chicken broth, fresh spinach, and tomatoes. Bring to a boil, cover, and cook just until spinach wilts. Sprinkle with balsamic vinegar. Serve over warm pasta and sprinkle with cheese.

Note: A good aged Parmesan cheese may be substituted for the Asiago cheese.

Serves 4

2 slices bacon, diced
1 cup chopped sweet onion
3 boneless, skinless chicken breasts, thinly sliced
Salt and pepper
2 teaspoons minced garlic
¼ cup chicken broth
1 package (10 ounces) fresh small-leaf spinach
2 medium fresh tomatoes, seeded and chopped
2 tablespoons balsamic vinegar
4 cups cooked pasta
⅓ cup shredded Asiago or aged Parmesan cheese

Nutritional information per serving:

Calories	430
Fat, gm.	10
Protein, gm.	35
Carbs, gm.	50
Cholesterol, mg.	70
Fiber, gm.	5.0

Meat and Potatoes Skillet Dinner

Serves 6

3 cups frozen shredded hash browns,
   thawed
1 teaspoon salt
1 teaspoon cumin
1 teaspoon chili powder
½ teaspoon pepper
1 egg white, lightly beaten
Butter spray
1 pound extra-lean ground beef
1 cup salsa
½ cup sliced black olives
¾ cup shredded Cheddar cheese
1 cup fat-free half-and-half
½ cup egg substitute or 2 eggs

Nutritional information per serving:

Calories	320
Fat, gm.	20
Protein, gm.	22
Carbs, gm.	13
Cholesterol, mg.	65
Fiber, gm.	0.9

This might be described as a real-man's quiche. It has a meaty filling with Southwestern seasoning in a potato crust. It is very attractive and colorful with the red tomatoes, black olives, and melted cheese.

❖ Preheat oven to 425°F. Butter a 10-inch, nonstick, ovenproof skillet or a deep 9-inch pie pan. Place thawed potatoes in a large bowl. In a small custard cup combine salt, cumin, chili powder, and pepper. Set aside. In a small bowl, mix egg white and add one-third of the spice mixture. Stir egg white mixture into potatoes. Press potatoes into bottom of skillet and up the sides. Lightly spray with butter spray. Bake for 20 to 25 minutes or until potatoes begin to brown. Remove from oven and put aside. While potatoes are in the oven, brown meat in a medium skillet. Sprinkle with one-third of the spice mixture. When potatoes are done, spoon meat on top of potatoes. Spoon salsa on top of meat. Sprinkle with olives and cheese. In a small bowl, combine half-and-half, egg substitute or eggs, and the remaining spice mixture. Mix well and pour into skillet. Reduce oven to 350°F and bake for 35 to 45 minutes or until set in the middle.

Note: *Choose your favorite mild or medium salsa to make it as hot as you like.*

Mushroom Stroganoff

This is an extraordinary meatless meal that is a real taste treat. The seasoning is perfect, but if you like it extra hot, add a dash of hot pepper sauce.

1. In a large skillet, heat 1 tablespoon of oil. Add onions and cook until lightly brown. Remove from pan. Add part of the mushrooms and cook until lightly brown. Remove from pan and add the next batch. Add oil as needed. Sprinkle each batch with salt and pepper. (Cooking is small batches will help the mushrooms brown better.) Combine all mushrooms, reserved onions, paprika, thyme, and red pepper flakes in the skillet. In a shaker, combine flour and ½ cup chicken broth. Shake to mix well. Pour into skillet. Add remaining chicken broth and mustard. Bring to a boil, stirring constantly. Reduce heat and simmer for 5 minutes. When ready to serve, add wine and sour cream. If mixture is too thick, add additional broth or wine. Heat through. Add hot pepper sauce to taste.

2. Serve on cooked noodles.

———

Choose a variety of mushrooms for this dish.

Serves 4

2 tablespoons canola oil, divided
2 cups chopped sweet onions
1½ pounds sliced mixed mushrooms (white, baby bellas, portabella mushrooms)*
Salt and pepper
½ teaspoon paprika
¼ teaspoon thyme
Dash red pepper flakes
3 tablespoons flour
2 cups fat-free chicken broth, divided
1 tablespoon Dijon mustard
¼ cup white wine, optional
½ cup fat-free sour cream
Hot pepper sauce to taste

Nutritional information per serving (without the noodles):

Calories	195
Fat, gm.	8
Protein, gm.	6
Carbs, gm.	25
Cholesterol, mg.	5
Fiber, gm.	3.6

Serves 6

Sauce:

3 tablespoons butter or margarine
¼ cup flour
2 cups fat-free milk*
¾ cup shredded Parmesan cheese
4 ounces Neufchatel cheese (reduced-fat
   cream cheese)
⅛ teaspoon white pepper
⅓ cup white wine
Salt and pepper to taste

Added Ingredients:

16 ounces frozen or fresh mixed vegetables, cooked
½ pound cooked chicken, shrimp,
   or scallops

**Nutritional information per serving
(without the pasta):**

Calories	235
Fat, gm.	13
Protein, gm.	17
Carbs, gm.	13
Cholesterol, mg.	95
Fiber, gm.	1.8

Pasta Alfredo—Create Your Own

This tastes so rich and creamy, you won't believe it is very low in fat and calories compared to the usual Alfredo sauce.

1. In a medium, heavy saucepan, melt butter. Add flour and cook over medium heat, stirring constantly, for 2 minutes. Add milk and bring to a boil, stirring constantly. Add Parmesan cheese, Neufchatel cheese, white pepper, and wine. Heat through. Add salt and pepper to taste. Add cooked vegetables and chicken or seafood as desired. Heat through. If sauce is too thick, add extra milk to thin.

2. Serve on cooked pasta of your choice.

_____

Other milk such as 2% or whole milk would work well in this recipe.

Pasta with Broccoli and Red Peppers in Peanut Sauce

The sauce tastes like you worked all day to prepare it. There is a hint of peanut flavor that is not overwhelming. The sesame oil is the secret ingredient.

❖ In a small saucepan, combine chicken broth, peanut butter, soy sauce, sesame oil, and garlic. Bring to a boil over medium heat. In a small cup, mix cornstarch in water. Add to saucepan and bring to a boil, stirring constantly. Add red pepper flakes. Remove from heat but keep warm. Cook pasta in boiling salted water. Drain and set aside. Cook vegetables in boiling salted water until tender-crisp. In a large bowl, combine peanut sauce, pasta, and vegetables. Top with peanuts.

*Any combination of colorful mixed vegetables may be used. This dish is also good with chicken added.

Serves 4

Sauce:
2 cups fat-free chicken broth
½ cup creamy peanut butter
3 tablespoons soy sauce
1 teaspoon sesame oil
½ teaspoon minced garlic
1½ teaspoons cornstarch
1 tablespoon water
⅛ teaspoon red pepper flakes, optional

Pasta and Vegetables:
6 ounces linguine or pasta of your choice
4 cups frozen broccoli and red pepper mix*
¼ cup chopped peanuts

Nutritional information per serving:

Calories	635
Fat, gm.	23
Protein, gm.	34
Carbs, gm.	74
Cholesterol, mg.	0
Fiber, gm.	8.0

Pasta with Spinach, Olives, and Pine Nuts

There are major health benefits to eating more spinach, olives, olive oil, nuts, and tomatoes. This recipe has them all!

❖ In a small jar, combine vinegar, honey, and 3 tablespoons olive oil. Set aside. In a large saucepan, cook pasta in boiling salted water until al dente. Drain and place in serving bowl. While pasta is cooking, heat 1 tablespoon oil in large skillet. Add tomatoes and garlic and cook 1 minute over medium heat. Add spinach to the skillet in batches. Cook each batch just until it begins to wilt. Sprinkle each batch of spinach lightly with salt and pepper. Transfer spinach to serving bowl when it is done. Add reserved pasta, olives, pine nuts, and cheese. Add reserved vinegar and honey mixture. Toss to coat. Season with salt and pepper.

Serves 4

3 tablespoons balsamic vinegar
2 teaspoons honey
4 tablespoons olive oil, divided
1½ cups pasta shells or small penne
  pasta
½ cup chopped sun dried tomatoes
1 teaspoon minced garlic
12 ounces fresh baby spinach
Salt and pepper to taste
½ cup sliced black olives
¼ cup pine nuts, toasted
1 cup freshly shredded Parmesan cheese
Salt and pepper to taste

Nutritional information per serving:

Calories	425
Fat, gm.	24
Protein, gm.	20
Carbs, gm.	33
Cholesterol, mg.	15
Fiber, gm.	3.9

Pasta with Tomato and White Bean Sauce—A Build Your Own Pasta Dish

You can build your own pasta sauce with this great pasta base. Add a variety of optional ingredients to create your own unique dish.

1. Cook pasta in a pot of boiling salted water until al dente. Drain and rinse. Set aside. In a large skillet, heat oil. Add onion and cook until translucent. Add garlic and cook 1 minute. Add tomatoes, beans, Italian seasoning, basil, and red pepper flakes. Cook for 10 to 20 minutes or until mixture reaches desired consistency. Add any of the optional ingredients. Heat through. Add salt and pepper to taste. Add pasta to the sauce in the pan or serve sauce over the pasta on individual plates.

2. Top with Parmesan cheese right before serving.

Serves 4

1½ cups pasta shells or penne pasta
1 tablespoon olive oil
1 medium onion, chopped
2 teaspoons minced garlic
1 can (28 ounces) garlic-seasoned diced tomatoes
1 can (15 ounces) great northern white beans, partially drained
1 teaspoon Italian seasoning
1 teaspoon dried basil or ¼ cup chopped fresh basil
¼ teaspoon red pepper flakes

Optional Ingredients:
1 cup sliced mushrooms, sautéed
2 cups fresh broccoli florets or asparagus tips, blanched
2 cups cooked vegetables of your choice
½ pound cooked low-fat Italian sausage
½ cup black or green olives
½ pound cooked shrimp or scallops
Salt and pepper to taste
⅓ cup freshly grated Parmesan cheese

Nutritional information per serving (without the sausage or shrimp):

Calories	415
Fat, gm.	7
Protein, gm.	20
Carbs, gm.	68
Cholesterol, mg.	10
Fiber, gm.	10

Pork and Noodles

Serves 4

4 ounces thin noodles
1 tablespoon canola oil
1 pound pork loin, cut in thin slices
1 medium onion, thinly sliced
4 cups shredded cabbage
1 cup finely chopped carrots
½ cup fat-free chicken broth
¼ cup soy sauce
⅛ teaspoon ground ginger
2 teaspoons sugar
1 teaspoon cornstarch
Dash red pepper flakes
½ cup peanuts, optional

Nutritional information per serving:

Calories	360
Fat, gm.	15
Protein, gm.	23
Carbs, gm.	33
Cholesterol, mg.	55
Fiber, gm.	3.6

Instead of picking up Chinese fast food, try this recipe. It is easy if you buy the shredded cabbage and carrots.

❖ In a medium saucepan, cook pasta in boiling salted water until al dente. Drain, rinse under cold water, and set aside. Rewarm pasta under hot water when ready to serve. In a large skillet, heat oil. Add pork and cook over medium-high heat until brown. Cook the pork in several small batches to help it brown better. Add onion and cook until translucent. Add cabbage and carrots. Cook until vegetables are tender. In a cup, mix broth, soy sauce, ginger, sugar, cornstarch, and pepper flakes. Stir into skillet. Bring to a boil to thicken. Add reserved pasta and heat through. Add peanuts if desired.

Reuben Casserole

You have to love sauerkraut to enjoy this fast and easy-to-assemble casserole.

1. Preheat oven to 350°F. Grease a 9" × 13" baking pan. Spoon sauerkraut into baking pan. Arrange slices of pastrami on top. Sprinkle with 1 cup of cheese. Drizzle with salad dressing. Top with bread cubes. Spray lightly with butter spray. Sprinkle with remaining ½ cup of cheese. Bake for 30 minutes or until heated through.

2. Serve extra Thousand Island dressing on the side if desired.

Serves 6

1 can (27 ounces) sauerkraut, drained
8 ounces thin deli-sliced lean pastrami
1½ cups shredded Swiss cheese, divided
½ cup reduced-fat Thousand Island salad dressing
6 slices (6 ounces) rye bread, cubed
Butter spray

Nutritional information per serving:

Calories	275
Fat, gm.	11
Protein, gm.	19
Carbs, gm.	25
Cholesterol, mg.	45
Fiber, gm.	5.4

Russian Beef, Mushrooms, and Noodles

Kids will love this mild-flavored noodle dish. It is one of those casserole-type dishes that you keep taking "just one more spoonful" of.

Serves 4

1 pound extra-lean ground beef
Salt and pepper
1 medium onion, finely chopped
1 medium green or red pepper, thinly
  sliced
½ pound sliced mushrooms, optional
2 cups tomato-vegetable juice
1 tablespoon Worcestershire sauce
½ teaspoon celery salt, optional
4 ounces (3 cups) uncooked medium
  noodles
½ cup fat-free sour cream

❖ In a large skillet, cook beef over medium-high heat until brown. Sprinkle with salt and pepper. Add onion and cook until translucent. Add pepper and mushrooms. Cook until tender. Add tomato-vegetable juice, Worcestershire sauce, and celery salt. Stir to mix and simmer for 15 to 20 minutes. While sauce is simmering, cook noodles in boiling salted water until al dente. Drain. Add noodles to meat mixture. When ready to serve, stir in sour cream. Heat through.

Nutritional information per serving:

Calories	440
Fat, gm.	21
Protein, gm.	28
Carbs, gm.	35
Cholesterol, mg.	110
Fiber, gm.	2.9

Seafood and Red Pepper Couscous

Couscous is a coarsely ground durum wheat that is a staple in North African cuisines. It has the shape of very tiny beads and is similar in texture and flavor to rice. Best of all, it cooks in only 5 minutes.

1. In a medium saucepan, heat olive oil. Add onion and cook until translucent. Add carrots, celery, and pepper. Cook until tender. Add chicken broth and bring to a boil. Stir in couscous. Cover pan and remove from heat. Let stand for 5 minutes. Fluff couscous with a fork. Add seafood.

2. In a small jar, combine wine vinegar, balsamic vinegar, olive oil, basil, mustard, and sugar. Cover jar and shake until mixed. Add to couscous. Stir gently until mixed. Add salt and pepper to taste.

Other seafood choices that would be good in this recipe are grilled salmon or tuna, cut into bite-sized pieces. This dish can be served warm or chilled.

Serves 4

1 tablespoon olive oil
1 medium onion, finely chopped
1 cup finely diced carrots
½ cup finely diced celery
1 medium red pepper, thinly sliced
1¼ cups fat-free chicken broth
1 cup couscous
¾ pound shrimp, cooked and shelled, or bay scallops

Dressing:
2 tablespoons white wine vinegar
1 tablespoon balsamic vinegar
2 tablespoons extra-virgin olive oil
2 teaspoons dried or 2 tablespoons fresh basil
2 tablespoons Dijon mustard
½ teaspoon sugar
Salt and freshly ground pepper to taste

Nutritional information per serving:

Calories	370
Fat, gm.	11
Protein, gm.	28
Carbs, gm.	39
Cholesterol, mg.	20
Fiber, gm.	3.9

Serves 6

6 ounces (2 cups) penne pasta
2 tablespoons butter or margarine
3 tablespoons flour
1 teaspoon minced garlic
2 cups fat-free half-and-half
1 medium red pepper, thinly sliced
¼ teaspoon white pepper
¼ teaspoon salt
1½ cups (6 ounces) shredded Swiss or
   Gruyère cheese, divided
¼ cup dry white wine
1 pound cooked shrimp, peeled and
   deveined
2 cups frozen peas
1 cup fat-free chicken broth, as needed to
   thin
Freshly ground pepper to taste
Chopped parsley to garnish

Nutritional information per serving:

Calories	420
Fat, gm.	14
Protein, gm.	33
Carbs, gm.	40
Cholesterol, mg.	190
Fiber, gm.	3.2

Shrimp and Pasta in Creamy Swiss Cheese Sauce

This looks and tastes like it would be decadent in calories and fat, but you will be surprised. If you like a creamy shrimp dish, you will love this.

❖ Preheat oven to 375°F. Butter a 2-quart casserole dish. In a large saucepan, cook pasta in boiling salted water until al dente. Drain and rinse under cold water. Set aside. In a large skillet, melt butter. Add flour and garlic. Cook, stirring constantly, for 1 minute. Add half-and-half and bring to a boil, stirring constantly. Add red pepper, white pepper, salt, 1 cup cheese, and wine. Heat through. Add shrimp, peas, and reserved pasta. Stir to mix. Add broth to thin to desired consistency. Add pepper to taste. Spoon into baking dish.* Top with remaining cheese. Bake for 10 minutes or until cheese is melted and casserole is heated through. Top with finely chopped parsley.

You can skip the baking step if you prefer. Heat the cheese sauce, shrimp, pasta and peas completely through and spoon into serving dish. Garnish with shredded cheese and chopped parsley.

Spaghetti and Italian Sausage Pie

Use a jar of spaghetti sauce and create a dish of your own. This recipe works well, and part of the secret is the eggs, which hold the sauce and spaghetti noodles together. It is a good make-ahead meal.

❖ Preheat oven to 350°F. Butter a 9-inch pie pan. Sprinkle with bread crumbs. In a large saucepan, cook spaghetti in boiling salted water until al dente. Drain and rinse under cold water. Set aside. In a small skillet, cook sausage over medium heat until brown and thoroughly cooked. Drain and discard any fat. Crumble meat. In a large bowl, combine meat, reserved cooked spaghetti, spaghetti sauce, eggs, and ½ cup of cheese. Stir to mix. Spoon into bread crumb–coated pan. Sprinkle top with remaining cheese. Bake for 30 to 35 minutes or until middle is set and top is brown. Let cool 5 to 10 minutes before cutting.

Serves 4

1 tablespoon dry bread crumbs
4 ounces spaghetti, broken in half
½ pound low-fat bulk Italian sausage
2 cups spaghetti sauce
2 large eggs, lightly beaten
1 cup shredded fresh Parmesan cheese, divided

Nutritional information per serving:

Calories	445
Fat, gm.	17
Protein, gm.	31
Carbs, gm.	42
Cholesterol, mg.	100
Fiber, gm.	4.9

Spaghetti with Beef and Bacon Tomato Sauce

Serves 4

¾ pound lean ground beef
4 slices turkey or pork bacon, diced
Salt and pepper
1 teaspoon Italian seasoning
1 cup chopped onion
½ cup shredded carrot
1 can (28 ounces) seasoned diced
*   tomatoes*
⅓ cup red wine
1 teaspoon sugar, optional
8 ounces spaghetti
¼ cup grated Parmesan cheese, optional

Nutritional information per serving:

Calories	485
Fat, gm.	10
Protein, gm.	38
Carbs, gm.	61
Cholesterol, mg.	75
Fiber, gm.	4.2

Once you make this one, you will know why you should bother making your own spaghetti sauce. The flavor is extra special. And shredded carrots add extra nutrients and make the sauce taste even better.

❖ In a large, heavy skillet, combine ground beef and bacon. Cook over medium-high heat until meat is brown. Sprinkle with salt and pepper. Add Italian seasoning, onion, and carrot. Cook until onion is translucent. Add tomatoes and wine. Bring to a boil, reduce heat, and boil gently for 10 to 30 minutes or until sauce reaches desired consistency. Add sugar if desired. While sauce is simmering, cook spaghetti in a large pot of salted water until al dente. Drain well. Place spaghetti in serving bowl and sauce in another serving bowl. Top individual servings with grated cheese if desired.

Spanish Rice with Chicken and Red Peppers

This is for the family that loves old-fashioned casseroles. It is not exceptionally attractive, but it is full of good flavor.

❖ In a large, heavy skillet, heat oil. Add chicken and cook over medium-high heat until browned. Sprinkle with salt and pepper. Remove chicken from pan and set aside. Add onion and cook until translucent. Add pepper, mushrooms, garlic, chili powder, cumin, and Worcestershire sauce. Cook until tender. Add rice, broth, and tomatoes. Bring to a boil. Reduce heat, cover, and simmer for 20 to 30 minutes or until rice is tender and most of the liquid has been absorbed. Add reserved chicken, sugar, and black olives. Stir to mix. Garnish with chopped green onions.

Serves 4

1 tablespoon canola oil
3 boned and skinned chicken breast
   halves, thinly sliced
Salt and pepper
1 medium onion, chopped
1 large red pepper, thinly sliced
¼ pound sliced mushrooms, optional
1 teaspoon minced garlic
1 teaspoon chili powder
¼ teaspoon cumin
½ teaspoon Worcestershire sauce
¾ cup long-grain white rice
1 cup fat free chicken broth
1 can (15 ounces) seasoned diced
   tomatoes
½ teaspoon sugar
½ cup sliced black olives
Chopped green onions to garnish

Nutritional information per serving:

Calories	260
Fat, gm.	6
Protein, gm.	18
Carbs, gm.	33
Cholesterol, mg.	40
Fiber, gm.	2.7

Spicy Seafood Rice

Serves 4

1 tablespoon olive oil
1 medium onion, finely chopped
2 teaspoons minced garlic
½ teaspoon cumin
½ teaspoon chili powder
¼ teaspoon cinnamon
2 teaspoons hot curry powder*
1 cup basmati rice**
1 pound cooked shrimp, peeled and
  deveined
2 cups fat-free chicken broth
1 cup frozen or canned corn
1 cup frozen peas
1 tablespoon lime juice

Nutritional information per serving:

Calories	390
Fat, gm.	5
Protein, gm.	32
Carbs, gm.	54
Cholesterol, mg.	220
Fiber, gm.	4.2

The flavor will change depending on the curry powder you choose. Use your favorite hot one.

❖ In a large, heavy skillet, heat oil. Add onion and cook until translucent. Add garlic, cumin, chili powder, cinnamon, and curry powder. Stir to mix. Add rice and shrimp. Cook for 2 to 3 minutes, stirring constantly, to coat the rice with spices. Remove the shrimp and set aside. Add broth to skillet and bring to a boil. Reduce heat, cover, and simmer for 20 minutes or until rice is tender. Add corn, peas, shrimp, and lime juice. Stir to mix and heat through.

―――

*Curry powder is actually a combination of spices. It has been said that there are as many different curry powder combinations as there are Indian cooks. The one ingredient always part of the combination is turmeric, which gives curry its yellow color. Other spices that may be in the mix include cardamom, cumin, pepper, cloves, cinnamon, nutmeg, and ginger. Chilies give it heat, and garlic enhances the flavor.

―――

**The directions on some packages or boxes of basmati rice recommend rinsing the rice before cooking it. When I rinsed the rice for this recipe, the rice became gummy. I found the dish turned out much better when I did not rinse the rice.

Tamale Pie

This may look like a dish you worked on for hours, but it can be put together very quickly. It is a complete meal with lots of flavor. If you like it hot, add some hot chili peppers.

❖ Preheat oven to 375°F. Lightly butter a 2-quart casserole dish. In a large skillet, cook ground beef over medium-high heat until brown. Sprinkle with salt and pepper. Add chili powder, oregano, onion, and pepper. Cook until onion is tender. Add tomatoes, chili beans, and corn. Heat through. Spoon into casserole dish and top with cheese. Combine muffin mix with egg and milk. Stir to mix. Using a tablespoon, drop batter on top of casserole. Bake for 20 to 30 minutes or until muffins are cooked through and lightly brown on top.

Note: You do not need to transfer the beef-and-bean mixture into a casserole if you are using an ovenproof skillet. Place muffin batter on top of beef-and-bean mixture and bake right in the skillet.

Serves 6

1 pound lean ground beef
Salt and pepper
1 tablespoon chili powder
½ teaspoon oregano
1 medium onion, chopped
½ medium red pepper, thinly sliced
1 can (15 ounces) Mexican-seasoned
   petite-cut diced tomatoes
1 can (15 ounces) chili beans, undrained
1 cup corn
1 cup shredded reduced-fat Monterey jack
   cheese

Topping:
1 package (8½ ounces) corn muffin mix
1 egg
⅓ cup milk

Nutritional information per serving:

Calories	460
Fat, gm.	15
Protein, gm.	34
Carbs, gm.	48
Cholesterol, mg.	85
Fiber, gm.	2.7

Tortilla and Bean Casserole

Serves 4

1 can (15 ounces) black beans, drained
   and rinsed
1 can (15 ounces) seasoned diced
   tomatoes
1 can (11 ounces) corn, drained
1 can (4 ounces) green chilies
2 teaspoons chili powder
½ teaspoon cumin
6 (6 inch) corn tortillas, divided
1½ cups shredded Monterey jack cheese,
   divided

Nutritional information per serving:

Calories	410
Fat, gm.	14
Protein, gm.	21
Carbs, gm.	50
Cholesterol, mg.	40
Fiber, gm.	11

This is an attractive, flavorful, and filling meal. There is no chopping or cooking involved in this recipe.

❖ Preheat oven to 375°F. Butter a 7" × 11" baking pan. In a large bowl, combine beans, tomatoes, corn, chilies, chili powder, and cumin. Stir to mix. In bottom of casserole, place 3 tortillas. Spoon half of the bean mixture on top. Sprinkle with ½ cup cheese. Repeat the layers with remaining tortillas, bean mixture, and remaining cheese. Bake for 30 to 40 minutes or until cheese is melted and casserole is heated through.

Note: *This may be served with salsa and sour cream on the side.*

Tuna Noodle Casserole

Do you remember this one? My mother used to put potato chips on top, but the bread crumbs are a good, healthful substitute.

❖ In a large saucepan, cook noodles in boiling salted water until al dente. Set aside. Preheat oven to 375°F. Butter a 2-quart casserole. In a large bowl, combine soup and milk. Stir to mix. Add tuna, peas, lemon juice, white pepper, and reserved noodles. Stir to mix. Add salt and pepper to taste. Spoon into casserole dish. Sprinkle bread crumbs on top of casserole. Lightly spray with butter spray. Bake for 30 to 40 minutes or until heated through.

Serves 4

6 ounces (3 cups) egg noodles
1 can (10 ounces) cream of mushroom soup
1 cup fat-free milk
1 large can (12 ounces) tuna in water, drained
1½ cups frozen green peas
1 tablespoon lemon juice
¼ teaspoon white pepper
Salt and pepper to taste
½ cup bread crumbs
Butter spray

Nutritional information per serving:

Calories	475
Fat, gm.	11
Protein, gm.	36
Carbs, gm.	58
Cholesterol, mg.	70
Fiber, gm.	4.7

Turkey and Dressing Casserole

Serves 6

1 tablespoon butter or margarine
1 medium onion, finely chopped
3 cups dry herb-seasoned stuffing cubes
½ cup fat-free chicken broth
6 ounces diced cooked turkey breast meat
2 eggs
½ cup fat-free mayonnaise
1½ cups fat-free milk
½ teaspoon salt
¼ teaspoon pepper
¼ teaspoon sage or poultry seasoning

Nutritional information per serving:

Calories	345
Fat, gm.	7
Protein, gm.	20
Carbs, gm.	50
Cholesterol, mg.	90
Fiber, gm.	0.5

You will want to make extra dressing with your turkey just to have enough to prepare this comfort-food casserole. You can also make this recipe quickly from scratch with purchased stuffing cubes.

1. Preheat oven to 350°F. Grease a deep 9-inch pie pan or a 7" × 11" baking pan. In a large skillet, heat butter. Add onion and cook over medium heat until lightly browned. Add stuffing cubes and broth. Stir to mix. Spoon into baking pan. Top with turkey. In a small bowl, combine eggs, mayonnaise, milk, salt, pepper, and sage. Beat well. Pour over turkey and dressing. Bake for 45 to 50 minutes or until middle is set. Let stand 10 minutes before serving.

2. This can be made ahead and refrigerated until ready to bake.

Note: *Leftover dressing may be used in place of the onion, stuffing cubes, and broth.*

CHAPTER 8
Side Dishes

Apple Apricot Bread Dressing
BLT Mashed Potatoes
Colcannon—Irish Mashed Potatoes and Cabbage
Cornbread
Grilled Potato Salad
Hot German Potato Salad
Irish Soda Bread
Mediterranean Rice with Pine Nuts and Dried Cranberries
Mexican Rice
Orange Persian Barley
Orzo with Parmesan and Basil
Oven Roasted Red Potatoes with Rosemary
Parmesan Potatoes
Pasta with Pesto Sauce
Pilaf with Spinach and Walnuts
Spice It Up with Lentils
Tuscan White Beans with Herbs
Wild Rice with Cranberries and Cashews
Yellow Rice with Golden Raisins

Side Dishes Cooking Tips

A great seasoning that complements potato or pasta side dishes is white pepper. The white peppercorns are milder than black peppercorns yet they have a distinctive bite and flavor. The white pepper is made from fully ripe pepper berries from which the outer hull has been removed. Once you use white pepper in a dish like mashed potatoes, you will never want to make the dish without it.

When using cheese in a sauce, processed cheese is a good choice. Processed cheese is made from blending together many different cheeses, heating it, and adding emulsifiers to hold the mixture together. (The most familiar brand is Velveeta.) The advantage of processed cheese is that it melts easily and smoothly.

When cooking with cheese, cook at a low temperature. High heat causes cheese to become rubbery. It is best to shred the cheese or cut it into small pieces when adding it to a hot liquid. It will melt more quickly and with very little extra heat.

It is convenient to keep a container of purchased bread crumbs in your cupboard but you can make your own with toasted bread or crumbled breadsticks.

The equivalent of 1 ounce of cheese is ¼ cup shredded cheese.

Some recipes call for capers. They are the brine-cured, unopened flower buds of a shrub native to the Mediterranean. Capers are usually sold soaking in brine. They add potent flavor to side dishes, salads, and sauces. If you are in the middle of a recipe and do not have capers, you might substitute chopped dill pickles or green olives.

When using evaporated milk, shake the can well. Milk solids often settle to the bottom of the can.

Apple Apricot Bread Dressing

This has a wonderful combination of flavors and it is lower in fat and calories than most bread dressings or stuffings are.

❖ Preheat oven to 350°F. Butter a 2-quart ovenproof bowl. In a medium skillet, heat oil. Add onion and cook over medium heat until lightly browned. Add apricot pieces, apple, cinnamon, cloves, savory, and salt. Cook 5 minutes. Add chicken broth. Bring to a boil. Reduce heat and simmer for 10 minutes. In a large bowl, combine fruit mixture and stuffing cubes. Gently mix with a spoon. Place mixture in ovenproof bowl. Cover and bake for 40 to 50 minutes or until heated through and slightly brown on the bottom.

Serves 6

1 tablespoon canola oil
1 large onion, finely chopped
½ cup dried apricot halves, each cut into quarters
1 large apple, peeled, cored, and chopped
½ teaspoon cinnamon
¼ teaspoon cloves
½ teaspoon savory or thyme
¼ teaspoon salt
2½ cups fat-free chicken broth
4 cups herb-seasoned stuffing cubes

Nutritional information per serving:

Calories	210
Fat, gm.	3
Protein, gm.	6
Carbs, gm.	39
Cholesterol, mg.	0
Fiber, gm.	2.1

BLT Mashed Potatoes

Serves 6

5 large russet potatoes, peeled and diced
½ cup fat-free or 2% milk
½ cup fat-free sour cream
⅛ teaspoon white pepper
Salt to taste
¼ pound bacon, diced
1 large leek, white part only, thinly sliced
¼ cup minced sun-dried tomatoes

Nutritional information per serving:

Calories	180
Fat, gm.	9
Protein, gm.	8
Carbs, gm.	17
Cholesterol, mg.	20
Fiber, gm.	1.3

BLT—Bacon, Leek, and Tomato. You will love the unique flavor twist of these mashed potatoes. They are also special because you can make them a day or two before serving and they still taste like you just made them.

1. In a large saucepan, cook potatoes in boiling salted water until tender. Drain well. Add milk, sour cream, and white pepper. Beat with electric mixer. Add extra milk if necessary to make potatoes light and fluffy. Add salt to taste.

2. While potatoes are boiling, cook bacon in a small skillet. Cook over medium-high heat until bacon is crisp. Add leek and tomatoes. Cook until leek is tender. Drain and discard any excess bacon fat. When potatoes have been mashed, add bacon mixture. Stir to mix.

_____

Note: *If you make these ahead, cover and refrigerate. Warm potatoes in the oven or microwave before serving.*

Colcannon—
Irish Mashed Potatoes and Cabbage

Traditional Irish country-comfort food. Be sure to serve it for St. Patrick's Day, but it is also a good way to enjoy potatoes anytime and to get the cancer-fighting phytochemicals in cabbage.

❖ In a large saucepan, cook potatoes in boiling salted water until tender. While potatoes are cooking, place cabbage in a large saucepan. Cover pan and cook in boiling salted water for 10 minutes or until tender. Drain and set aside. When potatoes are done, drain well. Add milk and beat with electric mixer until smooth. Add sour cream, cream cheese, and white pepper. Beat until smooth. Add additional milk if necessary to make potatoes light and fluffy. Add cabbage and stir to mix. Adjust seasoning with salt and pepper to taste.

Serves 8

2½ pounds (6 large) potatoes, peeled and quartered
½ pound (4 cups) shredded cabbage
½ cup fat-free milk
½ cup fat-free sour cream
4 ounces fat-free cream cheese
¼ teaspoon white pepper
Salt and pepper to taste

Nutritional information per serving:

Calories	125
Fat, gm.	0
Protein, gm.	6
Carbs, gm.	25
Cholesterol, mg.	5
Fiber, gm.	1.7

Cornbread

Serves 12

1 box (8 ounces) corn muffin mix
1 can (8 ounces) drained canned corn
1 can (8 ounces) creamed-style corn
1 cup fat-free sour cream
2 large eggs, lightly beaten
¼ cup butter or margarine, melted

Nutritional information per serving:

Calories	175
Fat, gm.	7
Protein, gm.	3
Carbs, gm.	25
Cholesterol, mg.	45
Fiber, gm.	0.9

This recipe is for me, and you, too, if you do not like cornbread because it is too dry. You will be pleasantly surprised because this one is so moist and good. It will convert you into being a cornbread lover!

❖ Preheat oven to 350°F. Butter a 7" × 11" baking pan. In a large mixing bowl, combine all ingredients. Stir until well mixed. Spoon mixture into pan. Bake 40 to 45 minutes or until set in the middle and lightly browned.

Grilled Potato Salad

The flavor of this special potato salad prepared on the grill is fantastic. You may never buy deli salad again.

❖ Heat grill to medium-hot temperature. Grease a vegetable grill pan. Place potatoes in a large, shallow bowl. Add 1 tablespoon water and cover with plastic wrap. Microwave on high for 7 to 10 minutes or until potatoes are almost tender. (It may be better to microwave in two batches. Unwrap plastic wrap carefully to prevent burning fingers with hot steam.) Drain potatoes. Place potatoes in grill pan. Add onions, red pepper, and bacon. Sprinkle with seasoned salt and lightly spray with olive oil spray. Place on grill. Close cover and grill until potatoes are browned and tender. Stir frequently to prevent burning. While potatoes are grilling, combine dressing ingredients in a small jar. Shake to mix and set aside. Remove potatoes from grill. Place in large bowl and add dressing. Stir until well mixed. Let stand 10 minutes before serving.

Serves 4

2 pounds small red potatoes, cut into 1½-inch cubes (about 5 cups cubed potatoes)
2 large sweet onions, cut into chunks
1 medium red pepper, cut into strips
2 slices bacon, cut into quarters
¼ teaspoon seasoned salt
Olive oil spray

Dressing:
¼ cup cider vinegar
¼ cup fat-free chicken broth
2 tablespoons olive oil
2 cloves garlic, minced
¼ teaspoon white pepper
½ teaspoon salt
½ teaspoon dry mustard
½ teaspoon dill weed

Nutritional information per serving:

Calories	235
Fat, gm.	8
Protein, gm.	5
Carbs, gm.	36
Cholesterol, mg.	3
Fiber, gm.	3.8

Hot German Potato Salad

Serves 6

6 medium potatoes (about 2½ pounds)
6 slices bacon, diced
½ cup chopped onion
2 tablespoons flour
½ cup water
⅔ cup cider vinegar
2 tablespoons sugar
1 teaspoon celery seeds, optional
Salt and pepper to taste

Nutritional information per serving:

Calories	190
Fat, gm.	3
Protein, gm.	5
Carbs, gm.	36
Cholesterol, mg.	5
Fiber, gm.	2.8

I served this family favorite for my father's eighty-ninth birthday and he loved it. We will savor the memories.

❖ In a large saucepan, cook unpeeled potatoes in boiling salted water until tender. Drain and cool until easy to handle. Remove peels and discard. Slice potatoes and place in a large bowl. In a medium skillet, cook bacon until crisp. Drain all but 2 tablespoons of bacon grease from the pan. Discard excess grease. Add onion and cook until tender. Add flour to skillet. Cook, stirring constantly, over medium heat for 2 minutes. Add water and vinegar. Bring to a boil, stirring constantly, until mixture thickens. Add sugar and celery seeds. If mixture is too thick, thin with additional water. Combine dressing and potatoes. Stir gently to coat potatoes. Add salt and pepper to taste. Serve warm.

Irish Soda Bread

I always thought that soda bread was dry and tasteless, but this one is a real surprise. It has a touch of sweetness and a nice texture. Put it together in just a few minutes and enjoy the aroma of freshly baking bread.

❖ Preheat oven to 375°F. Grease a baking sheet. In a large bowl, combine flour, sugar, baking soda, baking powder, and salt. Add butter and cut in with two knives or a pastry blender until mixture resembles coarse cornmeal. Stir in currants and caraway seeds. Combine egg and buttermilk in a cup. Pour into flour mixture and stir until mixed. Form into 2 rounded loaves and place on baking sheet. Cut an X in the top of each. Bake for 20 to 30 minutes or until lightly brown. Cool on a rack.

Serves 12

4 cups flour
½ cup sugar
1 teaspoon baking soda
2 teaspoons baking powder
2 teaspoons salt
½ cup butter or margarine
1 cup dried currants or golden raisins
1 tablespoon caraway seeds, optional
1 large egg
1 cup low-fat buttermilk

Nutritional information per serving:

Calories	290
Fat, gm.	8
Protein, gm.	5
Carbs, gm.	50
Cholesterol, mg.	35
Fiber, gm.	0.5

Mediterranean Rice
with Pine Nuts and Dried Cranberries

Serves 6

1 tablespoon olive oil
1 large onion, finely chopped
1 cup basmati rice or
  long-grain white rice
½ teaspoon ground sage
¼ teaspoon coriander
⅛ teaspoon cinnamon
½ teaspoon salt
2 cups fat-free chicken broth
¼ cup pine nuts, toasted
½ cup dried cranberries
¼ cup chopped chives

Nutritional information per serving:

Calories	205
Fat, gm.	5
Protein, gm.	4
Carbs, gm.	36
Cholesterol, mg.	0
Fiber, gm.	1.6

This recipe uses sage and an interesting blend of spices. Sage is a flavorful herb that comes primarily from the Mediterranean. British cooking is partial to sage. The Chinese drink sage tea, and many people believe that sage helps promote a long and healthy life.

❖ In a large, heavy saucepan, heat oil. Add onion and cook until translucent. Add rice, sage, coriander, cinnamon, and salt. Stir over medium-high heat until rice is lightly browned. Remove from heat and carefully add broth. Return to heat and bring to a boil. Reduce heat and cover pan. Boil gently for 20 minutes or until rice is tender and liquid has been absorbed. Remove from heat. Stir in pine nuts, dried cranberries, and chives.

Mexican Rice

I am always looking for a way to be a little creative with side dishes.

❖ Preheat oven to 350°F. Spray a 1½-quart casserole with cooking spray. In a small, covered saucepan, cook rice in broth for 20 minutes or until tender and liquid has been absorbed. In a large bowl, combine cooked rice, corn, cottage cheese, sour cream, chilies, roasted red peppers, and ½ cup shredded cheese. Add salt and pepper to taste. Spoon into casserole dish. Sprinkle with remaining cheese. Bake for 30 to 35 minutes or until casserole is heated through and cheese is melted.

Note: Another cheese of your choice can be used in this recipe.

Serves 6

½ cup basmati rice or white rice
1 cup fat-free chicken broth or water
1 can (11 ounces) corn, drained
½ cup low-fat cottage cheese
½ cup fat-free sour cream
1 can (4 ounces) chopped green chilies
½ cup diced roasted red peppers, optional
1 cup (4 ounces) shredded Monterey Jack
  cheese, divided
Salt and pepper to taste.

Nutritional information per serving:

Calories	190
Fat, gm.	6
Protein, gm.	10
Carbs, gm.	24
Cholesterol, mg.	20
Fiber, gm.	1.8

Orange Persian Barley

Serves 6

1 cup pearl barley
3 cups fat-free chicken broth or water
1 teaspoon olive oil
½ cup chopped pitted dates
½ cup dried apricots, chopped
¼ cup sugar-free orange marmalade
½ teaspoon ground cumin
¼ teaspoon cinnamon
½ teaspoon salt
¼ teaspoon pepper to taste
⅓ cup slivered almonds, toasted

Nutritional information per serving:

Calories	265
Fat, gm.	5
Protein, gm.	6
Carbs, gm.	49
Cholesterol, mg.	0
Fiber, gm.	7.0

Barley has a mild, nutty flavor. It is a rich source of soluble fiber. Pearl barley has been processed to have the outer hull removed, but unlike most grains, in which fiber is found mostly in the outer layer (bran) of the kernel, barley contains fiber throughout the grain.

❖ In a large, heavy saucepan, combine barley and broth. Bring to a boil. Reduce heat, cover pan, and boil gently for 45 to 55 minutes or until barley is tender and liquid is absorbed. While barley is cooking, heat oil in a small skillet. Add dates, apricots, marmalade, cumin, cinnamon, salt, and pepper. Cook over low heat until fruit softens. When barley is done, stir sauce into cooked barley. Add additional salt and pepper to taste, if desired. Spoon into serving dish and top with almonds.

Orzo with Parmesan and Basil

Orzo is a pasta that is shaped like rice. It is bland tasting on its own but this recipe makes it good.

1. In a large skillet, heat oil. Add leek and cook over medium heat until translucent. Add mushrooms and cook until tender. Add garlic and zucchini and cook until zucchini softens. Remove from heat and set aside. In a large saucepan, cook orzo in salted water for 6 to 10 minutes or until al dente. Drain well. Add orzo to the vegetable mixture. Return to stove and heat through. Add cheese and basil, stir to mix, and heat through. Add salt and pepper to taste.

2. Pass additional Parmesan cheese at the table if desired.

Serves 6

1 tablespoon extra-light olive oil
1 large leek, white part only, thinly sliced
8 ounces mushrooms, finely chopped
2 teaspoons minced garlic
2 cups chopped zucchini
1 cup orzo
½ cup freshly grated Parmesan cheese
¼ cup finely chopped fresh basil
Salt and pepper

Nutritional information per serving:

Calories	120
Fat, gm.	4
Protein, gm.	6
Carbs, gm.	15
Cholesterol, mg.	5
Fiber, gm.	1.5

Oven Roasted Red Potatoes with Rosemary

Serves 4

2 pounds small red potatoes
¼ cup olive oil
1 teaspoon minced garlic
2 teaspoons dried rosemary
¼ teaspoon salt
¼ teaspoon pepper
2 tablespoons chopped parsley
Fresh rosemary for garnish, optional

Nutritional information per serving:

Calories	170
Fat, gm.	9
Protein, gm.	2
Carbs, gm.	20
Cholesterol, mg.	0
Fiber, gm.	1.9

What a great, easy way to make potatoes special!

❖ Preheat oven to 325°F. Grease a 9" × 13" baking pan. In a large plastic bag or bowl, combine potatoes, oil, garlic, rosemary, salt, and pepper. Toss to mix well. Pour into baking pan. Bake for 1 hour or until potatoes are tender. Garnish with fresh parsley and fresh rosemary sprigs.

———

Note: *If potatoes vary in size, cut the larger ones in half.*

Parmesan Potatoes

This recipe was adapted from a very high-calorie, high-fat recipe and it works! Everyone loves these potatoes.

❖ Preheat oven to 350°F. Butter a 7" × 11" baking pan. In a large skillet, melt butter. Add onion and cook until translucent. Add flour and cook, stirring constantly, for 1 minute. Add half-and-half, white pepper, and garlic powder. Bring to a boil and remove from heat. Add salt to taste. Add hash browns and ½ cup Parmesan cheese. Stir to mix. Spread potatoes evenly in baking pan. Cover with foil and bake 30 minutes. Uncover and top with remaining cheese. Sprinkle with paprika. Place under broiler until cheese is melted.

Note: Additional herbs such as rosemary, thyme, dill weed, or oregano may be added, if desired.

Serves 4

4 tablespoons butter or margarine
1 large onion, thinly sliced
1 tablespoon flour
1 cup fat-free half-and-half
¼ teaspoon white pepper
¼ teaspoon garlic powder, optional
Salt to taste
12 ounces frozen hash browns
1 cup grated Parmesan cheese, divided
Dash paprika

Nutritional information per serving:

Calories	300
Fat, gm.	17
Protein, gm.	13
Carbs, gm.	24
Cholesterol, mg.	45
Fiber, gm.	1.6

Pasta with Pesto Sauce

Serves 4

1 cup fresh basil
1 teaspoon minced garlic
¼ cup pine nuts
½ cup shredded Parmesan cheese
⅓ cup olive oil
6 ounces linguine
Salt and pepper to taste

Nutritional information per serving:

Calories	400
Fat, gm.	25
Protein, gm.	11
Carbs, gm.	33
Cholesterol, mg.	10
Fiber, gm.	1.4

This simple but very flavorful pasta makes an interesting side dish, but it also may be served in a larger quantity as a main entree.

1. Wash basil leaves and pat dry. In a small food processor, combine basil leaves, garlic, pine nuts, and Parmesan cheese. Blend. Add oil gradually, with food processor running. Process until smooth. Set aside. Cook linguine in boiling salted water until al dente. Drain well. Toss pasta with pesto sauce. Add salt and pepper to taste.

2. Pass additional Parmesan cheese at the table if desired.

Pilaf with Spinach and Walnuts

This makes an interesting side dish, but cooked poultry, meat, or seafood could be added to make it a substantial meal. Use leftover meat or purchase a rotisserie chicken.

❖ In a large saucepan, heat oil. Add onion and carrots and cook over medium heat until onion is translucent. Add rice and cook 1 minute, stirring constantly. Add broth and cinnamon stick. Bring to a boil. Reduce heat, cover pan, and boil gently for 20 minutes or until rice is tender and liquid has been absorbed. Add spinach and continue to cook for about 3 minutes or just until spinach is wilted. Remove cinnamon stick. Add salt and pepper to taste. Sprinkle with walnuts when ready to serve.

Serves 6

1 tablespoon canola oil
1 medium onion, finely chopped
1 cup diced carrots
1½ cups basmati rice or white rice
3 cups fat-free chicken broth
1 cinnamon stick
6 ounces fresh spinach, torn into bite sized pieces
Salt and pepper to taste
½ cup chopped walnuts

Nutritional information per serving:

Calories	225
Fat, gm.	4
Protein, gm.	5
Carbs, gm.	43
Cholesterol, mg.	0
Fiber, gm.	2.7

Spice It Up with Lentils

Serves 14 (½ cup servings)

1 tablespoon olive oil
1 large onion, finely chopped
1 teaspoon ground thyme
¼ teaspoon cumin
¼ teaspoon turmeric
¼ teaspoon salt
4 cloves garlic, minced
1 pound (2½ cups) dried green lentils*
4 cups fat-free chicken broth
1 cup shredded carrots
¼ teaspoon cayenne pepper, optional

Nutritional information per serving:

Calories	125
Fat, gm.	1
Protein, gm.	9
Carbs, gm.	20
Cholesterol, mg.	0
Fiber, gm.	10.3

Surprise your family with something a little different. The spice combination makes this a really tasty side dish. This recipe makes a lot of lentils. Cut it in half if cooking it for a small family meal or you will be eating lentils all week.

❖ In a large, heavy pan, heat oil. Add onion, thyme, cumin, turmeric, and salt. Cook until onion is translucent. Add garlic and cook 1 minute. Add lentils and chicken broth. Bring to a boil. Reduce heat, cover pan, and boil gently for 20 to 30 minutes or until lentils are tender. Add carrots and cook an additional 5 minutes or until carrots are tender. Add cayenne pepper if desired.

_____

Note: *To save time, you may want to use the chopped onions and shredded carrots that are usually available in the produce section of grocery stores.*

_____

Choose green lentils for this recipe. Some other lentils, such as the orange-colored lentils, turn to mush when cooked. They can be used for soups, but for this dish, you will prefer to have lentils that are tender but still look like lentils.

Tuscan White Beans with Herbs

This is a very traditional side dish that is served in the Tuscany region and throughout Italy. It makes a great side dish but could also be used for a vegetarian meal. Check out the fiber in this dish!

❖ In a large skillet, add olive oil and onion. Cook over medium heat until onion is translucent. Add garlic and cook 1 minute. Add beans, tomatoes, thyme, basil, vinegar, and lemon juice. Stir to mix. Bring to a boil, reduce heat, and boil gently for 10 to 15 minutes or until mixture thickens to desired consistency. Add chicken broth to thin if needed. Add salt and pepper to taste. Garnish with green onions. Serve warm or at room temperature.

This recipe is even better if you can use fresh thyme and basil; however, a good substitute is the ready to-use basil in a jar. It is usually found in the produce section of grocery stores.

Serves 6

1 tablespoon olive oil
1 medium onion, finely chopped
2 teaspoons minced garlic
2 cans (15 ounces each) great northern beans, drained
1 can (15 ounces) basil- or Italian-seasoned diced tomatoes
½ teaspoon ground thyme
2 teaspoons basil (ready-to-use basil in a jar)*
2 tablespoons red wine vinegar
1 tablespoon lemon juice
½ cup chicken or vegetable broth, optional
Salt and freshly ground pepper to taste
¼ cup chopped green onions

Nutritional information per serving:

Calories	215
Fat, gm.	3
Protein, gm.	12
Carbs, gm.	36
Cholesterol, mg.	0
Fiber, gm.	8.2

Wild Rice with Cranberries and Cashews

Serves 10

1¼ cups wild rice
6 cups water
2 teaspoons salt
1 cup sliced green onions
1½ cups dried cranberries
½ cup chopped cashews

Dressing:

⅓ cup extra-virgin olive oil
¼ cup white wine vinegar
½ teaspoon dried thyme
1 teaspoon dried rosemary, crushed
2 tablespoons honey
½ teaspoon salt
¼ teaspoon pepper

Nutritional information per serving:

Calories	245
Fat, gm.	10
Protein, gm.	4
Carbs, gm.	35
Cholesterol, mg.	0
Fiber, gm.	2.8

This is so full of flavor and healthy too!

❖ In a large saucepan, combine rice, water, and salt. Bring to a boil. Reduce heat, cover, and gently boil for 45 to 60 minutes or until rice is tender-crisp. Drain and chill quickly with cold running water. Drain well and place in large mixing bowl. Add onions and cranberries. Set cashews aside. In a small jar, mix dressing ingredients. Combine with rice mixture. Cover and refrigerate until ready to serve. Spoon into serving bowl and top with cashews.

Yellow Rice with Golden Raisins

This yellow rice is mildly seasoned with turmeric.

❖ In a large, heavy saucepan, heat oil. Add rice, cloves, cardamom, cinnamon, turmeric, and salt. Cook over medium-high heat, stirring constantly, until rice is lightly browned. Add garlic and cook 1 minute. Remove from heat and carefully add chicken broth. Return to heat and bring to a boil. Reduce heat, cover pan, and boil gently for 20 minutes or until rice is tender and liquid has been absorbed. Add raisins and chives. Stir to mix.

Serves 6

1 tablespoon olive oil
1 cup basmati rice or long-grain white rice
¼ teaspoon ground cloves
¼ teaspoon ground cardamom
¼ teaspoon cinnamon
¼ teaspoon ground turmeric
½ teaspoon salt
1 teaspoon minced garlic
2 cups fat-free chicken broth or vegetable broth
½ cup golden raisins
¼ cup chopped chives

Nutritional information per serving:

Calories	175
Fat, gm.	2
Protein, gm.	3
Carbs, gm.	36
Cholesterol, mg.	0
Fiber, gm.	1.0

CHAPTER 9

Vegetables

Asparagus Blue Cheese Bundles
Asparagus with Black Olives and Bacon
Baked Stuffed Sweet Potatoes
Broccoli with Honey Sesame Topping
Brussels Sprouts in Creamy Dijon Sauce
Brussels Sprouts with Apricot Glaze
Carrots with Dried Cranberries and Walnuts
Green Beans with Blue Cheese and Bacon Dressing
Green Beans with Pecans
Green Beans with Tomatoes and Onions
Honey and Parmesan Topped Asparagus
Marmalade Glazed Carrots
Roasted Red and Yellow Peppers with Green Beans
Sweet Potatoes and Apples in Ginger Orange Sauce
Swiss Spinach Soufflé
Wilted Spinach with Balsamic Mustard Sauce
Zucchini Bake

Vegetable Cooking Tips

Are sweet potatoes really yams? Actually, sweet potatoes are a root of the morning glory family. Real yams are not grown in this country and are truly a different vegetable; however, since there is confusion about the name, many canned sweet potatoes are also called yams on the label.

To remove the seeds from the inside of a squash that has been cut in half, use an ice cream scoop.

There are hundreds of varieties of chili peppers. Some of the most common are:

- **Anaheim chilies**—They are light green in color with a mild flavor. They are usually 4 to 6 inches long, 2 inches wide, and have a rounded tip.

- **Chipotle chilies**—These peppers have a strong, distinctive flavor. They are actually smoked, dried red jalapeño peppers. They have a smoky flavor and are very hot.

- **Jalapeño peppers**—These are the well-known small, dark green chilies. They are only 2 to 3 inches long and ½ inch wide. They are usually very hot.

- **Poblano peppers**—These are a larger dark green pepper, about 4 to 5 inches long. They are usually fairly mild.

- **Serrano peppers**—Watch out. These are very hot. They are very small and medium green or red in color.

When dicing peppers for a dish, always discard the seeds and white membrane.

Chili-garlic sauce is made from red chilies and garlic with a variety of additional ingredients, including vinegar, salt, ginger, or fermented soybeans. Use it to spice up vegetables or to add heat to meat or poultry marinades.

To peel a whole tomato, cut out the core and score a cross in the rounded bottom of the tomato. Place tomatoes in a pan of boiling water for 15 to 20 seconds. Remove from the pan and immerse in cold water. The skin will split and can then be easily pulled off with your fingers.

Plum tomatoes are sometimes called Italian tomatoes. They are smaller and firmer than most other varieties of tomatoes. They are a good choice when you need diced fresh tomatoes.

When a recipe calls for diced fresh tomatoes, remove the seeds and excess juice from the inside of the tomatoes. To remove the seeds, cut the tomatoes in quarters. Using one of your fingers or the back of a spoon, scrape out the seeds. If you do not remove the seeds, your dish may be too thin and runny.

If a recipe calls for a small amount of tomato paste and you don't use the whole can, remove the remaining paste from the can and freeze it in a small resealable plastic bag.

Green onions are also called scallions. They are harvested before the bulbs grow large and mature. All other onions are dry onions, meaning that they are harvested when mature and allowed to dry until their skins are papery.

Mushrooms are used to add flavor in many dishes in this book. They are nutritionally different from fruits and vegetables since they are botanically fungi. They are very low in calories and are an excellent source of B vitamins, potassium, and some trace minerals. Clean mushrooms quickly under running water and dry them. Do not soak mushrooms because they readily absorb water and this will prevent flavor from being infused into the mushrooms. It is best to sauté mushrooms when the mushrooms are dry and the fat is hot. Don't overcrowd the skillet or the mushrooms will steam rather than brown. Cook, stirring occasionally, until golden brown and any released juices have evaporated.

Mushrooms can be frozen to keep on hand for later use. Line a baking sheet with wax paper or parchment and place unwashed mushrooms on the pan. Place them in the freezer until they are hard and then transfer to a plastic freezer bag. To use, remove dirt by rubbing lightly with a paper towel.

Olives, considered a fruit, often have a bad reputation for being high in calories. Actually, that is not true. Four large olives contain only about 25 calories. Most of the fat in olives is the healthy monounsaturated fat. Freshly picked olives are too hard and bitter to eat. They must have their skins softened and seasoned by soaking them in a salted brine solution. It is interesting that olive trees can live more than 1,500 years.

Roasted red peppers make a tasty addition to many dishes. They add a special sweet, smoky flavor that cannot be duplicated with raw peppers. You can roast them yourself or buy them in a jar already roasted. If you decide to prepare them, cut the peppers into quarters. Remove seeds and white membrane from the middle. Place pepper pieces on a greased baking sheet. Press down to flatten. Place a few inches under a preheated broiler. If using an electric oven, keep the door partially open. Broil until the skin is blistered and completely blackened. Place hot pieces in a small brown bag to steam 5–10 minutes. Using your fingers, pull blackened skin from the peppers. Discard the skin and slice peppers into pieces of desired size.

To roast fresh garlic, use a sharp knife to cut off the top one-third of the bulb. Do not peel the bulb. Place it in a nest of aluminum foil to prevent it from tipping over. Drizzle 1 tablespoon of olive oil on top of each bulb. Cover with foil and bake at 300°F for 1½ to 2 hours or until cloves are very soft. Squeeze the cloves out of the bulb. Spread them on crusty bread or mash them into potatoes or other dishes.

Onions should be stored in a cool, dark place where air can circulate around them.

Potatoes should be stored separately from the onions. Storing the onions and potatoes together will shorten the shelf life of the potatoes.

Potatoes should never be stored in the refrigerator. Cold temperatures cause some of the starch to turn into sugar, which will change the taste of the potatoes.

Vegetables taste best when cooked al dente, which means a little crisp. The term tender-crisp is often also used.

If a recipe calls for blanching a vegetable, put it in boiling water for 30 to 60 seconds and then chill it very quickly under cold running water. This is done to firm the flesh, loosen the skin, and bring out the color of the vegetable. Note the brighter, deeper color of blanched broccoli compared to raw broccoli. Most vegetables are blanched before freezing.

Asparagus Blue Cheese Bundles

Impress your guests with this fancy way to serve asparagus, but don't let them know how easy it is. The asparagus rolls can even be assembled ahead of time and refrigerated until ready to serve.

❖ Preheat oven to 425°F. Butter a 7" × 11" baking pan. In a medium skillet, cook asparagus in boiling salted water for 3 to 5 minutes or just until tender. Chill under cold running water and pat dry. Set aside. In a small bowl, combine cream cheese, blue cheese, and hot pepper sauce. Stir to mix. Spread each slice of bread with ¼ of the cream cheese mixture. Cut each slice in half on the diagonal. Place 3 spears of asparagus on each of the diamond-shaped pieces of bread. Roll bread around the asparagus, pressing bread thin as you roll. Place in baking pan and spray with butter spray. Bake for 8 to 12 minutes or just until bread is lightly toasted.

_____

Grated Parmesan cheese or another cheese of your choice can be substituted for the blue cheese.

Serves 4

24 spears asparagus
2 ounces reduced-fat cream cheese
2 tablespoons crumbled blue cheese*
Dash hot pepper sauce
4 slices bread, crust removed
Butter spray

Nutritional information per serving:

Calories	130
Fat, gm.	6
Protein, gm.	5
Carbs, gm.	15
Cholesterol, mg.	15
Fiber, gm.	1.9

Asparagus with Black Olives and Bacon

Serves 4

3 slices bacon
1 pound fresh asparagus
1 tablespoon butter or margarine, melted
1 tablespoon balsamic vinegar
¼ cup grated Parmesan cheese
¼ cup sliced black olives

Nutritional information per serving:

Calories	95
Fat, gm.	7
Protein, gm.	5
Carbs, gm.	3
Cholesterol, mg.	15
Fiber, gm.	1.3

Add a little color and flavor to fresh asparagus.

❖ In a small skillet, cook bacon until crisp. Crumble and set aside. In a large saucepan, cook asparagus in boiling salted water just until tender-crisp. (Do not overcook.) Drain and discard water. Add butter, vinegar, and cheese to the pan. Stir gently until asparagus is coated and cheese is melted. Place on serving plate and top with olives and bacon.

Baked Stuffed Sweet Potatoes

Just as easy as baked white potatoes but more nutritious.

❖ Preheat oven to 350°F. Wash sweet potatoes and prick with a fork. Bake for 1 to 1¼ hours or until tender. Cut ⅓ off the top of each potato lengthwise. Carefully scoop pulp from the shells and place in a large mixing bowl. Set skins aside. Add orange juice, butter, and crushed pineapple to the bowl. Beat with electric mixer until fluffy. Add more orange juice if needed. Add salt and pepper to taste. Stuff shells with sweet potato mixture and sprinkle with pecans. Refrigerate if not serving immediately. When ready to serve, warm in preheated 350°F oven for 10 to 15 minutes.

Serves 6

6 small (about 3 pounds) sweet potatoes
½ cup orange juice
1 tablespoon butter or margarine
1 can (8 ounces) crushed pineapple, drained
Salt and pepper to taste
¼ cup chopped pecans

Nutritional information per serving:

Calories	240
Fat, gm.	4
Protein, gm.	3
Carbs, gm.	48
Cholesterol, mg.	5
Fiber, gm.	5.4

Broccoli with Honey Sesame Topping

Serves 4

4 cups broccoli florets
Salt and pepper

Topping:
2 tablespoons honey
⅛ teaspoon ground ginger
1 teaspoon lemon juice
1 teaspoon sesame oil
1 tablespoon toasted sesame seeds*

Nutritional information per serving:

Calories	110
Fat, gm.	3
Protein, gm.	4
Carbs, gm.	17
Cholesterol, mg.	0
Fiber, gm.	4.7

Entice your family to eat their broccoli with this simple, but tasty, sesame topping.

❖ In a medium saucepan, cook broccoli in boiling salted water until tender-crisp. Drain well and place in serving bowl. Sprinkle with salt and pepper to taste. While broccoli is cooking, combine all remaining ingredients. Stir to mix and spoon over warm broccoli. Toss gently.

_____

To toast sesame seeds, place seeds in a small nonstick skillet. Cook over medium heat for 2 to 5 minutes, stirring constantly, until lightly brown.

Brussels Sprouts in Creamy Dijon Sauce

When is the last time you asked for a second serving of Brussels sprouts? This is the recipe that will make that happen. The sauce is wonderful and it complements the stronger flavor of this vegetable.

❖ In a medium saucepan, cook Brussels sprouts in boiling salted water for 6 to 10 minutes or just until tender-crisp. Drain well and set aside. In a small saucepan, melt butter. Add flour and cook, stirring constantly, for 1 minute. Add milk and continue to stir until mixture comes to a boil and thickens. Add white pepper, tarragon, mustard, and sour cream. Adjust seasoning with salt and pepper. Add sauce to the Brussels sprouts and heat through.

Serves 4

*10 ounces fresh or frozen Brussels
    sprouts*
1 tablespoon butter or margarine
1 tablespoon flour
¾ cup fat-free milk
Dash white pepper
⅛ teaspoon dried tarragon
½ tablespoon Dijon mustard
¼ cup fat-free sour cream
Salt and pepper to taste

Nutritional information per serving:

Calories	95
Fat, gm.	3
Protein, gm.	5
Carbs, gm.	12
Cholesterol, mg.	10
Fiber, gm.	2.7

Brussels Sprouts with Apricot Glaze

Serves 6

1 package (20 ounces; 5 cups) frozen
   Brussels sprouts*
1 can (8 ounces) water chestnuts,
   drained
½ cup sugar-free apricot preserves
1 teaspoon dill weed
1 teaspoon lemon juice
¼ cup sliced almonds, toasted

Nutritional information per serving:

Calories	115
Fat, gm.	3
Protein, gm.	5
Carbs, gm.	17
Cholesterol, mg.	0
Fiber, gm.	5.3

If you think Brussels sprouts are a little bitter, sweeten them with this appealing glaze.

❖ In a large saucepan, cook Brussels sprouts in boiling salted water just until tender-crisp. Drain well. Add water chestnuts, apricot preserves, dill weed, and lemon juice to the pan. Stir to mix and heat through. Place in serving bowl and top with almonds.

———

*Fresh Brussels sprouts can also be used. Choose small Brussels sprouts. If some are larger than others, cut the larger ones in half.

Carrots with Dried Cranberries and Walnuts

These are so good that you might wish they were your main course.

❖ In a medium saucepan, cook carrots in salted water until tender-crisp. Drain and set aside. In a small bowl, combine brown sugar, cinnamon, dry mustard, orange juice, and cornstarch. Return carrots to saucepan. Add butter, orange juice mixture, and dried cranberries. Cook over medium heat for 2 to 3 minutes, stirring gently, until mixture thickens and carrots are coated and heated through. Spoon into serving bowl. Top with walnuts.

Serves 6

1 pound baby carrots
2 tablespoons brown sugar
1 teaspoon cinnamon
1 teaspoon dry mustard
½ cup orange juice
1 teaspoon cornstarch
2 tablespoons butter or margarine
½ cup orange-flavored dried cranberries
⅓ cup chopped walnuts

Nutritional information per serving:

Calories	135
Fat, gm.	5
Protein, gm.	1
Carbs, gm.	22
Cholesterol, mg.	10
Fiber, gm.	2.7

Green Beans
with Blue Cheese and Bacon Dressing

Serves 6

2 pounds fresh green beans, ends snipped

Dressing:
6 slices bacon
¼ cup finely chopped onion
¼ cup cider vinegar
1 teaspoon Dijon mustard
1 teaspoon dry mustard
¼ cup olive oil

Topping:
½ cup blue cheese, crumbled
⅓ cup dried cranberries, optional

Nutritional information per serving:

Calories	200
Fat, gm.	15
Protein, gm.	6
Carbs, gm.	11
Cholesterol, mg.	10
Fiber, gm.	4.7

Some people will eat their vegetables if you entice them with blue cheese.

❖ In a large saucepan, cook beans in boiling salted water just until tender-crisp. Drain well and pat dry. Set aside. In a small skillet, cook bacon until crisp. Remove from pan and crumble. Set aside. Drain and discard all but 1 tablespoon of bacon fat. Add onion and cook until translucent. Add vinegar, Dijon mustard, dry mustard, olive oil, and reserved bacon. Heat through. Pour over beans and toss to coat. Place in serving dish and top with blue cheese. Add cranberries if desired.

Green Beans with Pecans

Sometimes simple is best.

❖ In a large saucepan, cook green beans in salted water until tender-crisp. Drain well. In a small skillet, melt butter. Add pecans, parsley, tarragon, salt, and pepper. Cook over low heat for 3 to 5 minutes or until pecans are lightly toasted. Pour butter mixture over beans in serving dish and stir to coat.

Serves 4

1 pound frozen or fresh whole green beans
1 tablespoon butter or margarine
⅓ cup chopped pecans
2 teaspoons dried parsley
2 teaspoons dried tarragon
Salt and pepper to taste

Nutritional information per serving:

Calories	100
Fat, gm.	6
Protein, gm.	2
Carbs, gm.	10
Cholesterol, mg.	10
Fiber, gm.	3.6

Green Beans with Tomatoes and Onions

Serves 8

2 pounds fresh green beans, cut into
  2-inch pieces
1 tablespoon olive oil
1 large onion, thinly sliced
1 teaspoon minced garlic
1 teaspoon oregano
¼ cup red wine vinegar
1 tablespoon sugar
3 medium fresh tomatoes, seeded and
  chopped
¼ cup fresh chopped parsley
Salt and freshly ground pepper to taste

Nutritional information per serving:

Calories	75
Fat, gm.	2
Protein, gm.	2
Carbs, gm.	12
Cholesterol, mg.	0
Fiber, gm.	4.2

Dress up your beans with this colorful tomato-and-onion topping.

❖ Cook beans, covered, in a large saucepan in boiling salted water. Cook just until tender-crisp. Do not overcook. Drain and chill quickly under cold running water. Set aside. In a medium skillet, heat oil. Add onion and cook until translucent and just beginning to brown. Add garlic and cook 1 minute. Add oregano, vinegar, sugar, tomatoes, and parsley. Cook about 5 minutes, until tomatoes are hot and liquid is partially reduced. Adjust seasoning with salt and pepper. Arrange beans in a large serving dish. Top with tomato-and-onion mixture. Serve warm or at room temperature.

Honey and Parmesan Topped Asparagus

Use a touch of honey and freshly shredded Parmesan to make asparagus special.

❖ In a large skillet, cook asparagus in boiling water for 3 to 6 minutes or just until tender-crisp. Drain well, pat dry, and sprinkle with salt and pepper. Place in serving bowl. Add honey and cheese. Toss to mix.

Serves 4

1 pound asparagus
Salt and pepper
1 tablespoon honey
¼ cup shredded Parmesan cheese

Nutritional information per serving:

Calories	50
Fat, gm.	1
Protein, gm.	3
Carbs, gm.	7
Cholesterol, mg.	5
Fiber, gm.	1.3

Marmalade Glazed Carrots

Serves 4

4 cups baby carrots
3 tablespoons sugar-free apricot
   marmalade*
1 tablespoon butter or margarine
1 tablespoon brown sugar
2 tablespoons chopped fresh parsley
Salt and pepper to taste

Nutritional information per serving:

Calories	130
Fat, gm.	3
Protein, gm.	2
Carbs, gm.	24
Cholesterol, mg.	5
Fiber, gm.	0.2

It is interesting to note that although raw carrots are good to eat, you actually absorb the nutrients better from carrots that are cooked. This will make the carrots taste even better.

❖ In a medium covered saucepan, cook carrots in boiling salted water about 8 minutes or until tender. Drain well and add all remaining ingredients. Toss to mix and serve.

―――

Use the fruit marmalade of your choice, such as peach or orange.

Roasted Red and Yellow Peppers with Green Beans

This is a recipe for make-your-own roasted peppers. They have a unique smoky flavor that can't be duplicated with raw peppers.

❖ Preheat broiler. Line a baking pan with foil and spray foil with cooking spray. Cut red and yellow peppers into quarters and remove seeds. Press down flat on baking sheet with skin side up. Place pan a few inches below broiler and broil until the skin is totally blackened. Remove and place in a small paper or plastic bag for 10 minutes. Remove peppers from bag and peel off blackened skin. Discard the skin. Cut the peppers into thin strips. While peppers are being broiled, cook green beans in a large saucepan of salted water until tender-crisp. Drain well and set aside. In a medium skillet, heat oil. Add garlic and cook 1 minute. Add black pepper, lemon juice, peppers, and green beans. Cook over medium heat just until heated through. Top with grated cheese and cover pan for 1 minute until cheese is melted. Place in serving bowl and top with pine nuts.

Note: *Roasted red peppers can be purchased in a jar if you prefer not to make them.*

Serves 4

1 medium red pepper
1 medium yellow pepper
1 pound fresh green beans, ends trimmed
1 teaspoon olive oil
1 clove garlic, minced
¼ teaspoon freshly ground pepper
1 teaspoon lemon juice
2 tablespoons grated Parmesan cheese
2 tablespoons pine nuts, toasted

Nutritional information per serving:

Calories	75
Fat, gm.	3
Protein, gm.	3
Carbs, gm.	9
Cholesterol, mg.	0
Fiber, gm.	3.5

Serves 6

Sauce:
1 cup orange juice
1 tablespoon cornstarch
2 tablespoons brown sugar
½ teaspoon allspice
¼ teaspoon ground ginger
¼ teaspoon salt
½ cup diced mixed dried fruit

2 large sweet potatoes, peeled and diced
3 large carrots, peeled and diced
1 tablespoon butter or margarine
1 large sweet onion, chopped
2 large Granny Smith apples, peeled, cored, and sliced
Salt and pepper to taste

Nutritional information per serving:

Calories	155
Fat, gm.	2
Protein, gm.	2
Carbs, gm.	33
Cholesterol, mg.	5
Fiber, gm.	3.3

Sweet Potatoes and Apples in Ginger Orange Sauce

This is a delightful combination of flavors. You may want to prepare it ahead for a company meal.

1. In a small saucepan, combine all sauce ingredients. Stir until cornstarch is mixed with the juice. Cook over medium heat, stirring constantly, until mixture comes to a boil and thickens. Remove from heat and set aside.

2. In a medium saucepan, cook sweet potatoes and carrots in boiling salted water until tender. When done, drain well and set aside.

3. While potatoes are cooking, melt butter in a large nonstick skillet. Cook onion over medium-high heat until lightly browned. Add apples and cook just until tender-crisp. Remove from heat. Add cooked potatoes and carrots. Add sauce and stir gently. Heat through, or, if dish is made ahead, cover and refrigerate. Heat through when ready to serve. Add salt and pepper to taste.

Swiss Spinach Soufflé

Spinach is loaded with healthful nutrients. You might want to eat it often after you try this recipe. Spinach never tasted so good!

❖ Preheat oven to 325°F. Butter an 8" × 8" baking pan. Heat oil in medium skillet. Add onion and cook over medium heat until lightly browned. Add garlic and cook 1 minute. Remove from heat and set aside. In a large bowl, combine cream cheese, flour, salt, pepper, and nutmeg. Beat until smooth. Gradually add milk and egg substitute or eggs. Beat until smooth. Stir in spinach and reserved onion. Spoon into baking pan. Bake 40 to 45 minutes or until knife inserted in the middle comes out clean. Sprinkle with cheese and return to oven. Place under broiler and broil 4 to 5 minutes or until cheese is melted and lightly brown. Sprinkle with paprika. Let stand 5 minutes before serving.

Serves 8

½ tablespoon canola oil
1 medium onion, finely chopped
2 teaspoons minced garlic
8 ounces Neufchatel cheese (reduced-fat cream cheese)
2 tablespoons flour
½ teaspoon salt
½ teaspoon pepper
¼ teaspoon nutmeg
¾ cup fat-free milk
⅓ cup egg substitute or 2 eggs
2 packages (10 ounces each) frozen spinach, thawed and squeezed dry
1 cup shredded Swiss cheese
Dash paprika

Nutritional information per serving:

Calories	200
Fat, gm.	13
Protein, gm.	12
Carbs, gm.	9
Cholesterol, mg.	35
Fiber, gm.	2.6

Wilted Spinach with Balsamic Mustard Sauce

Serves 4

2 tablespoons olive oil
6 shallots, finely chopped
¼ cup water
2 tablespoons balsamic vinegar
1 tablespoon Dijon mustard
1 tablespoon granular Splenda or sugar
⅛ teaspoon salt
⅛ teaspoon freshly ground pepper
1 package (10 ounces) fresh baby spinach*

Nutritional information per serving:

Calories	100
Fat, gm.	7
Protein, gm.	2
Carbs, gm.	8
Cholesterol, mg.	0
Fiber, gm.	1.5

This simple sauce makes spinach so good!

❖ In a large skillet, heat olive oil. Add shallots and cook until tender. Add water, vinegar, mustard, Splenda, salt, and pepper. Bring to a boil. Add spinach and cook, stirring occasionally, for about 2 to 5 minutes, just until spinach begins to wilt. Serve immediately.

*If baby spinach is not available, tear large spinach leaves into smaller pieces.

Zucchini Bake

Chose an attractive baking dish or pie pan and bring this great vegetable right to the table from the oven.

❖ Preheat oven to 350°F. Heavily butter an 8" × 8" baking dish or pie pan. In a large bowl, combine zucchini, onion, cheese, garlic, salt, and pepper. Stir to mix. Add biscuit mix, eggs, and butter. Stir to mix. Pour into baking pan. Bake for 40 to 50 minutes or until set.

Serves 6

6 cups chopped fresh zucchini
1 cup chopped onion
½ cup shredded Swiss cheese
1 teaspoon minced garlic
1 teaspoon salt
¼ teaspoon white pepper
1 cup reduced-fat biscuit mix
4 eggs, lightly beaten
½ cup butter or margarine, melted

Nutritional information per serving:

Calories	315
Fat, gm.	22
Protein, gm.	9
Carbs, gm.	20
Cholesterol, mg.	170
Fiber, gm.	2.0

CHAPTER 10

Snacks

Avocado Olive Dip
Banana Oatmeal Bread
Bean Salsa Dip
Black Bean and Red Pepper Dip
Bruschetta and Crostini
Feta and Red Pepper Cheesecake
Light Guacamole
Mushroom Bacon Spread
Rhubarb Bread
Roasted Red Pepper and Olive Tapenade
Spinach and Artichoke Dip

Avocado Olive Dip

Serves 6

2 medium very ripe avocados, peeled and
    mashed
½ cup chopped green olives
1 tablespoon olive oil
1 tablespoon lemon juice
½ cup chopped roasted red peppers*
¼ cup chopped fresh basil or 1 teaspoon
    dry basil
Salt and pepper to taste

Nutritional information per serving:

Calories	120
Fat gm.	11
Protein, gm.	1
Carbs, gm.	5
Cholesterol, mg.	0
Fiber, gm.	3.1

It is very hard to stop eating this healthful dip. The mild avocado is complemented by the subtle flavor of the roasted peppers and the stronger flavor of the olives. It can be made hours ahead of time.

❖ In a large bowl, combine all ingredients. Stir to mix. Cover and refrigerate until ready to serve.

❖ Serve with fresh vegetables, crackers, toasted baguette slices, or corn chips.

*Roasted red peppers are available canned in jars. They are usually stocked in the aisle with the olives or with the vegetables in the grocery store.

Banana Oatmeal Bread

Add some healthy oatmeal and make your banana bread even better with this recipe.

❖ Preheat oven to 350°F. Butter a 5" × 9" loaf pan. In a large bowl, combine oil, sugar, eggs, vanilla, baking soda, salt, and cinnamon. Beat well. Add flour and oats. Stir to mix. Add bananas and milk. Stir to mix. Add walnuts if desired. Bake for 50 to 60 minutes or until lightly browned and set in the middle.

Serves 16

½ cup canola oil
1 cup sugar
2 eggs
1 teaspoon vanilla
1 teaspoon baking soda
½ teaspoon salt
½ teaspoon cinnamon
1 cup flour
1 cup quick-cooking oats
1½ cups mashed banana (about 3 medium bananas)
¼ cup milk
½ cup chopped walnuts, optional

Nutritional information per serving:

Calories	180
Fat, gm.	8
Protein, gm.	2
Carbs, gm.	25
Cholesterol, mg.	30
Fiber, gm.	0.9

Bean Salsa Dip

Serves 12

1 can (15 ounces) fat-free refried beans
1 can (15 ounces) black beans, drained and rinsed
8 ounces reduced-fat cream cheese, room temperature
⅓ cup fat-free sour cream
1 cup salsa
2 tablespoons canned jalapeño peppers
½ cup shredded Cheddar cheese

Nutritional information per serving:

Calories	140
Fat, gm.	7
Protein, gm.	7
Carbs, gm.	12
Cholesterol, mg.	20
Fiber, gm.	3.8

Everyone likes this dip. Since it makes quite a large amount, you might make it ahead of time and divide it up into smaller baking dishes. Use it as a quick, healthful snack to hold you or your kids over while preparing supper.

❖ Preheat oven to 325°F. Grease a 9-inch round baking dish or pie pan. In a medium bowl, combine refried beans, black beans, cream cheese, sour cream, salsa, and jalapeño peppers. Stir to mix. Spoon into baking pan. Sprinkle with shredded cheese. Bake for 15 to 20 minutes or until heated through and cheese is melted.

❖ Serve with corn chips or tortilla chips.

Black Bean and Red Pepper Dip

You can feel good about enjoying this snack. It is full of healthful ingredients.

❖ Combine all ingredients except salt and pepper in food processor. Blend to the desired consistency. Taste and adjust seasoning with salt and pepper. Add extra hot sauce if desired.

❖ Serve with baked tortilla wedges or corn chips.

Note: These ingredients will fit into a small food processor. The roasted red peppers are available in jars. You could also roast them yourself, if you prefer.

If you enjoy spicy-hot foods, add a small chopped jalapeño pepper.

Serves 8

1 medium roasted red pepper, diced
1 can (15 ounces) black beans, drained and rinsed
⅓ cup fresh chopped cilantro
⅓ cup chopped onion
1 teaspoon minced garlic
1 tablespoon lime juice
1 tablespoon balsamic vinegar
¼ teaspoon allspice
¼ teaspoon cumin
Dash hot sauce
Salt and freshly ground pepper to taste

Nutritional information per serving:

Calories	60
Fat, gm.	0
Protein, gm.	4
Carbs, gm.	11
Cholesterol, mg.	0
Fiber, gm.	4.3

Bruschetta and Crostini

Bruschetta is made from thin slices of fresh bread, and crostini is made from thin slices of toasted bread. Both may be dressed with olive oil, garlic, and a variety of vegetables and cheeses.

1.   Cut bread into thin slices. Lightly brush or spray olive oil on both sides of each piece. Place on baking sheet and broil in the oven until lightly browned. Watch carefully to prevent burning. Turn each slice to brown the other side.
2.   There are many ways to create toppings for an appealing appetizer.

1.   **Traditional:** Alternate slices of fresh mozzarella cheese and thinly sliced tomato on top of the toasted bread. Sprinkle with Pinch of Herbs* or your choice of herbs. Drizzle with small amount of olive oil.
2.   **Blue Cheese and Walnut:** Mix 2 ounces blue cheese with ½ cup fat-free sour cream. Stir in 2 tablespoons chopped walnuts. Place spinach leaf on toasted bread. Top with dollop of blue cheese mixture.
3.   **White Beans and Herbs:** In a small skillet, sauté 1 small chopped onion and 2 cloves minced garlic. Place in food processor. Add 1 can (15 ounces) great northern beans, drained and rinsed; 2 teaspoons balsamic vinegar; 1 teaspoon lemon juice; and ½ teaspoon Pinch of Herbs.* Blend until smooth. Add salt, pepper, and hot pepper sauce to taste. Spread small amount of bean mixture on toasted bread.

One brand of a good herb mixture is Lawry's Pinch of Herbs. It is an aromatic blend of oregano, thyme, basil, rosemary, and sesame seeds.

Feta and Red Pepper Cheesecake

Treat yourself to a slice of this healthy cheesecake for lunch. Spread it on thinly sliced French bread or crackers. It is also great served as an appetizer at a dinner party. I like to keep some on hand for a quick snack while I am cooking supper. It keeps very well in the refrigerator for at least a week.

❖ Preheat oven to 350°F. In a 9-inch springform pan or a 9-inch pie pan, combine crushed pretzels and butter. Mix well and press in bottom of the pan. In a large bowl, combine feta, ricotta, Neufchatel, and sour cream. Stir to blend. Add eggs and garlic. Beat with electric mixer until smooth. Stir in red peppers and 3 tablespoons of chopped basil. Add hot pepper sauce. Pour mixture into baking pan. Bake for 35 to 40 minutes or until center is just about set. (The center should jiggle slightly.) Cool 30 minutes. Loosen edges with knife. If a springform pan was used, remove sides of pan and place base of pan and cheesecake on serving plate. Sprinkle top with remaining finely chopped basil. Cut into thin wedges and serve with crackers or baguette slices. Serve warm or chilled.

In place of the fresh basil, you can use 1 teaspoon of your favorite dried herbs. I like Lawry's Pinch of Herbs, which is a classic herb blend that includes basil, oregano, rosemary, thyme, and sesame seeds.

Serves 12

1 cup (2 ounces) crushed pretzels
2 tablespoons butter or margarine, melted

Filling:

4 ounces reduced-fat feta cheese, crumbled
1 cup part-skim ricotta cheese
8 ounces Neufchatel cheese (reduced-fat cream cheese)
½ cup fat-free sour cream
2 large eggs
1 teaspoon minced garlic
½ cup chopped roasted red peppers
4 tablespoons chopped fresh basil*, divided
Dash hot pepper sauce

Nutritional information per serving (without the crackers):

Calories	145
Fat, gm.	10
Protein, gm.	7
Carbs, gm.	7
Cholesterol, mg.	60
Fiber, gm.	0.3

Light Guacamole

Serves 8

2 large avocados*, peeled, divided
1 tablespoon lemon juice
½ cup fat-free sour cream
¼ cup finely chopped onion
¼ teaspoon cumin
½ teaspoon Spike seasoning**, optional
Salt to taste
Hot pepper sauce to taste
3 small Roma tomatoes, seeded and
   chopped

Nutritional information per serving (without the chips):

Calories	85
Fat, gm.	6
Protein, gm.	1
Carbs, gm.	7
Cholesterol, mg.	0
Fiber, gm.	2.7

Avocados are a rich source of the good monounsaturated fats, but they are fairly high in calories. In this recipe, the calories are reduced, without changing the wonderful taste of fresh avocados, by adding fat-free sour cream.

❖ Remove pits from avocados. In a food processor, combine 1 avocado, lemon juice, sour cream, onions, cumin, and Spike seasoning. Process until smooth. Adjust seasoning with salt and hot pepper sauce to taste. Spoon into small bowl. Mash remaining avocado with a fork and stir into pureed avocado mixture. (If you prefer a smooth guacamole, blend both avocados in the food processor.) Spoon into serving bowl and top with chopped tomatoes. Serve with tortilla chips.

———

*The guacamole is best when made with very ripe avocados.

———

**Spike seasoning is a mixture of many spices that adds a lot of flavor to many dishes. It is available in an original mixture and a salt-free mixture (Modern Products, Inc., Milwaukee, Wisconsin).

Mushroom Bacon Spread

This is a taste treat you can make ahead and keep in the refrigerator. It can be served warm or cold.

❖ In a medium skillet, cook bacon until crisp. Remove all but 2 tablespoons of bacon grease and discard. Add mushrooms, onions, and thyme to the skillet and cook over medium heat until tender. Add all remaining ingredients. Stir over medium heat until heated through. Spoon into a food processor and blend until smooth.* Refrigerate until ready to serve. Serve with crackers or small pieces of toasted bread.

---

*If the mushrooms are finely chopped, you may choose not to blend the mixture in the food processor.

Serves 10

4 slices bacon, diced
1 pound fresh mushrooms, finely chopped
4 small green onions, finely chopped
¼ teaspoon thyme
⅓ cup sherry
1 tablespoon Worcestershire sauce
8 ounces low-fat cream cheese
1 tablespoon soy sauce
½ cup fat-free sour cream
Dash Tabasco sauce, optional

Nutritional information per serving:

Calories	100
Fat, gm.	4
Protein, gm.	5
Carbs, gm.	10
Cholesterol, mg.	15
Fiber, gm.	2.1

Rhubarb Bread

Serves 8

1 cup rhubarb, cut into ½-inch pieces
1½ cups flour
¾ cup brown sugar
⅓ cup canola oil
1 egg
½ cup buttermilk
½ teaspoon salt
½ teaspoon baking soda
½ teaspoon cinnamon
⅛ teaspoon nutmeg
1 teaspoon vanilla

Topping:
1 teaspoon butter or margarine, melted
2 tablespoons sugar

Nutritional information per serving:

Calories	180
Fat, gm.	8
Protein, gm.	3
Carbs, gm.	24
Cholesterol, mg.	20
Fiber, gm.	0.2

Make this bread when rhubarb is in season and freeze a few loaves. I like to keep it on hand for a quick snack.

❖ Preheat oven to 325°F. Butter a 5" × 9" loaf pan. In a medium bowl, combine rhubarb and flour. Toss to coat rhubarb. Set aside. In a large bowl, combine all remaining ingredients. Beat to mix well. Add rhubarb and flour. Stir to mix. Spoon into baking pan. For Topping: Combine butter and sugar. Using your fingers, crumble mixture on top of batter in pan. Bake for 55 to 60 minutes or until lightly browned and set in the middle.

Roasted Red Pepper and Olive Tapenade

The fusion of flavors and the colors make this a wonderful Mediterranean snack or appetizer. Serve it for company or enjoy it while you wait for dinner. It keeps well in the refrigerator for days.

1. Combine all ingredients in a medium bowl. Cover and refrigerate until ready to serve, to blend flavors. Serve with crackers or toasted French bread.

2. To make an attractive appetizer for guests, spoon tapenade on top of soft goat cheese or on a round of Brie cheese. (Brie cheese should be at room temperature for easy spreading.)

Note: *Roasted red peppers are available in jars. They are usually stocked in the aisle with the olives or with the vegetables in the grocery store.*

Serves 8

2 large red peppers, roasted and diced
1 cup black olives, pitted and chopped
1 cup green olives, pitted and chopped
1 large tomato, seeded and chopped
½ cup finely chopped onion
⅓ cup drained capers, optional
2 tablespoons balsamic vinegar
1 tablespoon olive oil
Dash Tabasco sauce

Nutritional information per serving (without the crackers or bread):

Calories	70
Fat, gm.	5
Protein, gm.	1
Carbs, gm.	5
Cholesterol, mg.	0
Fiber, gm.	0.8

Spinach and Artichoke Dip

Serves 8

1 tablespoon canola oil
1 medium onion, finely chopped
1 package (10 ounces) frozen spinach,
  thawed and squeezed dry
4 ounces fat-free cream cheese
1½ cups fat-free sour cream
½ cup shredded Parmesan cheese
1 can (14 ounces) artichoke hearts,
  drained and chopped
¼ teaspoon pepper
Dash hot pepper sauce
Red pepper flakes to taste
Salt to taste

Nutritional information per serving:

Calories	120
Fat, gm.	2
Protein, gm.	10
Carbs, gm.	16
Cholesterol, mg.	10
Fiber, gm.	4.1

This is so good, it could be a meal.

❖ In a medium skillet, heat oil. Cook onion over medium heat until translucent. Add spinach and cream cheese. Cook, stirring constantly, until cream cheese melts. Stir in sour cream, Parmesan cheese, artichoke hearts, pepper, and pepper sauce. Heat through. Season with red pepper flakes and salt to taste. Serve with baguette slices or crackers.

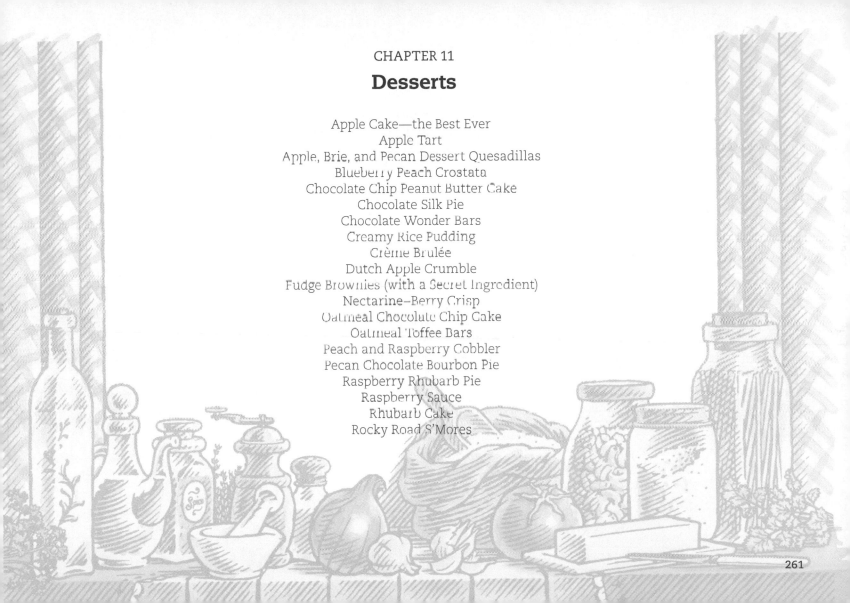

CHAPTER 11
Desserts

Apple Cake—the Best Ever
Apple Tart
Apple, Brie, and Pecan Dessert Quesadillas
Blueberry Peach Crostata
Chocolate Chip Peanut Butter Cake
Chocolate Silk Pie
Chocolate Wonder Bars
Creamy Rice Pudding
Crème Brulée
Dutch Apple Crumble
Fudge Brownies (with a Secret Ingredient)
Nectarine–Berry Crisp
Oatmeal Chocolate Chip Cake
Oatmeal Toffee Bars
Peach and Raspberry Cobbler
Pecan Chocolate Bourbon Pie
Raspberry Rhubarb Pie
Raspberry Sauce
Rhubarb Cake
Rocky Road S'Mores

Desserts Cooking Tips

In traditional baking, fat is creamed with sugar to form tiny air cells in the batter, which gives the baked goods a fine, light texture. When a traditional recipe is changed to be lower in fat, the baked product may lack moisture and flavor. The texture will also be heavier.

Sugar provides sweetness and flavor and aids in the browning of baked goods. It is essential to the creaming process, which incorporates air into the batter, making it lighter. When combined with flour, sugar also helps make baked goods tender. Because sugar serves these important functions, it cannot always be replaced by sugar substitutes in baked goods.

Splenda is a sugar substitute that can be used in cooking and in some baked products. It starts out with the same chemical structure as sugar but a little tinkering goes on. Several chlorine atoms are added and that is enough to make the body refuse to burn it for calories. But the taste buds still believe it is sugar. Sounds like magic? Yes, but not so fast. Splenda may taste like sugar but it does not bake like sugar. Use it to sweeten a sauce or put it on your grapefruit, but if you make a cake with it you may throw it out. You can't fool Mother Nature because real sugar makes a cake moist, light in texture, and helps it brown. But never fear, the Splenda company (McNeal Nutrtionals) has come up with a Sugar Splenda Baking Blend. It is a great compromise made up of half sugar and half Splenda. Now you can keep some of the baking qualities of sugar yet get rid of half the sugar calories. I like this new product. That means in a piece of cake you would be able to save about 50 calories.

When using plain Splenda, it works best when you need just the sweet taste in a cooked product or sauces. Measure it spoon for spoon like sugar. When baking, use the Splenda Sugar Blend for Baking and use only ½ the amount of the sugar called for in your recipe. If you forget, the information is on the label.

Measure flour by gently spooning the flour into the cup and use a knife to even off the top. If you use the measuring cup to scoop out the flour from the container or bag, the flour will be packed too tightly in the cup; therefore, too much flour may be added to your recipe.

Brown sugar is measured much differently than flour. Measure brown sugar by pressing the sugar firmly into the measuring cup. When a recipe calls for brown sugar, it usually means light brown sugar. Dark brown sugar has more molasses flavor and is best used for baked beans, gingerbread, and other dishes with a hearty flavor.

When baking custard-type desserts, recipes usually recommend baking them in a water bath. The water bath technique is called *bain-marie* in French. This cooking technique helps assure that delicate sauces, custards, and pudding dishes do not curdle or fall apart. Place your baking dish in a larger, shallow pan of warm water. This wraps the food in warm, gentle heat. Use caution in removing the pan of water from your oven.

To make your own cinnamon-sugar mixture, combine ½ cup sugar with 1–2 teaspoons cinnamon. Adjust the amount of cinnamon to suit your taste. It is handy to keep this mixture in a covered shaker.

Toasting nuts before using them in baking intensifies their wonderful flavor. Another bonus is that they are less likely to sink to the bottom of cake or bread batters if they are toasted.

To prevent ice crystals from forming in ice cream, place a piece of plastic wrap directly on the surface of the ice cream before covering the partially used container.

When cutting sticky foods such as marshmallows or dried fruit, spray your knife or scissors with cooking spray.

Avoid using cooking spray on nonstick baking sheets and baking pans. The spray causes a dark, gummy residue to build up on the pans and the pans will lose their nonstick capability.

When baking in a glass or nonstick baking pan, lower the recommended oven temperature by 25 degrees. Foods baked in dark-colored pans bake more quickly than in light colored pans.

Avoid overbaking, especially if baked goods are lower in fat. Reduced fat baked goods tend to bake more quickly than those made with full fat. Try lowering the oven temperature by 25 degrees and check for doneness a few minutes before the end of the usual baking time. A toothpick test does not always work with reduced-fat baking. Look for lightly browned edges that are beginning to pull away from the pan.

The best news of all in this dessert section is that dark chocolate has been found to be a good source of antioxidants. Perhaps we should consider it a health food.

Serves 15

¼ cup canola oil
½ cup fat-free vanilla yogurt
1 cup sugar
1 large egg
½ teaspoon baking soda
½ teaspoon baking powder
½ teaspoon salt
½ teaspoon cinnamon
¼ teaspoon nutmeg
¼ teaspoon ginger
1 teaspoon vanilla
1¼ cups flour
3 medium apples, peeled, cored, and
  chopped

Topping:
⅓ cup butter or margarine
½ cup brown sugar
¼ cup fat-free evaporated milk
1 cup coconut
½ teaspoon cinnamon
½ cup chopped walnuts, optional

Nutritional information per serving:

Calories	255
Fat, gm.	12
Protein, gm.	3
Carbs, gm.	34
Cholesterol, mg.	30
Fiber, gm.	1.6

Apple Cake—the Best Ever

You will love this super-moist, wonderfully flavored cake. It is very hard to eat just one piece! The ingredient list looks long (many are spices), but believe me, this recipe is worth it!

❖ Preheat oven to 325°F. Butter a 7" × 11" baking pan. Combine all cake ingredients except apples. Beat until well blended. Stir in apples. Spoon batter into pan. Bake for 30 minutes or until lightly browned and set in the middle. While cake is baking, combine topping ingredients in a small saucepan. Heat over low heat until butter is melted. When cake is done, gently spread topping evenly over the cake. Place cake under oven broiler and broil until topping is bubbling and lightly brown.

Apple Tart

I knew the recipe was a keeper, when my husband asked for a second piece. He is not a dessert lover, but he really liked this one.

❖ Preheat oven to 375°F. Place pie crust on large baking sheet and lift the edges to form a crust. Combine the sugar, Splenda, cinnamon, and nutmeg. Sprinkle 3 tablespoons of the sugar mixture on the pie crust dough. Arrange apple slices in a single layer, in a circle, on top of the dough, working from the outside edge of the dough to the center. Sprinkle apple slices with remaining sugar mixture. Spray lightly with butter spray. Bake for 30 to 40 minutes or until apples are tender and crust is brown. While apples are baking, combine honey and vanilla. If honey is thick, warm it briefly in the microwave. When tart is done, remove from oven and brush honey mixture on top. This is best served warm.

Note: *Choose a good baking apple such as Golden Delicious for this recipe.*

Serves 8

1 (9 inch) prepared pie crust, such as
  Pillsbury
¼ cup sugar
¼ cup granular Splenda or sugar
¾ teaspoon cinnamon
¼ teaspoon nutmeg
3 large or 6 small (about 2 pounds)
  baking apples, cored, peeled,
  and thinly sliced
Butter spray
¼ cup honey
1 teaspoon vanilla

Nutritional information per serving:

Calories	182
Fat, gm.	6
Protein, gm.	1
Carbs, gm.	31
Cholesterol, mg.	0
Fiber, gm.	1.4

Apple, Brie, and Pecan Dessert Quesadillas

Serves 6

6 (6 inch) flour tortillas
Oil spray
4 ounces Brie cheese, room temperature
⅓ cup chopped pecans
1 medium apple, peeled, cored, and
* grated*
Cinnamon-sugar mixture, optional

Nutritional information per serving:

Calories	160
Fat, gm.	8
Protein, gm.	5
Carbs, gm.	17
Cholesterol, mg.	20
Fiber, gm.	1.8

Would you like a dessert to serve on the patio? These grilled quesadillas are surprisingly delicious and are fun to make.

❖ Preheat charcoal grill. Lightly spray one side of each tortilla with oil spray. Place 3 tortillas, oiled-side down, on baking sheet. Spread each with ⅓ of the Brie cheese. Top each with ⅓ of the pecans and grated apple. Top with remaining tortillas, keeping oiled side on top. Place each quesadilla on grill and cook until lightly browned. Turn over and brown remaining side. Cut each quesadilla into wedges and serve warm. If desired, sprinkle with cinnamon-sugar mixture.

Blueberry Peach Crostata

Crostata is a rustic, free-formed tart that is a popular Italian dessert. I was given this recipe to make for our gourmet group, and it was the hit of the party.

❖ Preheat oven to 375°F. Place piece of parchment sheet on a baking pan. Place prepared pie crust on baking pan. In a large bowl, combine blueberries, peaches, and lemon juice. In a small bowl, combine sugar, cornstarch, allspice, and cinnamon. Sprinkle over fruit and stir until well mixed. Spoon fruit mixture in center of pie dough, leaving 2-inch border of dough. Brush egg white around the border with a pastry brush. Lift up edges of the dough, pinching seam every 2 to 3 inches to form a standing border. Fold border down over fruit. The center 4 to 5 inches of fruit will remain uncovered. Brush 1 tablespoon apricot preserves over the exposed fruit and around the top edge of the pastry crust. Bake 50 to 60 minutes or until crust is golden brown and the fruit filling is bubbling. Remove from oven. Brush with remaining apricot preserves. Serve warm or at room temperature.

Note: *Frozen peach slices can be used in place of the fresh peaches. If the slices are thick, slice them in half.*

Serves 6

1 (9 inch) pie crust
1 cup fresh blueberries
4 fresh peaches, peeled and sliced
2 teaspoons lemon juice
¼ cup sugar
2 teaspoons cornstarch
¼ teaspoon allspice
¼ teaspoon cinnamon
1 egg white, lightly beaten
2 tablespoons apricot preserves, warmed, divided

Nutritional information per serving:

Calories	225
Fat, gm.	8
Protein, gm.	3
Carbs, gm.	35
Cholesterol, mg.	0
Fiber, gm.	1.7

Chocolate Chip Peanut Butter Cake

My friend who gave me this recipe has been making this dessert for years, and every time she takes it to an event, she makes copies of the recipe before she goes. She tells me that she has never made this cake without people asking for the recipe. A bonus is that it has its own topping and you don't have to frost it.

Serves 20

1 package yellow cake mix
1 cup peanut butter
½ cup brown sugar
3 eggs
¼ cup canola oil
1 cup water
1 cup chocolate chips
¾ cup chopped nuts, optional

Nutritional information per serving:

Calories	265
Fat, gm.	14
Protein, gm.	5
Carbs, gm.	32
Cholesterol, mg.	25
Fiber, gm.	1.3

❖ Preheat oven to 350°F. Butter and flour one 9" × 13" baking pan or two 9" × 9" baking pans. In a large mixing bowl, combine dry cake mix, peanut butter, and brown sugar. Beat with an electric mixer until well mixed. Remove ⅔ cup of the mixture and set aside. Add eggs, oil, and water to the cake mixture in the bowl. Stir to blend and beat with an electric mixer a full 2 minutes. Pour into baking pan(s). Sprinkle with reserved crumb mixture and top with chocolate chips. Sprinkle with nuts if desired. Bake 30 to 40 minutes or until lightly brown and set in the middle.

Chocolate Silk Pie

You won't believe how smooth and good this pie is until you try it yourself. Do not tell anyone about the tofu. When the tofu is blended with the melted chocolate, it makes a rich-tasting chocolate mousse.

❖ In an 8-inch pie pan or a 7" × 11" pan, mix graham cracker crumbs, sugar, and melted butter. Mix with a fork and press firmly in the bottom of the pan and partly up the sides. In a small non stick skillet, melt chocolate chips and butter over the lowest heat. Meanwhile in a food processor, blend tofu, honey, powdered sugar, butter, and vanilla. Blend until very smooth. Add melted chocolate mixture and blend again until smooth. Pour into pie pan and refrigerate.

Serves 10

1 cup graham cracker crumbs
¼ cup granular Splenda or sugar
3 tablespoons butter or margarine
1 cup chocolate chips, melted
1 tablespoon butter or margarine
1 box (12 ounces) firm low-fat tofu, drained
1 tablespoon honey
2 tablespoons powdered sugar
1 tablespoon butter or margarine, melted
1 teaspoon vanilla

Nutritional information per serving:

Calories	190
Fat, gm.	10
Protein, gm.	1
Carbs, gm.	21
Cholesterol, mg.	10
Fiber, gm.	1.6

Serves 24

Crust:
½ cup butter or margarine
1 egg yolk
2 tablespoons water
1¼ cups flour
1 tablespoon sugar
1 teaspoon baking powder

Middle:
6 ounces (1 cup) chocolate chips

Topping:
2 large eggs
¾ cup sugar
6 tablespoons butter or margarine,
   melted
2 teaspoons vanilla
1 cup chopped pecans

Nutritional information per serving:

Calories	170
Fat, gm.	11
Protein, gm.	2
Carbs, gm.	16
Cholesterol, mg.	40
Fiber, gm.	1

Chocolate Wonder Bars

Everyone loved these decadent tasting, soft chocolate bars when I served them at a taste-testing buffet. I found this recipe on an old, yellowed recipe card in a file I had not touched for twenty years. When I made them again, they really did taste as good as I remembered.

❖ Preheat oven to 350°F or 325°F if using a glass or nonstick baking pan. Butter a 7" × 11" baking pan. In a small bowl, combine all crust ingredients. Beat to mix well. Press mixture into bottom of baking pan. Bake for 8 minutes. Remove from oven and sprinkle with chocolate chips. Return to oven for 1 minute. Remove from oven and smooth out chocolate with a knife. In a small bowl, beat eggs until thick. Add all remaining ingredients. Beat to mix well. Spread over top. Bake for an additional 25 to 35 minutes or until golden brown.

Creamy Rice Pudding

I have been testing rice pudding recipes for years and this is the best. It's creamy and tasty but not super-high in calories.

1. In a large, heavy saucepan, combine rice, water, salt, and butter. Bring to a boil. Reduce heat, cover pan, and boil gently for 10 minutes. Combine warm milk and Splenda. Pour into rice. Cover pan and continue to boil gently for 20 to 30 minutes or until rice is very tender and most of the liquid has been absorbed. (Some liquid will be absorbed as rice cools.)

2. While rice is cooking, combine raisins, brandy, and brown sugar in a custard cup. Warm in the microwave and set aside. After rice is done cooking, add raisin mixture, vanilla, allspice, and cinnamon. Cool to room temperature. Fold in whipped topping. Serve at room temperature or chilled.

_____

Note: *The rice-and-milk mixture can easily boil over and make a mess on your stove. If you want to save yourself a lot of trouble, be sure to use a large saucepan. When I used only a 1½-quart pan, it boiled over twice before I was smart enough to put it in a larger, 3-quart pan.*

_____

*The recipe will work with any milk, including fat-free milk, but it is slightly better with 2% or whole milk.

Serves 8

¾ cup Arborio rice
1 cup water
½ teaspoon salt
3 tablespoons butter or margarine
2½ cups 2% milk*, warmed
⅓ cup granular Splenda or sugar
½ cup golden raisins
2 tablespoons brandy
1 tablespoon brown sugar
1 teaspoon vanilla
¼ teaspoon allspice
¼ teaspoon cinnamon, optional
½ cup low-fat whipped topping

Nutritional information per serving:

Calories	175
Fat, gm.	5
Protein, gm.	4
Carbs, gm.	28
Cholesterol, mg.	15
Fiber, gm.	0.4

Crème Brulée

Serves 8

½ cup milk
1 tablespoon cornstarch
1 can (12 ounces) fat-free evaporated
    milk
½ cup sugar
¾ cup fat-free half-and-half
2 egg yolks
½ cup Egg Beaters 99% egg substitute
1 tablespoon vanilla extract
1 tablespoon brandy

Topping:
¼ cup sugar

Nutritional information per serving:

Calories	155
Fat, gm.	2
Protein, gm.	6
Carbs, gm.	28
Cholesterol, mg.	60
Fiber, gm.	0

This is an extreme make over recipe. Crème brulée is usually very high in calories and fat. This is a super-slim version.

❖ Preheat oven to 350°F. Place eight 6-ounce ramekins or custard cups in two large pans. In a medium, heavy saucepan, combine milk and cornstarch. Mix until smooth. Add evaporated milk and sugar. Cook over medium heat until mixture comes to a boil. Remove from heat. In a small bowl, combine fat-free half-and-half with the egg yolks and Egg Beaters. Beat lightly. Add a small amount of the hot milk to the egg mixture while stirring. Pour the warmed egg mixture into the saucepan. Add vanilla and brandy. Stir to mix. Divide mixture into the 8 ramekins. Pour hot water into the large pans to make a water bath for the custard. Carefully place pans in oven. Bake for 30 minutes or until custard is set. Remove ramekins from water bath. Refrigerate for several hours or until completely cold. When ready to serve, sprinkle 1 to 2 teaspoons of sugar on top of each ramekin. Using a small butane-fuel torch, heat sugar until it caramelizes and turns light brown.

Note: *This can also be baked in a 9-inch pie pan in place of the individual ramekins. Place pie pan in water bath to bake. Increase baking time to about 40 minutes.*

Dutch Apple Crumble

Calories are kept as low as possible with the substitution of Splenda for some of the sugar, but you can use all sugar if you prefer.

❖ Preheat oven to 350°F. Butter a 9-inch deep pie pan. Place apples in large bowl. In a small bowl, combine brown sugar, Splenda, cinnamon, nutmeg, and salt. Stir to mix. Pour into bowl with apples and toss to mix. Spoon apples into pie pan. In a small bowl, combine all topping ingredients. Using two knives or a pastry blender, cut butter into flour, sugar, and Splenda until mixture resembles cornmeal. Sprinkle on top of apples. Bake for 60 to 75 minutes or until apples are tender and topping is lightly browned.

_____

Note: *Choose a cooking apple such as Golden Delicious or Macintosh for this recipe.*

Serves 6

6 cups sliced apples, peeled and cored
⅓ cup brown sugar
¼ cup granular Splenda or sugar
½ teaspoon cinnamon
¼ teaspoon nutmeg
¼ teaspoon salt

Topping:
½ cup flour
¼ cup sugar
¼ cup granular Splenda or sugar
½ cup butter or margarine

Nutritional information per serving:

Calories	300
Fat, gm.	15
Protein, gm.	1
Carbs, gm.	41
Cholesterol, mg.	40
Fiber, gm.	2.9

Fudge Brownies (with a Secret Ingredient)

Serves 16

½ cup (3 ounces) chocolate chips
3 tablespoons butter or margarine
3 tablespoons fruit-based fat substitute*
3 tablespoons cocoa powder
1 cup sugar
2 eggs
1 teaspoon vanilla
¾ cup flour

Nutritional information per serving:

Calories	130
Fat, gm.	4
Protein, gm.	2
Carbs, gm.	22
Cholesterol, mg.	25
Fiber, gm.	0.6

Don't panic if you need a dessert at the last minute and don't have a baking mix. Try these easy brownies—they will definitely satisfy your chocolate craving. Another bonus is that these particular brownies keep well for days. I actually served them to company when they were three days old.

❖ Preheat oven to 350°F, or 325°F if using a glass or nonstick pan. Butter an 8" × 8" baking pan. In a small nonstick skillet, melt chocolate chips and butter over the lowest heat. In a large bowl, combine melted chocolate mixture, fruit-based fat substitute, cocoa powder, sugar, eggs, and vanilla. Beat well. Stir in flour. Bake for 20 to 30 minutes or just until a toothpick comes out with moist crumbs adhering to it. Do not overbake. Cool before cutting (if you can resist eating them hot).

*The products I used in testing this recipe were Smucker's Baking Healthy Oil and Shortening Replacement for Baking and Sunsweet's Lighter Bake. Both are found in the grocery-store aisle with cooking oils and fats. They keep for months in the refrigerator after opening.

Nectarine-Berry Crisp

A fantastic way to eat your fruit.

1. Preheat oven to 350°F. Butter a 7" × 11" casserole dish. In a food processor, pulse the flour and butter until they have the texture of coarse cornmeal. Remove to a bowl and toss with remaining topping ingredients until mixed. (This can be refrigerated for 1 week.)

2. To prepare filling, combine all ingredients in a bowl. Stir to mix well. Place the fruit filling in the casserole dish. Cover the filling with the topping. Bake 35 to 45 minutes or until bubbling and the fruit in the middle is tender. Serve warm for the best flavor.

Note: *This is best when made with fresh fruit. If you use frozen fruit, you will need to increase the amount of cornstarch in the recipe to 2 or 3 tablespoons or the dessert will be too runny. The dessert must be cooked long enough for the fruit to bubble so the cornstarch can thicken the mixture.*

Serves 8

Topping:
¼ cup flour
¼ cup butter or margarine
¼ cup rolled oats
¾ cup brown sugar
¾ teaspoon cinnamon
½ teaspoon nutmeg
½ cup chopped walnuts

Filling:
2½ cups blackberries or blueberries
2½ cups raspberries
2½ cups nectarine slices
¼ teaspoon ground ginger
½ cup granular Splenda or sugar
2 tablespoons cornstarch

Nutritional information per serving:

Calories	200
Fat, gm.	7
Protein, gm.	2
Carbs, gm.	33
Cholesterol, mg.	15
Fiber, gm.	5.0

Serves 18

1¾ cups boiling water
1 cup quick-cooking oats
½ cup butter or margarine
1 cup white sugar*
1 cup brown sugar
2 eggs
1¾ cups flour
1 teaspoon baking soda
1 teaspoon salt
1 tablespoon cocoa
1 cup chocolate chips

Topping:
1 cup chocolate chips
½ cup chopped walnuts
¼ cup sugar

Nutritional information per serving:

Calories	280
Fat, gm.	12
Protein, gm.	3
Carbs, gm.	46
Cholesterol, mg.	35
Fiber, gm.	1.7

Oatmeal Chocolate Chip Cake

Once you taste this chocolate cake, it may turn out to be your all-time favorite.

❖ Preheat oven to 350°F, or 325°F if using a glass or nonstick pan. Butter a 9" × 13" baking pan. In a large bowl, combine boiling water and oats. Let stand for 5 minutes. Add butter, 1 cup sugar, brown sugar, and eggs. Beat well. Add flour, baking soda, salt, cocoa, and 1 cup of chocolate chips. Stir to mix well. (Batter will be thin.) Pour into pan. Sprinkle with 1 cup chocolate chips and nuts. Sprinkle with ¼ cup sugar. Bake for 35 to 40 minutes or until toothpick comes out clean when inserted in the middle of the cake.

_____

*Splenda works well in this cake and it cuts out a few calories and carbohydrates. Replace half of the sugar with Splenda. In this recipe, use ½ cup white sugar and ½ cup Splenda.

Oatmeal Toffee Bars

Be careful. These are addictive!

1. Preheat oven to 400°F. Butter a 9" × 9" or a 7" × 11" baking pan. In a medium bowl, combine melted butter and rolled oats. Mix well. Add brown sugar, corn syrup, salt, and vanilla. Stir to mix. Press mixture in baking pan. Bake for 7 to 12 minutes or just until mixture is bubbling and is beginning to turn brown. Watch carefully. Do not overbake. Remove from oven. Using a knife, loosen around the edges of the pan.

2. While bottom is baking, combine chocolate chips and peanut butter in a small nonstick skillet. Melt over the lowest heat. Spoon melted chocolate chip mixture on top of oatmeal bottom. Sprinkle with nuts, if desired.

3. Cut into bars while still warm.

――――

Note: *To set the top more quickly, put it in the refrigerator for a few minutes. Cover and store at room temperature.*

Serves 20

½ cup butter or margarine, melted
2 cups rolled oats
½ cup brown sugar
¼ cup corn syrup
½ teaspoon salt
2 teaspoons vanilla

Topping:
6 ounces (1 cup) chocolate chips
½ cup peanut butter
½ cup chopped pecans or peanuts, optional

Nutritional information per serving:

Calories	175
Fat, gm.	10
Protein, gm.	3
Carbs, gm.	18
Cholesterol, mg.	10
Fiber, gm.	1.7

Serves 10

Filling:
1 cup sugar
2 large eggs, lightly beaten
2 tablespoons flour
¼ teaspoon nutmeg
¼ teaspoon allspice
1 bag (16 ounces) frozen peach slices
1 bag (16 ounces) frozen loose-packed
  raspberries

Topping:
1½ cups flour
¼ cup granular Splenda or sugar
1 teaspoon baking powder
½ teaspoon salt
⅓ cup butter or margarine, cut into small
  pieces
1 large egg, lightly beaten
¼ cup fat-free milk
1 teaspoon vanilla
3 tablespoons sugar

Nutritional information per serving:

Calories	345
Fat, gm.	7
Protein, gm.	4
Carbs, gm.	63
Cholesterol, mg.	70
Fiber, gm.	2.7

Peach and Raspberry Cobbler

The combination of peaches and raspberries with a light crumb topping is irresistible. It will bring back memories of Grandmother's house.

❖ Preheat oven to 375°F. Butter a 9" × 13" baking pan. For the filling, combine sugar, 2 eggs, flour, nutmeg, and allspice in a large bowl. Mix well. Add peaches and raspberries. Stir gently to mix. Spoon mixture into baking dish. In a small bowl, combine flour, Splenda, baking powder, salt, and butter. Using two knives or a pastry blender, cut in butter until mixture resembles coarse cornmeal. Combine 1 egg, milk, and vanilla. Pour into dry ingredients. Stir just until moistened. Crumble mixture over the fruit. Sprinkle 3 tablespoons sugar on top. Bake for 40 to 45 minutes or until lightly browned on top.

Pecan Chocolate Bourbon Pie

Enjoy this soft, sumptuous, and delicious pie. It is a lightened adaptation of the famous Derby Pie.

❖ Preheat oven to 350°F. In a 9-inch pie pan, combine graham cracker crumbs, Splenda, and butter. Mix well with a fork. Press crumb mixture firmly on bottom and sides of the pan. Spray lightly with butter spray. Arrange pecan halves on bottom of the pie crust. Sprinkle with chocolate chips. In a medium bowl, combine corn syrup, brown sugar, bourbon, vanilla, and eggs. Beat with hand mixer. Pour into crust. Bake for 25 to 35 minutes or until set in the middle.

Serves 8

Crust:
1 cup graham cracker crumbs
¼ cup granular Splenda or sugar
3 tablespoons butter or margarine, melted
Butter spray

Filling:
¾ cup pecan halves
⅓ cup chocolate chips
⅔ cup dark or light corn syrup
½ cup brown sugar
¼ cup bourbon
1 teaspoon vanilla
3 eggs

Nutritional information per serving:

Calories	335
Fat, gm.	13
Protein, gm.	51
Carbs, gm.	4
Cholesterol, mg.	80
Fiber, gm.	1.3

Raspberry Rhubarb Pie

Serves 8

1 (9 inch) pie crust
3 cups fresh or frozen rhubarb
2 cups fresh or frozen loose-packed
  raspberries
½ cup granular Splenda or sugar
¼ cup brown sugar
3 tablespoons flour
1 egg, lightly beaten
1 teaspoon vanilla
¼ teaspoon nutmeg

Topping:
⅓ cup flour
⅓ cup brown sugar
¼ cup butter or margarine

Nutritional information per serving:

Calories	250
Fat, gm.	12
Protein, gm.	3
Carbs, gm.	32
Cholesterol, mg.	40
Fiber, gm.	2.7

I love this pie! This is definitely one of my favorite recipes in this book. If you have a sweet tooth, and like rhubarb and raspberries, this is the recipe for you.

❖ Preheat oven to 350°F. Place prepared pie crust into pie pan and set aside. In a large bowl, combine rhubarb, raspberries, Splenda, brown sugar, and flour. Stir to mix. In a small bowl, combine egg, vanilla, and nutmeg. Pour into bowl with rhubarb. Stir to mix. Spoon mixture into pie shell. In a small bowl, combine topping ingredients. Using two knives or a pastry blender, cut butter into flour and sugar until mixture resembles coarse corn meal. Sprinkle on top of pie. Bake for 35 to 45 minutes or until crust is brown and it is set in the middle.

Note: *If using frozen rhubarb or raspberries, do not thaw the fruit before mixing it in this recipe. Baking time may be increased if the fruits are frozen.*

Raspberry Sauce

This is a sauce you might see served in a gourmet restaurant. It adds an elegant touch to simple desserts such as rice pudding, custard, and ice cream.

❖ In a heavy saucepan, combine raspberries, corn syrup, water, cornstarch, lemon juice, and salt. Cook over medium heat, stirring constantly, until mixture comes to a boil. Continue to boil gently for 2 minutes. Remove from heat. Pour sauce in small amounts through a strainer to remove the raspberry seeds. Discard seeds. Add Splenda and vanilla to the strained sauce. Taste and add additional Splenda or sugar for more sweetness.

_____

Note: *This is a super-simple recipe except for the straining of the sauce. It takes some time to press the sauce through a strainer. It also tends to be messy. Be careful not to get raspberry sauce on your clothes. This recipe will yield about 1 cup of strained sauce.*

Serves 8

1 package (10 ounces) frozen raspberries
¼ cup corn syrup
2 tablespoons water
1 tablespoon cornstarch
1 tablespoon lemon juice
½ teaspoon salt
1 tablespoon granular Splenda or sugar
½ teaspoon vanilla

Nutritional information per serving:

Calories	70
Fat, gm.	0
Protein, gm.	0
Carbs, gm.	18
Cholesterol, mg.	0
Fiber, gm.	0

Rhubarb Cake

Serves 8

4 cups fresh or frozen rhubarb, cut into ½-inch slices
1 cup granular Splenda or sugar

Topping:
⅓ cup butter or margarine
⅔ cup sugar
1 egg
1 tablespoon milk
¼ teaspoon cinnamon
⅛ teaspoon nutmeg
¼ teaspoon salt
1 teaspoon baking powder
1 teaspoon vanilla
1 cup flour

Nutritional information per serving:

Calories	215
Fat, gm.	8
Protein, gm.	3
Carbs, gm.	33
Cholesterol, mg.	40
Fiber, gm.	0.9

A good rhubarb dessert is one of the best parts of spring—but now frozen rhubarb is available all year. If you like rhubarb, you will love this recipe.

❖ Preheat oven to 350°F. Butter a 9" × 9" baking pan. Combine rhubarb and Splenda in a large bowl. Spoon into baking pan. In the same large bowl, combine butter and sugar. Beat until smooth. Add egg, milk, cinnamon, nutmeg, salt, baking powder, and vanilla. Beat well. Stir in flour. Spoon batter over rhubarb. (Batter will be very thick.) Bake for 35 to 45 minutes or until lightly browned.

———

Note: *This cake is especially good topped with fat-free half-and-half, milk, or whipped cream.*

Rocky Road S'Mores

This could be a fun rainy-day treat to make with the kids. However, they are so good, you will not want to wait until a rainy day.

❖ Preheat oven to 375°F, or 350°F if using a glass or nonstick pan. Butter an 8" × 8" or 9" × 9" baking pan. In a medium bowl, beat together butter and sugar until light and fluffy. Add flour and graham cracker crumbs. Beat with electric mixer until crumbly. Press firmly into baking pan. Sprinkle with marshmallows, chocolate chips, and walnuts. Bake for 15 to 20 minutes. Do not overbake.

Serves 16

½ cup butter or margarine
½ cup brown sugar
1 cup flour
½ cup graham cracker crumbs
2 cups miniature marshmallows
6 ounces (1 cup) chocolate chips
½ cup chopped walnuts

Nutritional information per serving:

Calories	175
Fat, gm.	9
Protein, gm.	2
Carbs, gm.	22
Cholesterol, mg.	15
Fiber, gm.	0.8

Recipe Index

A

Alcohol, xiv
Apple and Kraut Pork Chops, 93
Apple Apricot Bread Dressing, 207
Apple, Brie, and Pecan Dessert Quesadillas, 266
Apple Butternut Squash Soup with Brandy, 4
Apple Cake—The Best Ever, 264
Apple Glazed Salmon, 151
Apple Raisin Rum Stuffed Chicken Breasts, 125
Apple Tart, 265
Apricot Chicken with Pecans, 126
Artichoke and Mushroom Chicken Bake, 127
Artichoke and Red Pepper Pie, 77
Asparagus Blue Cheese Bundles, 231
Asparagus with Black Olives and Bacon, 232
Avocado Olive Dip, 250

B

Bacon and Egg Pizza, 78
Bacon and Potato Soup, 5
Bacon Corn Chowder, 6
Bacon, Swiss, and Grape Salad, 48
Bacon Wrapped Scallops in Brandy Marinade, 152
Baked Sea Bass with Walnut Crumb Crust, 153
Baked Stuffed Sweet Potatoes, 233
Banana Oatmeal Bread, 251
Bean Salsa Dip, 252

Beef
Beef Fillets Crusted with Blue Cheese, 94
Beef Merlot, 95
Beef Strip Steak with Soy Maple Mustard Glaze, 96
Beef Stroganoff with Mushrooms and Peppers, 97
Beef Tenderloin with Soy Ginger Marinade, 98
Burger Stuffed Bundles, 100
Chicken-Fried Steak, 101
Chilies and Refried Bean Casserole, 176
cooking tips, 92
Enchilada Casserole, 179
Hamburger Pie, 181
Hamburger Soup, 25
Honey and Soy Marinated Flank Steak, 105
Irish Stew with Stout Beer, 26
Italian Beef and Spinach Pie, 183
Lasagna with No-Cook Noodles, 184
Meat and Potatoes Skillet Dinner, 186
Mediterranean Beef Stew, 29
Minestrone-Style Stew, 32
Moroccan Beef Kabobs, 109
Oriental Beef and Noodle Soup, 34
Russian Beef, Mushrooms, and Noodles, 194
Santa Fe Soup, 37
Southwestern Chili, 40
Spaghetti with Beef and Bacon Tomato Sauce, 198

Spanish Beef and Mushrooms—Estofado, 118
Spicy Orange Marinated Beef Roast, 119
Swiss Steak, 120
Tamale Pie, 201
Beer, xiv
Beet and Orange Salad with Blue Cheese and Walnuts, 49
Black Bean and Red Pepper Dip, 253
Black Bean Soup with a Secret Ingredient, 7
BLT Mashed Potatoes, 208
Blueberry Peach Crostata, 267
Blueberry, Walnut, and Wild Rice Chicken Salad, 50
Breads, Dressing, and Stuffing
Apple Apricot Bread Dressing, 207
Banana Oatmeal Bread, 251
Chicken, Vegetables, and Stuffing Bake, 135
Cornbread, 210
Irish Soda Bread, 213
Orange Marmalade French Toast, 83
Rhubarb Bread, 258
Turkey and Dressing Casserole, 204
Breakfasts
Artichoke and Red Pepper Pie, 77
Bacon and Egg Pizza, 78
Cheesy Sausage Bake, 79
cooking tips, 76
Crustless Mexican Quiche, 80
Italian Egg Puff, 81

Mushroom and Artichoke Frittata Squares, 82
Orange Marmalade French Toast, 83
Sausage and Spinach Breakfast Casserole, 84
Scotch Eggs, 85
Strawberry Breakfast Salsa, 86
Swedish Pancakes, 87
Swiss Sweet Onion Pie, 88
Vegetable Frittata, 89
Broccoli Cheese Soup, 8
Broccoli, Roasted Red Peppers, and Artichoke Salad, 51
Broccoli with Honey Sesame Topping, 234
Broiled Shrimp and Cheese on French Bread, 154
Bruschetta and Crostini, 254
Brussels Sprouts in Creamy Dijon Sauce, 235
Brussels Sprouts with Apricot Glaze, 236
Burger Stuffed Bundles, 100

C
Cajun Chicken Soup, 9
Carrot Soup with Fresh Mint, 10
Carrots with Dried Cranberries and Walnuts, 237
Casseroles
    Chicken and Biscuit Casserole, 174
    Chicken Tetrazzini Casserole, 175
    Chilies and Refried Bean Casserole, 176
    cooking tips, 170–72
    Enchilada Casserole, 179
    Ham and Asparagus Casserole, 180
    Hamburger Pie, 181
    Italian Beef and Spinach Pie, 183
    Lasagna with No-Cook Noodles, 184
    Meat and Potatoes Skillet Dinner, 186
    Mushroom Stroganoff, 187

Pork and Noodles, 192
Reuben Casserole, 193
Russian Beef, Mushrooms, and Noodles, 194
Sausage and Spinach Breakfast Casserole, 84
Seafood and Red Pepper Couscous, 195
Spaghetti and Italian Sausage Pie, 197
Spaghetti with Beef and Bacon Tomato Sauce, 198
Spanish Rice with Chicken and Red Peppers, 199
Spicy Seafood Rice, 200
Tamale Pie, 201
Tortilla and Bean Casserole, 202
Tuna Noodle Casserole, 203
Turkey and Dressing Casserole, 204
Cheddar Veggie Pasta Toss, 173
Cheesy Sausage Bake, 79
Cherry Chicken Salad, 52
Chicken and Poultry
    Apple Raisin Rum Stuffed Chicken Breasts, 125
    Apricot Chicken with Pecans, 126
    Artichoke and Mushroom Chicken Bake, 127
    Cajun Chicken Soup, 9
    Chicken and Biscuit Casserole, 174
    Chicken Breast with Port Wine Plum Sauce, 128
    Chicken Breasts in Apricot Brandy Sauce, 129
    Chicken California Style, 130
    Chicken, Cashew, and Apple Stir-Fry, 134
    Chicken Chili, 11
    Chicken Noodle Soup with Spinach, 12
    Chicken Parmesan, 131
    Chicken, Sausage, and Bean Stew, 13

Chicken Tetrazzini Casserole, 175
Chicken, Vegetables, and Stuffing Bake, 135
Chicken with Brandy Orange Sauce, 132
Chicken with Mushrooms, Roasted Peppers, and Olives, 133
cooking tips, 124
Creamy Chicken Linguine, 178
Creamy Swiss Chicken Bake, 136
Grilled Chicken with Raspberry and Blueberry Grand Marnier Sauce, 137
Honey Mustard Chicken with Dried Cranberries, 138
Indian Chicken Curry, 139
Italian Chicken Rolls, 140
Jamaican Chicken Stew, 27
Linguine with Chicken, Spinach, and Tomatoes, 185
Maple Mustard Grilled Chicken, 141
Mexican Chicken Chili, 30
Orange Glazed Chicken Strips, 142
Pasta Alfredo—Create Your Own, 188
Pineapple Cranberry Chicken, 143
Posole, 36
Raspberry Chicken, 144
Soy Glazed Chicken and Dried Fruit Pilaf, 145
Spanish Rice with Chicken and Red Peppers, 199
Spicy Asian Chicken Noodle Soup, 41
Tortellini Soup, 44
Turkey and Dressing Casserole, 204
Turkey Piccata, 146
Turkey Tenderloins with Mustard Cranberry Sauce, 147
Tuscan Chicken with Pistachio Rice, 148
Chili Con Crazy, 14
Chilies and Refried Bean Casserole, 176
Chilled Spinach and Tarragon Soup, 15

Chocolate Chip Peanut Butter Cake, 268
Chocolate Silk Pie, 269
Chocolate Wonder Bars, 270
Chunky Gazpacho Garden Soup, 16
Cod Chowder with Black Beans and Corn, 17
Cod with Parmesan Dill Topping, 155
Colcannon—Irish Mashed Potatoes and
    Cabbage, 209
Colorful Bean and Cheddar Salad, 53
Cookies, Bars, and Brownies
    Chocolate Wonder Bars, 270
    Fudge Brownies (with a Secret
        Ingredient), 274
    Oatmeal Toffee Bars, 277
    Rocky Road S'Mores, 283
Cooking tips, xii–xiv. See also specific dishes
Cornbread, 210
Cornflake Crusted Cod, 156
Country Italian Penne, 177
Country Vegetable Soup, 18
Crab Bisque Florentine, 19
Crab Imperial, 157
Crab Potato Soup, 20
Cream of Spinach Soup, 21
Creamy Chicken Linguine, 178
Creamy Rice Pudding, 271
Creamy Swiss Chicken Bake, 136
Crème Brulée, 272
Crunchy Cole Slaw with Cashews, 54
Crustless Mexican Quiche, 80
Curried Lentil Soup, 22
Curried Pork and Rice, 102

D
Desserts, Cakes, and Pies
    Apple, Brie, and Pecan Dessert
        Quesadillas, 266
    Apple Cake—The Best Ever, 264

Apple Tart, 265
Blueberry Peach Crostata, 267
Chocolate Chip Peanut Butter Cake, 268
Chocolate Silk Pie, 269
Chocolate Wonder Bars, 270
cooking tips, 262–63
Creamy Rice Pudding, 271
Crème Brulée, 272
Dutch Apple Crumble, 273
Fudge Brownies (with a Secret
    Ingredient), 274
Nectarine-Berry Crisp, 275
Oatmeal Chocolate Chip Cake, 276
Oatmeal Toffee Bars, 277
Peach and Raspberry Cobbler, 278
Pecan Chocolate Bourbon Pie, 279
Raspberry Rhubarb Pie, 280
Raspberry Sauce, 281
Rhubarb Cake, 282
Rocky Road S'Mores, 283
Dips, Sauces, and Spreads
    Avocado Olive Dip, 250
    Bean Salsa Dip, 252
    Black Bean and Red Pepper Dip, 253
    Lemon Tuna Spread, 160
    Light Guacamole, 256
    Mushroom Bacon Spread, 257
    Raspberry Sauce, 281
    Spinach and Artichoke Dip, 260
    Strawberry Breakfast Salsa, 86
Dutch Apple Crumble, 273

E
Eggs
    Bacon and Egg Pizza, 78
    Cheesy Sausage Bake, 79
    cooking tips, 76
    Crustless Mexican Quiche, 80

Italian Egg Puff, 81
Sausage and Spinach Breakfast Casserole,
    84
Scotch Eggs, 85
Vegetable Frittata, 89
Enchilada Casserole, 179

F
Festive Apple Pear Salad, 55
Feta and Red Pepper Cheesecake, 255
Fish and Seafood
    Apple Glazed Salmon, 151
    Bacon Wrapped Scallops in Brandy
        Marinade, 152
    Baked Sea Bass with Walnut Crumb
        Crust, 153
    Broiled Shrimp and Cheese on French
        Bread, 154
    Cod Chowder with Black Beans and Corn, 17
    Cod with Parmesan Dill Topping, 155
    cooking tips, 150
    Cornflake Crusted Cod, 156
    Crab Bisque Florentine, 19
    Crab Imperial, 157
    Crab Potato Soup, 20
    Grilled Tuna Steak with Roasted
        Vegetables, 158
    Honey Mustard Haddock, 159
    Lemon Tuna Spread, 160
    Orange Glazed Salmon, 161
    Pasta Alfredo—Create Your Own, 188
    Pecan Crusted Sea Bass, 162
    Salmon Loaf with Creamy Dill Sauce, 163
    Salmon Mousse, 64
    Scallop, Mushroom, and Potato Soup, 38
    Seafood and Red Pepper Couscous, 195
    Shrimp and Feta with Italian Tomato
        Sauce, 164

Shrimp and Pasta in Creamy Swiss Cheese Sauce, 196
Shrimp Basil Soup, 39
Shrimp in Tomato Cream Sauce on Linguine, 165
Shrimp with Couscous, Roasted Red Peppers, and Pine Nuts, 166
Smoked Salmon with Sun-Dried Tomatoes on Fettuccine, 167
Southwestern Tuna with Avocado Butter Sauce, 168
Spicy Seafood Rice, 200
Tuna Noodle Casserole, 203
Fudge Brownies (with a Secret Ingredient), 274

G
Gingered Carrot Soup, 23
Green Beans with Blue Cheese and Bacon Dressing, 238
Green Beans with Gorgonzola, 56
Green Beans with Pecans, 239
Green Beans with Tomatoes and Onions, 240
Grilled Chicken with Raspberry and Blueberry Grand Marnier Sauce, 137
Grilled Ham Steak with Raisin Sauce, 103
Grilled Potato Salad, 211
Grilled Tuna Steak with Roasted Vegetables, 158

H
Ham and Asparagus Casserole, 180
Ham and Bean Soup for Two, 24
Ham with Maple Syrup, Pineapple Ginger Sauce, 104
Hamburger Pie, 181
Hamburger Soup, 25
Honey and Parmesan Topped Asparagus, 241

Honey and Soy Marinated Flank Steak, 105
Honey Apricot Glazed Ham, 106
Honey Mustard Chicken with Dried Cranberries, 138
Honey Mustard Haddock, 159
Hot German Potato Salad, 212
Hungarian Pork Chops, 107

I
Indian Chicken Curry, 139
Irish Soda Bread, 213
Irish Stew with Stout Beer, 26
Italian Baked Mostaccioli, 182
Italian Beef and Spinach Pie, 183
Italian Chicken Rolls, 140
Italian Egg Puff, 81

J
Jamaican Chicken Stew, 27

L
Lasagna with No-Cook Noodles, 184
Lazy Day White Bean Chili, 28
Lemon Tuna Spread, 160
Light Guacamole, 256
Linguine with Chicken, Spinach, and Tomatoes, 185
Liquors, xiv

M
Make Ahead Coleslaw, 57
Maple Mustard Grilled Chicken, 141
Marmalade Glazed Carrots, 242
Meat and Potatoes Skillet Dinner, 186
Mediterranean Beef Stew, 29
Mediterranean Rice with Pine Nuts and Dried Cranberries, 214
Mexican Chicken Chili, 30

Mexican Macaroni Salad, 58
Mexican Pork Chili, 31
Mexican Rice, 215
Minestrone-Style Stew, 32
Molasses Grilled Pork Chops with Horseradish Sauce, 108
Moroccan Beef Kabobs, 109
Moroccan Rice Salad with Feta, 59
Mushroom and Artichoke Frittata Squares, 82
Mushroom Bacon Spread, 257
Mushroom Stroganoff, 187

N
Nectarine-Berry Crisp, 275

O
Oatmeal Chocolate Chip Cake, 276
Oatmeal Toffee Bars, 277
Old-Fashioned Sweet Brandy Pork Medallions, 99
Olive oil, 46–47
Orange and Yellow Pepper Soup, 33
Orange Glazed Chicken Strips, 142
Orange Glazed Salmon, 161
Orange Marmalade French Toast, 83
Orange Persian Barley, 216
Oriental Beef and Noodle Soup, 34
Orzo with Parmesan and Basil, 217
Oven Roasted Red Potatoes with Rosemary, 218

P
Parmesan Potatoes, 219
Pasta
    Cheddar Veggie Pasta Toss, 173
    cooking tips, 170–72
    Country Italian Penne, 177
    Creamy Chicken Linguine, 178

Pasta—*continued*
    Hamburger Pie, 181
    Italian Baked Mostaccioli, 182
    Italian Beef and Spinach Pie, 183
    Lasagna with No-Cook Noodles, 184
    Linguine with Chicken, Spinach, and
       Tomatoes, 185
    Pasta Alfredo—Create Your Own, 188
    Pasta with Broccoli and Red Peppers in
       Peanut Sauce, 189
    Pasta with Pesto Sauce, 220
    Pasta with Spinach, Olives, and Pine
       Nuts, 190
    Pasta with Tomato and White Bean
       Sauce—A Build Your Own Pasta Dish,
       191
    Pork and Noodles, 192
    Russian Beef, Mushrooms, and Noodles,
       194
    Shrimp and Pasta in Creamy Swiss
       Cheese Sauce, 196
    Spaghetti and Italian Sausage Pie, 197
    Spaghetti with Beef and Bacon Tomato
       Sauce, 198
Peach and Raspberry Cobbler, 278
Peanut Raisin Slaw, 60
Pecan Chocolate Bourbon Pie, 279
Pecan Crusted Sea Bass, 162
Pilaf with Spinach and Walnuts, 221
Pineapple Cranberry Chicken, 143
Pork
    Apple and Kraut Pork Chops, 93
    Cheesy Sausage Bake, 79
    cooking tips, 92
    Country Italian Penne, 177
    Country Vegetable Soup, 18
    Curried Pork and Rice, 102
    Grilled Ham Steak with Raisin Sauce, 103

Ham and Asparagus Casserole, 180
Ham and Bean Soup for Two, 24
Ham with Maple Syrup, Pineapple Ginger
    Sauce, 104
Honey Apricot Glazed Ham, 106
Hungarian Pork Chops, 107
Italian Baked Mostaccioli, 182
Lasagna with No-Cook Noodles, 184
Mexican Pork Chili, 31
Molasses Grilled Pork Chops with Horse-
    radish Sauce, 108
Old-Fashioned Sweet Brandy Pork Medal-
    lions, 99
Pork and Butternut Squash Stew, 35
Pork and Noodles, 192
Pork and Vegetable Stir-Fry on the Grill,
    110
Pork Chops and Apricots in Curry Sauce,
    111
Pork Chops, Potatoes, and Cabbage, 113
Pork Chops with Orange Cranberry Sauce,
    112
Pork Loin with Fruit Pilaf, 114
Pork Medallions with Port Wine Cherry
    Sauce, 115
Pork Ribs and Sauerkraut, 116
Pork Tenderloin with Cinnamon Apples,
    117
Sausage and Spinach Breakfast Casserole,
    84
Spaghetti and Italian Sausage Pie, 197
Split Pea Soup in an Hour, 42
Two-Meal Slow Roasted Pork Shoulder,
    121
Posole, 36
Poultry. *See* Chicken and Poultry

Q
Quinoa, Pepper, and Peanut Salad, 61

R
Raspberry Chicken, 144
Raspberry Pecan Spinach Salad, 62
Raspberry Rhubarb Pie, 280
Raspberry Sauce, 281
Red Cabbage and Apple Salad, 63
Reuben Casserole, 193
Rhubarb Bread, 258
Rhubarb Cake, 282
Roasted Red and Yellow Peppers with Green
    Beans, 243
Roasted Red Pepper and Olive Tapenade, 259
Rocky Road S'Mores, 283
Russian Beef, Mushrooms, and Noodles, 194

S
Salads
    Bacon, Swiss, and Grape Salad, 48
    Beet and Orange Salad with Blue Cheese
       and Walnuts, 49
    Blueberry, Walnut, and Wild Rice Chicken
       Salad, 50
    Broccoli, Roasted Red Peppers, and Arti-
       choke Salad, 51
    Cherry Chicken Salad, 52
    Colorful Bean and Cheddar Salad, 53
    Crunchy Cole Slaw with Cashews, 54
    Festive Apple Pear Salad, 55
    Green Beans with Gorgonzola, 56
    Make Ahead Coleslaw, 57
    Mexican Macaroni Salad, 58
    Moroccan Rice Salad with Feta, 59
    Peanut Raisin Slaw, 60
    preparation tips, 46–47
    Quinoa, Pepper, and Peanut Salad, 61

Raspberry Pecan Spinach Salad, 62
Red Cabbage and Apple Salad, 63
Salmon Mousse, 64
South of the Border Bean and Corn Salad, 65
Spinach, Kiwi, and Strawberry Salad with Poppy Seed Dressing, 69
Spinach Salad with Bacon Dressing, 66
Spinach Salad with Honey Cranberry Dressing, 67
Spinach Salad with Oranges and Pomegranates, 68
Strawberry and Spinach Salad with Apple Mustard Dressing, 70
Swiss Apple Grape Salad, 71
Tortellini and Shrimp Salad, 72
Tuscan Pasta Salad with Artichokes and Sun Dried Tomatoes, 73
Salmon Loaf with Creamy Dill Sauce, 163
Salmon Mousse, 64
Santa Fe Soup, 37
Sausage and Spinach Breakfast Casserole, 84
Scallop, Mushroom, and Potato Soup, 38
Scotch Eggs, 85
Seafood. See Fish and Seafood
Seafood and Red Pepper Couscous, 195
Shrimp and Feta with Italian Tomato Sauce, 164
Shrimp and Pasta in Creamy Swiss Cheese Sauce, 196
Shrimp Basil Soup, 39
Shrimp in Tomato Cream Sauce on Linguine, 165
Shrimp with Couscous, Roasted Red Peppers, and Pine Nuts, 166
Side Dishes
    Apple Apricot Bread Dressing, 207
    BLT Mashed Potatoes, 208

Colcannon—Irish Mashed Potatoes and Cabbage, 209
cooking tips, 206
Cornbread, 210
Grilled Potato Salad, 211
Hot German Potato Salad, 212
Irish Soda Bread, 213
Mediterranean Rice with Pine Nuts and Dried Cranberries, 214
Mexican Rice, 215
Orange Persian Barley, 216
Orzo with Parmesan and Basil, 217
Oven Roasted Red Potatoes with Rosemary, 218
Parmesan Potatoes, 219
Pasta with Pesto Sauce, 220
Pilaf with Spinach and Walnuts, 221
Spice It Up with Lentils, 222
Tuscan White Beans with Herbs, 223
Wild Rice with Cranberries and Cashews, 224
Yellow Rice with Golden Raisins, 225
see also Pasta; Vegetables
Smoked Salmon with Sun-Dried Tomatoes on Fettuccine, 167
Snacks
    Avocado Olive Dip, 250
    Banana Oatmeal Bread, 251
    Bean Salsa Dip, 252
    Black Bean and Red Pepper Dip, 253
    Bruschetta and Crostini, 254
    Feta and Red Pepper Cheesecake, 255
    Light Guacamole, 256
    Mushroom Bacon Spread, 257
    Rhubarb Bread, 258
    Roasted Red Pepper and Olive Tapenade, 259
    Spinach and Artichoke Dip, 260

Soups and Stews
    Apple Butternut Squash Soup with Brandy, 4
    Bacon and Potato Soup, 5
    Bacon Corn Chowder, 6
    Black Bean Soup with a Secret Ingredient, 7
    Broccoli Cheese Soup, 8
    Cajun Chicken Soup, 9
    Carrot Soup with Fresh Mint, 10
    Chicken Chili, 11
    Chicken Noodle Soup with Spinach, 12
    Chicken, Sausage, and Bean Stew, 13
    Chili Con Crazy, 14
    Chilled Spinach and Tarragon Soup, 15
    Chunky Gazpacho Garden Soup, 16
    Cod Chowder with Black Beans and Corn, 17
    cooking tips, 2–3
    Country Vegetable Soup, 18
    Crab Bisque Florentine, 19
    Crab Potato Soup, 20
    Cream of Spinach Soup, 21
    Curried Lentil Soup, 22
    Gingered Carrot Soup, 23
    Ham and Bean Soup for Two, 24
    Hamburger Soup, 25
    Irish Stew with Stout Beer, 26
    Jamaican Chicken Stew, 27
    Lazy Day White Bean Chili, 28
    Mediterranean Beef Stew, 29
    Mexican Chicken Chili, 30
    Mexican Pork Chili, 31
    Minestrone-Style Stew, 32
    Orange and Yellow Pepper Soup, 33
    Oriental Beef and Noodle Soup, 34
    Pork and Butternut Squash Stew, 35
    Posole, 36

Soups and Stews—*continued*
    Santa Fe Soup, 37
    Scallop, Mushroom, and Potato Soup, 38
    Shrimp Basil Soup, 39
    Southwestern Chili, 40
    Spicy Asian Chicken Noodle Soup, 41
    Split Pea Soup in an Hour, 42
    Squash Bisque with Rum, 43
    Tortellini Soup, 44
South of the Border Bean and Corn Salad, 65
Southwestern Chili, 40
Southwestern Tuna with Avocado Butter
    Sauce, 168
Soy Glazed Chicken and Dried Fruit Pilaf, 145
Spaghetti and Italian Sausage Pie, 197
Spaghetti with Beef and Bacon Tomato
    Sauce, 198
Spanish Beef and Mushrooms—Estofado, 118
Spanish Rice with Chicken and Red Peppers,
    199
Spice It Up with Lentils, 222
Spicy Asian Chicken Noodle Soup, 41
Spicy Orange Marinated Beef Roast, 119
Spicy Seafood Rice, 200
Spinach and Artichoke Dip, 260
Spinach, Kiwi, and Strawberry Salad with
    Poppy Seed Dressing, 69
Spinach Salad with Bacon Dressing, 66
Spinach Salad with Honey Cranberry
    Dressing, 67
Spinach Salad with Oranges and
    Pomegranates, 68
Split Pea Soup in an Hour, 42
Squash Bisque with Rum, 43
Strawberry and Spinach Salad with Apple
    Mustard Dressing, 70
Strawberry Breakfast Salsa, 86
Swedish Pancakes, 87

Sweet Potatoes and Apples in Ginger Orange
    Sauce, 244
Swiss Apple Grape Salad, 71
Swiss Spinach Soufflé, 245
Swiss Steak, 120
Swiss Sweet Onion Pie, 88

T
Tamale Pie, 201
Tortellini and Shrimp Salad, 72
Tortellini Soup, 44
Tortilla and Bean Casserole, 202
Tuna Noodle Casserole, 203
Turkey and Dressing Casserole, 204
Turkey Piccata, 146
Turkey Tenderloins with Mustard Cranberry
    Sauce, 147
Tuscan Chicken with Pistachio Rice, 148
Tuscan Pasta Salad with Artichokes and Sun
    Dried Tomatoes, 73
Tuscan White Beans with Herbs, 223
Two-Meal Slow Roasted Pork Shoulder, 121

V
Vegetable Frittata, 89
Vegetable oils, 46–47
Vegetables
    Asparagus Blue Cheese Bundles, 231
    Asparagus with Black Olives and Bacon,
      232
    Baked Stuffed Sweet Potatoes, 233
    Broccoli with Honey Sesame Topping, 234
    Brussels Sprouts in Creamy Dijon Sauce,
      235
    Brussels Sprouts with Apricot Glaze, 236
    Carrots with Dried Cranberries and
      Walnuts, 237
    cooking tips, 228–30

Green Beans with Blue Cheese and Bacon
    Dressing, 238
Green Beans with Pecans, 239
Green Beans with Tomatoes and Onions,
    240
Honey and Parmesan Topped Asparagus,
    241
Marmalade Glazed Carrots, 242
Roasted Red and Yellow Peppers with
    Green Beans, 243
Sweet Potatoes and Apples in Ginger
    Orange Sauce, 244
Swiss Spinach Soufflé, 245
Wilted Spinach with Balsamic Mustard
    Sauce, 246
Zucchini Bake, 247
see also Side Dishes

W
Wild Rice with Cranberries and Cashews,
    224
Wilted Spinach with Balsamic Mustard
    Sauce, 246
Wines, xiv

Y
Yellow Rice with Golden Raisins, 225

Z
Zucchini Bake, 247